Daughters, You Are Special

To Love and Be Loved by Our Heavenly Father

DR. SANDRA GATLIN WHITLEY

Ω Daughters, You Are Special

To Love and Be Loved by Our Heavenly Father

DR. SANDRA GATLIN WHITLEY

Copyright © 2020 Dr. Sandra Gatlin Whitley.

All rights reserved. No part of this book may be used or reproduced by any means, graphic, electronic, or mechanical, including photocopying, recording, taping or by any information storage retrieval system without the written permission of the author except in the case of brief quotations embodied in critical articles and reviews.

WestBow Press books may be ordered through booksellers or by contacting:

WestBow Press
A Division of Thomas Nelson & Zondervan
1663 Liberty Drive
Bloomington, IN 47403
www.westbowpress.com
1 (866) 928-1240

Because of the dynamic nature of the Internet, any web addresses or links contained in this book may have changed since publication and may no longer be valid. The views expressed in this work are solely those of the author and do not necessarily reflect the views of the publisher, and the publisher hereby disclaims any responsibility for them.

Any people depicted in stock imagery provided by Getty Images are models, and such images are being used for illustrative purposes only.
Certain stock imagery © Getty Images.

Scripture taken from the King James version of the Bible.
NKJV: Scripture taken from the New King James Version®. Copyright © 1982 by Thomas Nelson. Used by permission. All rights reserved.

Scripture quotations marked (NIV) are taken from the Holy Bible, New International Version®, NIV®. Copyright © 1973, 1978, 1984, 2011 by Biblica, Inc.™ Used by permission of Zondervan. All rights reserved worldwide. www.zondervan.com The "NIV" and "New International Version" are trademarks registered in the United States Patent and Trademark Office by Biblica, Inc.™

Scripture quotations marked MSG are taken from THE MESSAGE, copyright © 1993, 1994, 1995, 1996, 2000, 2001, 2002 by Eugene H. Peterson. Used by permission of NavPress. All rights reserved. Represented by Tyndale House Publishers, Inc.

Scripture quotations marked (NLT) are taken from the Holy Bible, New Living Translation, copyright ©1996, 2004, 2015 by Tyndale House Foundation. Used by permission of Tyndale House Publishers, Inc., Carol Stream, Illinois 60188. All rights reserved.

Scripture quotations are from the ESV® Bible (The Holy Bible, English Standard Version®), copyright © 2001 by Crossway, a publishing ministry of Good News Publishers. Used by permission. All rights re-served.

ISBN: 978-1-9736-7955-4 (sc)
ISBN: 978-1-9736-7957-8 (hc)
ISBN: 978-1-9736-7956-1 (e)

Library of Congress Control Number: 2019918083

Print information available on the last page.

WestBow Press rev. date: 4/7/2020

Quotes

While I know myself as a creation of God, I am also obligated to realize and remember that everyone else and everything else are also God's creation.
— Maya Angelou

To disrespect a person made in the image and likeness of God is a lot worse than desecrating a flag. We should be offended and repulsed in the same way when God's image bearers are desecrated – abused, beaten, neglected, discriminated against, and not loved and taken care of as they should be.
— James MacDonald, *Christ-Centered Biblical Counseling: Changing Lives with God's Changeless Truth*

Dedication

I dedicate this book to
God, the Most incredibly Loving Heavenly Father anyone can ever have. You kept watch over Your children, my parents, my sisters, my brothers, and me to bring us to the saving knowledge of Your firstborn Son, Jesus Christ. By faith, we believe, are growing, and becoming Your image-bearers.

Mom, for your strength and courage in taking risks, raising six children, and giving us the steadfast love only a true mother can give her children. The most important gift of all . . . us finding the God of the Bible in Sunday School and church.

Dad, for you loving and caring for your children, never letting us go, despite the circumstances. Our blended family is becoming a reflection of God working all things together for the good of those who love Him and are called according to His purpose.

Whit, my God-sent earthly bridegroom and husband . . . I love you!
Hallelujah! AMEN!

Contents

Acknowledgements xi
Prologue - A Pastoral Greeting xix
Introduction - Becoming His Bride on Earth as it is in Heaven xxvii

Part 1 – You Are Loved by God, Our Relationship with God and Family and Its Purpose

Chapter 1   Who Am I? Am I a Statistic? 1
Chapter 2   Who Am I? Growing Up Loved in a Traditional Family 15
Chapter 3   Who Am I? Growing up Loved in a Single-Parent Family 33

Part 2 – You Belong to God, Our Relationship with God Based on Gender and Purpose Outside the Family

Chapter 4   What's Right with Me? Love and Girlfriend Relationships 49
Chapter 5   What's Right with Me? Love and Right Relationship with Boys 73

Part 3 – You Are Valued by God, Our Relationship with God in Our Callings and Decisions

Chapter 6   What's Right with Me? Born with Dreams, Gifts, and Talents 101
Chapter 7   You Are Special…Born into Royalty! 137

Part 4 – You Are His Bride, Our Marriage Relationship … Becoming His Bride on Earth as it is in Heaven

Chapter 8   Marriage … Finally! Becoming A Bride on Earth 157

Epilogue - The Conclusion of the Matter . . . We are Our Sister's Keeper 187
Appendix - Poem 193
Chapter Sources and Notes 197
Author Bio 203

Acknowledgements

You are so amazing, Heavenly Father God. I just want to shout it from the rooftops and all around the world that You are Mighty marvelously, my Lord and Savior. After going to see the newly released Christian movie "War Room," I was in total awe of the real-life portrayal of the King James Version of Matthew chapter 6 verse 6, *"But thou, when thou prayest, enter into thy closet, and when thou hast shut thy door, pray to thy Father which is in secret; and thy Father which seeth in secret shall reward thee openly."* I was reminded of how I responded to this passage from the Bible after reading it in church at 15 years of age dealing with the emotional pain of my parents' separation and divorce. I thought, "I have a 'clothes closet.' I' will go in it and pray in private to ask the Father to bring my parents back together."

Thank You and thank You again, dear Heavenly Father for the mother of the Kendrick Brothers, who produced the movie. She was a woman of faith who raised and directed her children on the right path, and when they were older, they did not leave it (Proverbs 22:6 NIV). Because of You Lord guiding their mother, the Kendrick Brothers were able to identify and use their gifts and talents to bless other people. The movie "War Room" is just one example for me. Not only did the movie portray the revelation given to me to literally go in my "clothes closet" and pray, but the military analogy used also reminded me of how my childhood dream of joining the military came to pass. The movie confirmed for me that children too, do hear You when You speak. With our child-like faith, You will do the impossible and reward those who diligently seek you.

I can look back and see how You were at work in my life and for that reason I am truly grateful. You were that one constant in my life when others were not. Thank You for not rejecting, abandoning, or giving up on me. You saw pass all my faults and wretched sins and gave me just what I needed… *love unconditional!* Your incredible love would not let me go and for that again I am truly grateful. I love you very much, my Abba, Daddy God.

> *You put everything on the line for us, embracing our condition and exposing Yourself to the worst by sending Your own Son, Jesus. Is there anything else You would not gladly and freely do for us? Who is it that would dare tangle with You by messing with one of us, your chosen? Who would dare even point a finger? The one*

who died for us -who was raised to life for us is in the presence of You, our Most High God at this very moment! Is there anyone who thinks they can drive a wedge between us and Christ's love for us? There is no way! Not trouble, not hard times, not hatred, not hunger, not homelessness, not bullying threats, not backstabbing, not rejection, not abandonment, not nothing, not even the worst sins listed in Scripture (Romans 8:32-35 The Message Bible [MSG]). . . Hallelujah! Amen!

With thanksgiving in my heart, I also joyfully express my gratitude for You, our Creator orchestrating a cast of characters to be instrumental in You fulfilling Your purpose in our lives.

To my parents, Mom and Dad, may the Lord bless you tremendously for the sacrifices you made for your five, six, and eight children and teaching us right from wrong. Mom, while we were in your womb, God blessed us with a beautifully spirited mother full of love, nurture, and care from Him. I remember hearing of the times when we went outside to play that as soon as we got dirty, you brought us back in the house washed us up and put freshly cleaned clothes on us to go right back outside to play again. You took pride in your status as our mother, attentive to your children's every detail. Even in the midst of the changes in our family structure with you becoming a single parent mother, bless you for doing what was best for us first. We, now six of us, are all the better for your steadfast and immoveable spirit. It is true that when parents *"train up a child* (your six) *in the way they should go: and when they are old, they will not depart from it."* And you rose above your circumstances to successfully go back to school and complete your education. I love you dearly, Mom. You did it!

Dad, thank you for loving us, treating us like little princesses and princes, providing for and protecting us, while raising us to love and care for each other. Truly, you are a family man, who made sure we knew and visited our relatives on both sides of the family. You helped us to dream positively about getting an education and pursuing beneficial careers. After the divorce, although we did not immediately reciprocate your pursuits of staying in touch, thank you for not giving up on us and waiting until we came around. I remember the day you called your firstborn in desperation saying, "San, would you pray? Because I want this family to be a family." As I was about to hang up the phone to pray later, you said, "No, let's pray now." That was the first time we prayed aloud together. Another day you called in the nick of time, while I was in the middle of preparing a speech to present at a conference in 2005 when I was subconsciously wrestling with the "family incident" that I had not spoken to anyone about. As I began to respond to your question, uncontrollable tears welled up in my eyes as I asked your permission to share the incident. It was a definite breakthrough moment. A profound peace came over me when I heard you say, "The truth is the truth. If I had known better, I would have done things differently." And on another occasion years later on my birthday in October 2011, you affirmed me with these words, "I believe your calling is to minister to girls and young women." I love you, Dad.

To my beloved and very special sisters and brothers and their families, I love you very much, more than these words could possibly say. God only knew that each one of us would be the best sisters and brothers to each other. To all seven of you and your spouses and the parents of my nieces and nephews: Teresa (Kevin, Keisha, Trenton); Michele (Richard, Robert, Maya, Makayla); Buzzy (aka Ojay, Bernice, Jaylon, Charmaine); Ken (Amy, Khalil, Cameron, Lynn, Kendra), Andre (April, Andrea), Shawana (Nathaniel, Joshua), and Sancheleresa (Thomas, Harmony, Destiny) look how God brought us together with you being our last baby sister. Harmony, God allowed you to open my heart to see Him in a child-like way again.

To my friend and our step-mother Mona, Dad is blessed with your devoted love of him and his five children. Thank you so much for accepting, being patient with, loving and making sacrifices on our behalf as we grew to trust God in fitting our blended family together. Thanks be to God also for opening both you and mom's hearts to each other. I love you for being you, Mona!

To my deceased paternal grandparents Robert and Nina, who prayed for the right man to marry me. To my deceased maternal grandparents, Alfred and Jessie, for you "grandma" knowing that Whit was the one. And to my deceased god-parents Virginia, "Coach" Gary, and son Bill (Tanya, Janee, Jordan) and surviving son Brian (Helen, Claire & Duece) who trusted the Spirit of God enough to welcome me into your two-parent family, while adjusting to the transition in my own family. And also making Whit a part of the family, too.

To my family of relatives and the memories I do cherish: aunt Jessie Ruth "Tabu" (Melton, Melton Jr. Eric, Erica, Jailyn, Jody, Juelles)," uncle Sonny & Eloise, uncle V.C., uncle Foley (Bun, Kenneth, Cecilia, Richard), uncle Allen (Lois, Alfreda, Jessica), uncle W.T. (Margaret, Dale, Patrice, WT Jr.),

Aunt Ann (Debbie, Phyllis, Darryl), Auntee & George, uncle Vorice & aunt Frances (cousins Debbie, Spudnik, Regina, Anayah, Trey, Janice, Monae, Erica, Pete, Ken, Jeffrey), Brenda Faye, Paul "Tinkey" (Charlotte, Paula, Jamal), Clarence (Brenda), Sammy (Stephanie, Samaria), Hawkeye, Michael, aunt Gladys & uncle Harvey, Gill & Shirley (Chris, Vincent, Angela & Pam, Gill Jr.), Uncle Earl & Margaret (Susan Smith, Taylor), Wilfred (Ida); Aunt Imogene; Aunt Thelma; Squirt & Charlene (Tesha & Lyndon), uncle Charles & aunt Bettye (Bruce, Cynthia, LaReta, Mac, Arielle, Tyler, Hileigh), Frank & Frances, Linwood & Pearl (Venus, Lori), Mrs. Daniels, and to my cousin like sister, Felicia "LeeLee;" Special friends like, brothers Gary & "Mom" Kyle; Giles (Angelia, Simone).

To my special god–children and their families: Jamila Akilah (Jimmy, Ada, Issa) my firstborn so full of love and energy, Tia (Mark & Bonnie), Makayla (Richard & Michele), Marcus Love (Marcus & Linda, Latrice, Linda). To my special nieces, cousins, and their BFFs Makayla, JaDavia, Samequa, Erica, Katelyn, Jody, Jailyn Catalina, Taylar, Harmony, AJ, Jaeda, Shantri, and Kiana for our first "Day-Daydreaming to My Destiny" #DDMD Retreat; who are believing God will do the impossible in fulfilling your vision and dreams.

And to everyone along the journey and seasons God-sent you in my life of discovery and transformation to encourage, love, support, pray, inspire, and be accountable in preparing me to meet my husband:

To my Pastors, Chaplains, Spiritual Leaders: Sister Johnnie Calhoun (Debra, Diedre), Sister Terrell, Brother Adams (Debra), Pastor Robert & Nancy Castle (Robin, Chad), Mrs. Callie Young (Renee, Gail), Chaplain Armstrong, Pastor Wally and Marilyn Hickey, Mrs. Mary Sweitzer, Pastor Howie, Chaplain Layloni Craig, Chaplain John Wood, Bishop Vashti McKenzie, Pastor Charles & First Lady Nora Nobles (Shelley, Celia), Chaplain Matthew and Barbara Zimmerman, and my mentors and prayer warriors John & Jeanine Voorhees, "Mom V & Pop V" (David, Melanie, Eden, John Carter).

To my civilian and military bosses and friends, mentors, role models, marriage and ministry confidants, and family away from home: James Novak, Dennis & Maggie Coggburn, John & Johnnie Carter, Al Watson, Karen & Milt Nobles (Kim), Andrew & Callie Young (Gail, Renee), Paulette Wellington (Eric & Erica), Duke Wellington, Janice, Geneva & Fred Hunter (Terri, Sherri, Fred Jr.), Mary Davis, Paul & Beverly Warfield (Sonja, Malcolm); Daniel Flournoy, Robert Howe, Bryce Poe, James & Tina Barager,

Bob Drewes, Gary Cooper; Ellistene & Jeff, Norm & Carolyn, Alfred & Carrie Deas; Harrison & Beverly Benton; Earl & Lazelle Hunigan; Kathryn Ekberg, Melissa Rider, Jackie & Roger Gray, Howard & Beverly Dayton, Ed & Earline Briggs; Yoko Shannon, and Esther & Neil Pearson.

To my dearest friends, colleagues, line sisters, sorors, and mentor/mentees relationships God used to open my heart and eyes to a meaningful sisterhood of girlfriends and their daughters: Venus Little, Felicia Mack (deceased), Bonnie McCall, Sandra, Daisy Mae, Niecy, Andrea "Bitty," Jennifer Canty, Ruby, Dorothy, Marilyn, Mary B, Carolyn McKnight, Mae Ella (Lester, Eryn); Michelle Gardner, Cathy Morris, Carol Ware, Mary Mayer, Theresa Carroll, Millie Cooper, Jackie Nixon, Marcia Williams, Carolyn Walker, JoAnna Ogbomma (Makim, Howard, Tawanya), Bonnie Campbell (William, Noni), "Sistah" Carolyn Cohen, Cheryl Lohrman, Mary Lou, Margaret, Joyce, Bonnie Dawson, Dana 'Isake" Reed, Belindia Boyer, Mae Tanner, Marilyn Wills, Loreen (Chris, Naomi), Shirley (John, Kendra, Kelsey, Johnna), Marie (Donald, Rachel, and Naomi), Joyce (Al, Chari), Felicia Wiltz (Michael, Chris, Sean), Hosea & Natalie, Alycia Levels (Jonathan & Nuri), Lynda, Milna, Cheryl T-G, Cynthia, Natalie, Linda M, Tanisha, Renee, Jacqui, Tavina, Eva, Sandra B., Sandra M-L., Liz Walker, Gail-Lenora, Sabrina Gray, Sybille (Elliott), Kathy Schnepf (Craig, Chris, Danielle), and grateful for early in my military career God divinely reconnecting line sister Gwen and me in *not despising our humble beginnings and God making room for our gifts and friendship*; later Lynnita, Renay, Lillian and Washalyn, Mamie T, Hilda, Phylesia, Yolanda, "Liz" Elizabeth, Velma, Angela, and Alfreda.

To you who spurred me on to write and those interviewed. Praises to the Lord for first author friend Claire Cloninger; homegirl Patricia Ashley; the woman "angel" on the plane, Ann Abernathy; insightful and motivational Kris Johnson; Paula Batchelor Cable TV producer of "The Vision;" and consultant Cathy Fyock. Juan's daughter Melissa Gallego keep on believing in yourself, as a child of divorce, like me, both of your parents love you very much; Gladys V. & Saritin, thanks for allowing God to establish a bond of friendship through our ethnic lenses. Lois Collins Gwinn (Donald, Joshua, David) and Marjorie Jones grateful for your encouragement and editorial comments.

To my visionary professors, thanks for listening to God and letting Him use you to open my eyes to see beyond any insecurities. Dr. Aida and Dr. Bill Spencer presenting me with opportunities to write in published journals and a book. Dr. Karen Mason insightful and endearing teacher and counselor;

Pastor Randy Mathews & Dr. Alice Mathews "Ezer Commander" godly wisdom and motivation to pursue this ministry to girls and women; DMin Dr. Currie, Bridgett, Sara, and Ezer co-horts ... Sonja, Laurel, Cynthia, DeDe, Susan, Wanda, and Agnes.

To both sets of parents' in the ministry Pastor Grainger who married us and Pastor JoAnn Browning for your love, pastoral care, spiritual guidance, and the "Call to Ministry" and also Pastor Ray and Pastor Gloria-White-Hammond (Mariama, Adiyah, Ella) for your friendship, pastoral prayers, love, wisdom, divine revelation, and counsel in the call and ministry; Pastor Gregory & Rev. Barbara Groover for the encouragement, support, and guidance in answering the call "Launch into the Deep," and for Presiding Elder Herbert & Reverend Amelia Eddy's leadership, and my ordination and pastoral appointment from Bishop Richard Norris. To Bishop Gregory & Dr. Jessica Ingram and Presiding Elder Jocelyn Hart & Brother Eddie Lovelace for support in subsequent pastoral reappointments to our People's Chelsea A.M.E. Church family & the Beloved Community being transformed to reflect God's biblical marriage covenant. A member once shared with joy the revelation she received at a Lay Organization meeting, *"the relationship between the pastor and the lay is like a marriage." We are a body of believers being transformed and becoming the Bride of Christ* preparing to meet the head of the church and Bridegroom, Jesus Christ: Brother Ben, Beverly (Larry), Marcia (Philip), Sherree, Rhonda, Patricia, Tayjah, Carlene (deceased Mark; brother Ellis, Jaliyah, Nyarie, John, Yashonna, Manny, LaToya, Leia, LJ, Savannah, Robert), Willetta, Deborah, Jeanette, Nicole, Shirley, Roberto, Katherine, Alaina, Richelle (Larry, Maxwell, Krysten), Teresa (Mikhel, Mekhi, Mannix), Mishay, Seneeca (Dante, Michael), Dwight, Denise, Michael V, Sherry (Brian, Khyahjah), Michelle (Chayse), Monet (Senai), Mikhail, Evgeny, Cha Young, Jiri, Nadia, Ester, Amit & Ruet, Youngkyung, Amanda Y, Jocelyn, Jerome, Jaquari, Jarell, Joan & Kenneth (Jessy, Kyle, Kingsley, Jayde), Kelly & Phil, and Fatima & Mario. To the Youth and Young Adult Coalition (YYAC) and our divinely God-sent children Evan & Valarie (Aidan) for the mighty move of the Holy Spirit to *"Prepare Ye the Way of the Lord,"* Charlie, Jenny, Brian, Benjamin & Ruthy, Marina, Tania, Bobby, guardian Paul and also parents Thao & Chiely. For the YYAC "Girls Winter Ski Retreat sponsors, supporters, and facilitators - Charlene, Patrick, Allen Gordon, Sharon Caulfield, Beth Anderson, Patricia Mitchell, Laura Coolbaugh, Avalon, Kim, Janine, Duke Bradley, Ricky Velez, and so many others.

To my bridegroom, Prince Charming Kenneth, thank you for receiving me the day God presented me mysteriously to you during "the crisis project." Your strength to love me makes me for a better woman and wife that I am becoming. And of course, to the one who is responsible for your life, our loving centenarian 100-year old mother, Indiana Whitley, who lovingly welcomed and received me as your daughter.

To the meticulous staff of Westbow Publishing Jona Tate, Venus Gamboa, Anna and the Editorial Team, DeeAnna May, Teri Watkins, and Peter Le and the team of others.

We are in the Final Act, says the Lord!
To God be the Glory!

The beautiful thing about learning is that no one can take it away from you.
—B. B. King

The best teacher is the one whose life is the textbook.[1]

A Pastoral Greeting

A messenger of Jesus Christ and a helper of humankind ... Greetings to all God's children, all His daughters, girls, and young women everywhere in all the states in America and in countries around the world that I have either visited or lived in—Massachusetts, Maryland, Virginia, Ohio, Colorado, California, Japan, Texas, Alabama, Louisiana, Mississippi, Germany, Michigan, Illinois, Washington D.C., Bermuda, Bahamas, St. Maarten, Saint Thomas, Korea, Philippines, France, Czech Republic, Austria, Poland, Hungary, Aruba, Florida, Georgia, Hawaii, Kentucky, New Hampshire, Maine, Rhode Island, Connecticut, New York, Arizona, Pennsylvania, Israel, and beyond.

Dearest daughters, you are very special to God. This pastoral letter is written to you in order *that I may fulfill the ministry that I have received in the Lord* (Colossians 4:17 ESV). It is time to testify to the truth about what I know concerning girls and women. Our identity is formed in Christ Jesus, alone. God created you. God loves you. God chose you. God values you. You belong to God and you are one of His very special daughters,

> *God knew what he was doing from the very beginning. He decided from the outset to shape the lives of those who love him along the same lines as the life of his Son. The Son stands first in the line of humanity he restored. We see the original and intended shape of our lives there in Him. After God made that decision of what His children should be like, he followed it up by calling people by name. After he called them by name, he set them on a solid basis with Himself. And then, after getting them established, he stayed*

with them to the end, gloriously completing what He had begun (Romans 8:29, 30 NLT).

God is calling you to enter into a relationship with Him according to the Holy Bible. On a flight from Los Angeles to Boston during the summer of 2010, I was thoroughly interviewed by the woman sitting in the seat next to the window, where I usually like to sit when traveling. I shared with her how the high school my nephew graduated from was very accommodating to teenage girls and new mothers, unlike what I was familiar with seeing while growing up in public schools. In her questioning, I found by the end of the conversation that I had disclosed to a stranger a snapshot of my life's story. She encouraged me to write the book. She and I actually brainstormed on various titles for the book focus on the call to action, while also giving me names of prominent people I should connect with. Interestingly enough, she was the third person within two weeks to confirm it was time for me to write my story. I knew within my heart that this was the Lord's prompting and that I should obey and not be afraid. It was clear that God was giving me an urgent call to action. Finally, she disclosed, after giving her name, that she was a former television anchorwoman. No wonder she was able to get me to talk.

Your mere survival is at stake! With all the mixed messaging, pressures, abuses, temptations, relationship barriers, external stresses, and inner spiritual yearnings, girls and young women around the world are facing today, our Heavenly Father is calling His daughters back to Him. He is the transformer of *hurt, broken, rejected, wounded, neglected, fatherless, and motherless* daughters. This is why, more than ever before, our Creator is sounding the clarion call for His daughters to no longer be afraid, unsure, doubtful, guilt-stricken, and silenced.

Therefore, I am writing this pastoral letter to certify the truth about your identity according to the Bible and based on research, observations, and experiences from my own life. *"Jesus Christ is the way and the truth and the life and no one come to the Father except through Him"* (John 14:6 NIV). By reflecting on my own life, I am sharing with you the *truth* revealed to me about our identity. In knowing the truth, the truth sets us free. Our true identity is found in Jesus Christ alone. He is the living Son of God our Creator and Heavenly Father.

In every girls' DNA is her desire to be loved and to give love. God created you that way. He has established a divine order and purpose for how we are to be in relationship with Him, His Son Jesus Christ and other human beings. Since human beings were separated from God by an act of disobedience, we will discover how to gain direct access back to Him and the significance of your relationship with His Son. God created, chose, and purposed you to become His image-bearer just like His first-born Son Jesus Christ.

With that said and because *God does not show favoritism* (Romans 2:11 NIV), this is my loving assignment from God to edify, encourage, equip, and empower you to become all that He created you to be. You were made for love, affection, affirmation, acceptance, and support in committed relationships. Your first love relationship, other than with your parents and family, should be with God and second with all others. When you understand yourself, you will also better understand who you are and connect with others.[2] By knowing you are loved, you are valued, and you belong to God is the key to having positive self-esteem and be in healthy relationships with family and others at school, church, and the community. Your identity and real love are not found nor can it be found in any human girl-boy or girl-girl relationships. Researchers Josephs, Markus, and Tafarodi prove that positive self-esteem is the result of healthy relationships.[3] A lack of positive self-esteem and healthy relationships can affect your growth and thwart your dreams.

At this pivotal time in your life, you are growing, maturing, learning, and having fun dreaming about your future. God knows all the intricate details about your life. He is the one gently pursuing you to be in a relationship with Him and waiting for your response to His gentle "woos."

God has a special destiny for your life. His heart is reaching out to your heart for you to discover how special, royal, and valuable you are. The more you are self-aware of your basic and complex needs, the more likely you will be able to identify and find the sources to meet those needs for love in positive ways.

The Holy Bible is the foundation of Truth. There are 66 books of the Bible full of wisdom and knowledge. The Bible reveals the most beautiful story of God's *everlasting love*. The Bible guides and leads us to live right, have right relationships, and make right decisions with the love that God has instilled within our hearts. Therefore, by opening up the Holy Bible and discovering all of God's promises to you is the path to inner discovery about your female uniqueness. I believe the words of the Apostle Paul written in 2 Timothy 3:16, 17 (NIV): *"All Scripture is God-breathed and is useful for teaching, rebuking, correcting and training in righteousness, that the man (person) of God may be perfect, thoroughly furnished unto all good works."*

Each chapter in this book conveys a biblical, theological, and practical focus on the person and work of Jesus Christ in our personal lives.

Chapter One is the first discovery of knowing God's love. "Am I a Statistic? Who Am I?" exploring where and how our self-esteem originates from family relationships. Statistics can affect the way a girl positively or negatively sees herself. Who you are as female is not based on what others have reported in statistics.

Chapter Two is the second discovery of God's love by understanding He created you His image-bearer. "Who Am I? Growing Up Loved in a Traditional Family" is important in helping you to understand why you do what you do and knowing the source of your limitations. In traditional family relationships with two parents and siblings you will find and understand self-esteem, ethnic identity, and the effects of birth order in living your life. God's love for you is special. The biblical author of Isaiah writes about those He calls His.

> *That's how much you mean to me!*
> *That's how much I love you!*
> *I'd sell off the whole world to get you back,*
> *trade the creation just for you.*
> *(Isaiah 43:4 The Message Bible [MSG])*

Chapter Three is the third discovery of God's love with the question of "Who Am I? Growing Up Loved in a Single-Parent Family." God's love is also revealed in non-traditional families (i.e. separation, divorce) and how remarriage and blended-family relationship dynamics play out.

Chapter Four is the fourth discovery of belonging to God and finding "What's Right with Me? Love and Girlfriend Relationships," is about how God reveals His love in female friendships. You were created to belong in your girlfriend connections with peers and BFFs (best friends forever). The three areas of focus in these relationships are comparison, conformance, and competition.

Chapter Five explores the fifth discovery of belonging to God and finding "What's Right with Me? Love and Right Relationships with Boys." In these relationships, girls give their hearts with hopes of marriage. The "friends with benefits" (FWB) fad is a new form of dating. Many girls have been wronged in some way, such as through physical abuse or acquaintance / intimate partner rape. The pain can be healed.

Chapter Six is the sixth discovery of being valued by God in "What's Right with Me? Born with Gifts and Talents." You have purpose. This chapter explores discovering your gifts, talents, and passion, while identifying the dreams of who you will be—bride, wife, mother, athlete, lawyer, engineer, nurse, doctor, or president. Do limitations exist because of some painful past event in your life that is keeping you captive and from reaching your fullest potential? Discover how to rise above the challenges.

Chapter Seven is the seventh discovery being valued by God in your identity as royalty. "You are Special . . . Born into Royalty!" You are beautiful, set apart, and worth fighting for. You belong to God and have stolen His heart. This chapter gives you an understanding of how to grow in dignity and intimacy with God. You were bought for a price. He offers His gift of salvation in Jesus Christ.

Chapter Eight is the eighth discovery of becoming a bride of the bridegroom on earth as it is in heaven. God is the one who sends and presents His chosen mate in "Marriage ... Finally, Here Comes the Bride!" Childhood dreams come true. God designed marriage for companionship between male and female and Himself.

At the end of each of the eight chapters, I pray you will read and meditate on the words in the love letters from our Heavenly Father, God and be drawn to a deeply intimate relationship with Him. As Jesus prayed to His Father about you and me, *"I have given them the glory you gave me, so that they may be one as we are one. I am in them and you are in Me. May they experience such perfect unity that the world will know you sent me and you love them as much as you love me"* (John 17:22-23 NLT). This is also my prayer for us.

You will also have the opportunity at the end of each chapter to apply what you read. Please take the time to complete the self-discovery and self-reflection activities and questions, while creating your own vision board for your life. Therefore, you will need a poster board, ruler, glue, colorful pens, pencils, scissors, color construction paper, magazines, your photo album, and the Holy Bible. Invite your mother or a close adult female friend you admire to join you to both chat and share your reflections and responses to each question. The questions are designed to encourage you to take the lead on becoming self-aware and developing your inner self with the love and help of God. It requires examining how you see yourself and exploring your individual personality, personal interests, dreams, values, and beliefs. Therefore, seize the opportunity now to know, grow, and trust God's call to be in a relationship with His Son Jesus Christ and discovering your identity.

Finally, the epilogue is written for all the women parents, counselors, teachers, mentors, pastors, therapists, social workers, physicians, probation officers and all others, who are in daily contact with girls. The time is now. Our girls need the love and mentoring of other women and daughters of God, to learn and experience God's love through you. As God reveals His love to you personally, He will also express His love to the girls through mature women, such as yourselves.

In summary, the goal of this book is to provide understanding that will motivate girls and women to build healthy relationships with our Creator God, with yourself, and with others. Because before the day each one of us was born, our Heavenly Father had His eyes on all of His daughters, young girls and mature women. You were born in this world female and special for a reason. You are His masterpiece, born to be loved and to give love. God's divine purpose for all His children is to be prepared to return to our Heavenly home, to live with Him forever. All will hear of *"... the sounds of joy and gladness, the voices of the Bride and Bridegroom, and the voices of those who bring thank offerings to the house of the Lord, saying, "Give thanks to the Lord Almighty, for the Lord is good; His love endures forever"* (Jeremiah 33:11 NIV).

My prayerful hope is that the following pages will accomplish what the Lord intended for you to know about the significance of a relationship with Him. By writing this book, I testify the same as the Apostle John. *"He (she) testifies to what he (she) has seen and heard, but no one accepts his (her) testimony. The man (woman) who has accepted it has certified that God is truthful. For the one whom God has sent speaks the words of God, for God gives the spirit without limit. The Father loves the Son and has placed everything in His hands. Whoever believes in the Son has eternal life, but whoever rejects the Son will not see life, for God's wrath remains on him (her)"* (John 3:31–36 NIV).

This is my prayer for you:

Eternal God, our Heavenly Father, speak to Your daughter's heart and open her mind to understand what You are saying to her as she reads this book and what is recorded in Your Holy Scriptures. May she surrender to You and become all that You have created her to be. May all Your girls, regardless of age, ethnicity, hopes and dreams, hear You speak and receive Your gift of everlasting love from the pages of this book, the life of the author, and the Holy Bible by the power of the Holy Spirit. In Jesus' Holy and precious name, I pray. *Amen*!

Please pray this prayer aloud for yourself:

Heavenly Father, open my eyes to see You, my ears to hear You, my heart to know You, and my mind to understand what You are speaking to me through your Holy Spirit. Give me the desire to know You, to receive Your unconditional love, and to live out what You reveal to me. I need Your strength and will to seek a closer personal relationship with You. I pray I will be transformed by the power of Your Truth in what You reveal to me about me and the renewing of my mind and surrendering of my heart to You! *Amen*!

He will give a beauty for ashes, a joyous blessing instead of mourning, festive praise instead of despair!
—Isaiah 61:3 (NLT)

My Beloved is Mine and I am his.
—Song of Solomon 2:16 (NIV)

And without faith it is impossible to please God, because anyone who comes to Him must believe that He exists and that He rewards those who earnestly seek Him.
—Hebrews 11:6 (NIV)

INTRODUCTION

Becoming His Bride on Earth as it is in Heaven

It was a day to be remembered. A cold, wintery day in March in our nation's capital, her Prince Charming had arrived to join his bride in holy matrimony. Prayers were answered. Her dream was now becoming reality. Invited guests entered the sanctuary, were escorted and seated, and waited attentively for the ceremony to begin. All final wedding touches were completed. Musicians softly playing festive music in the background signaled the start of the ceremony. Parents were escorted to their seats by ushers to the music of Sebastian Bach, with "Jesu, Joy of Man's Desiring." At the front of the church along with the officiating pastor, stood Prince Charming with his nine groomsmen in black tuxedos and red bowties. With the Chancel Mass choir and soloist singing gospel love songs, liturgical dancers dancing, the ceremony began. Anticipation heightened as the bridal party led by the bride's sisters and matrons of honor Teresa and Michele and the seven other bride attendants strolled down the aisle in their red chiffon and sequined semi-formal dresses, while clutching their floral bouquets. Simone, the cute little flower girl nervously sprinkling rose petals on the runner for the bride.

Then a quiet pause was interrupted with an announcement. In their little-men tuxedos, both her six- and five-year-old nephews, Robert and Jaylon, paraded down the aisle, excitedly ringing bells with the six-year-old shouting to the top of his lungs, "The bride is coming! The bride is coming!" (The plan was for him to say, "Here comes the bride!").

The guests smiled as they stood to their feet for the grand entrance of the bride. Turning their faces to the center aisle and to the back of the church, the double-glass doors swung open at the sound of the bridal march "Real Love" sung by her line sister. The Bride dressed in a beautiful white mermaid-style wedding gown with a long veil and flowing train gracefully strolled down the aisle holding her father's left arm. Prince Charming made eye contact and gave her an affirming smile. The officiating Pastor asked, "Who gives this woman to be married to this man? "Her mother and I do," said her father. As she was given to the groom, the teary-eyed bride nervously grasped her groom's hand and proceeded to rhythmically brush his hand with her thumb throughout the entire ceremony.

Finally, they were making marriage vows before Almighty God and a host of witnesses from family, relatives, friends, co-workers, and bosses who traveled many miles to celebrate this joyous occasion. The bride and groom knew God had sent them to each other. It was a testament to the love in the air. *"I am my beloved's and my beloved is mine"* (Song 6:3).

The pastor stated, "Repeat after me: I, Kenneth, take you, Sandra, to be my beloved wife, and I, Sandra, take you, Kenneth (aka Whit), to be my beloved husband, to have and to hold from this day forward, for better or for worse, for richer or for poorer, in sickness and in health, to love and to cherish; from this day forward until death do us part."

He said, "I will." She said, "I will."

The Pastor then extended the invitation to the married guest couples, to come forward and join the newlyweds, Kenneth and Sandra at the altar, as they renew their marriage vows. As the ceremony was about to conclude, everyone gleefully waited for the sealing of the vows with the pronouncement of Mr. and Mrs., the kiss, and the jumping of the broom. The celebratory recessional was filled with joy by the choir with the couple making their grand exit under the six-man saber-bearers' arch.

Oh, what a day of rejoicing! God fulfilled His promise the bride's dream came true! He sent her the mate He chose for her. He was the right one, and she knew it. After their first date, as a reminder, God placed a rainbow in the sky to confirm what He had promised nine years before. Blushing while surrounded by love and hugs from family and friends. One commented, "You are a beautiful bride."

Despite the years of heartbreaks, broken and counterfeit relationships, and for each time she got impatient, she realized she would have missed this glorious blessing. In the moment, her flashbacks reminded her of the benefit of trusting God and what it means to *"Wait for the Lord; be strong and take heart and wait for the Lord"* (Psalm 27:14 NIV).

This was a remarkable and memorable day of unspeakable joy. This day, she was so very glad she finally gave the desires of her heart over to the Lord God and trusted Him to perform just what He said He would do. The bride and groom's real love was sealed on their wedding day. And God's unfailing love towards her and the groom made her feel very special. The song "Real Love," written by recording artist Kirk Franklin, expresses it all:

> Will you ever love somebody
> The way that Jesus loves you
> Over and over I ask myself
> Could there ever be anyone else …

Who would have imagined the bride had almost prematurely entered into marriage many years prior? *"Do not be anxious about anything, but in everything, by prayer and petition, with thanksgiving, present your requests to God" (Philippians 4:6 NIV).* Now the following pages are the rest of the story about how our Heavenly Father prepares all His daughters for *Becoming His Bride on Earth as it is in Heaven …*

Part One

You Are Loved by God, Our Relationship with God and Family and Its Purpose

*Do not put your faith in what statistics say until you
have carefully considered what they do not say.*
—William W. Watt

Have Faith in God, Jesus answered.
—Mark 11:22 (NIV)

Now faith is being sure of what we hope for and certain of what we do not see.
—Hebrews 11:1 (NIV)

CHAPTER 1

Who Am I? Am I a Statistic?

God's love for you is with purpose. You were born to be in relationships. And in those relationships, there is one key ingredient that your heart desires. It is *love!* You may have heard or possibly read about girls and their personal image and the negative outcomes of relationships in classes at school or college, seen on pop-ups on your phone or social media blogs, or even watched the television news or from following the #MeToo Movement. Most likely, the negative reporting is the result of a girls' broken heart and the love she once experienced or needed was gone... leaving her feeling rejected and abandoned.

Do you know of girls who were abandoned, rejected, and separated from their parents after their divorce or separation from each other? What about a family member who wrongfully treated a child and how the child ultimately acted out? Have you heard about a teenage girl who got pregnant and her boyfriend denied it or broke off the relationship and left her? Have you heard of a classmate who dropped out of school or committed suicide because she was mistreated and bullied by classmates or adults? Do you know of a classmate who was alienated by her peers because of a mental illness that caused her to act out with unacceptable behavior? You may also see or hear negative messages about peers who experienced rejection or separation from their parents by government officials or abandoned by their parents and placed in foster care, a juvenile detention center, or jail. What about the classmate whose boyfriend treated her violently in what is called date, acquaintance or intimate partner rape? Or you know of another teenage girl who does not like her body image, which causes her to either over-eat or under-eat and get sick.

Usually, the real cause and effect of the examples mentioned are not readily available from research. However, what we can find is statistics about girls and their lifestyle of low self-esteem, drugs, alcohol, gang involvement, violence, prostitution, and misguided promises by others. Such as boys or men who promise a better life that leaves her defenseless and possibly a victim of human trafficking.

Whatever the circumstances, girls tend to start forming ideas about who they are based on what they have either seen, read, heard about other girls or by no fault of their own have experienced on a personal and first-hand basis.

You may be thinking, yes, I can relate to one or more of these examples. Or on the other hand you may be thinking, no, I cannot personally relate to any of these examples. Whether you can or cannot, it is only the beginning of your life's journey. God cares and knows every detail about you. God wants you to search for Him and the meaning of your life. By discovering who He is, you will find love and come to trust God and experience His unconditional love. And by trusting in God, you will know He is always there for you no matter what.

You are a girl, whether you are born of a specific ethnic group, such as African, Latino, Asian, Indian, Pacific Islander, Native, or Caucasian, or a combination of various ethnic groups and cultures. And because of these variations of a girl's ethnicity and identity, the social and behavioral outcomes are usually negatively reported in statistics. Why? Because researchers only have pieces of data, which is usually negative. Negative data can influence how girls see themselves and how others see and respond to them.

Societal Views about Differences

Girls must become self-aware in order to understand what is going on within themselves and also with other girls. The first stage of identity awareness and self-esteem development is found in our family of origin. The process does not happen overnight or automatically. In fact, looking back over my life self-identity and the awareness of my ethnic identity evolved in phases. While a lot depends on what is going on in society at the time, the challenges, obstacles, trials, and tribulations are a normal part of life. But the way one responds to, reacts to, and internalizes their feelings is how character is built.

Being born the first daughter of a light-brown-skinned mother who attended segregated schools in Alabama and also a dark-brown-skinned father from Mississippi began the journey of my self-esteem and my ethnic identity in a society of negative social and behavioral outcomes. My mother, Lucy, is the third born of seven sisters and brothers who attended a segregated minority high school in Alabama. She met my Dad, Otha, at her high school football game. He was a young military man assigned to the military base in Montgomery, who was also a former football athlete. Standing at the gate of the stadium, he spotted this pretty majorette in the marching Wolverines band making their exit from the field. Lucy was looking good in her majorette outfit, stepping high and twirling her baton. After the game, everybody met at the Garden Patio restaurant. He gave the waitress a note, asking Lucy to come over to where he was. After chatting for a period of time and getting her name, he asked for her phone number, but she would not give it to him. She told him she was not allowed to date. He did not give up trying. After getting her phone number from her friend, he kept calling her.

Lucy was raised with both her father and mother in the home until her teenage years. One day, nervous Otha took a chance and went to her home where he met her mother, Jessie. She asked him a few questions to get to know a bit more about him. Before she would finally agree to let them go out on dates, she shared a few words of caution. She added to her stern words, that if anything happened to her daughter, he would be responsible for taking care of her. In their southern culture it was the norm for parents to be strict and protective of their daughters. The young Otha, a southerner from Mississippi was polite and a gentleman. He made a good impression on her. Grandmother believed he had a promising future. She then consented to her daughter dating him.

Otha's tour of duty came to an end. His next assignment was to a military base in Alaska. He had to leave his girlfriend behind in Alabama. Then one day he received a phone call with the news that Lucy was pregnant. He quickly took a leave of absence and flew back to Montgomery to take responsibility for their actions. He did not deny that Lucy was the mother of his child. In those days, the young man was expected to marry the mother of his child. The two were married on March 17th in the home of the bride.

The school system did not permit girls to continue their education while pregnant or even after the child was born. Lucy dropped out of her junior year of high school at the age of sixteen. The good news ... born to their union was a healthy seven-pound baby girl. The nurse at St. Jude Catholic Hospital asked, "What will be her name?" The couple was undecided about a name. The nurse began asking a series of questions that got them thinking about name possibilities suitable for their firstborn. They decided on the name Sandra. Later, I discovered my name meant "helper/defender of humankind."

Like my loving parents, my siblings and me entered a world of negative influences, such as prejudice, hatred, segregation, and injustice (two months before the civil rights movement began). However, with the love and nurturing of our parents, the affects were not as evident to their children as it was to them trying to raise and care for us. But God only knew the challenges of this ethnic group of people and in His timing Rosa Parks would have the strength and courage to become a trailblazer and hero. After a long day of work, Rosa Parks made the decision to not comply with the stereotype labeled her ethnic identity. The bus was filled to capacity and there were no remaining seats left in the white section for a white male passenger. She knew what was expected, to give up her seat in the front of the black section of the city bus, but this time she was just too tired to give up her seat for him. This was also not the first time she had been asked to move, and she complied. But this time was different, she chose not to comply.

Behavior and the Effect of Statistics

As a result of Rosa Parks' actions and the timing of an all-knowing God, He brought to the attention of America a young man named Reverend Dr. Martin Luther King Jr. The young 26 years old preacher and pastor Dr. King stepped up to the crisis and challenged the status quo to gain justice and equality for all peoples. Dr. King became the leader God chose to come to the aid of Rosa Parks and thus began the civil rights movement of liberty and justice for all those oppressed.

If the LORD delights in a man's (woman's) way, he makes his (her) steps firm; though he (she) stumble, he (she) will not fall, for the LORD upholds him (her) with his hand. (Psalm 37:23–24).

During the movement, Dr. King's dream was to bring equality and justice to all people, no matter the skin color. He led by example. He taught his followers the "strength to love" through non-violent actions.

Now married, the young sixteen-year-old Lucy and twenty-year-old Otha birthed five children into this world over a six- year period. The societal and behavioral outcomes are summed up in research data called statistics. The Oxford dictionary defines *statistic* as (1) a fact or piece of data from a study of a large quantity of numerical data or (2) an event or person regarded as no more than a piece of data. And the term *statistics* is the science of collecting, analyzing, and making inferences from that data.

A decade of statistics reflect that brown and black African and Latina girls are more than twice as likely as white girls to become pregnant in their adolescent years. Although teen pregnancies do occur and are not planned, researchers suggest that the usual causes are due more to racial and ethnic disparities than to religious or socioeconomic differences, such as poverty or where they live. Some researchers also report that the causes <u>may</u> be due to a lack of reproductive education and access to contraceptives.[4]

Statistics also revealed from another source based on a 2013 report about teenagers of African and Latina descent, girls are three times more likely than their white peers to get pregnant and have babies. What the research data does not include are responses to the questions: As it relates to the matters of the heart, do the girls and boys—young and old—(even with sex education) know how to abstain sexually and not confuse sex with love? Who is teaching girls and boys the difference between friendships or platonic relationships with each other and how to recognize adolescent amorous desires? Who is teaching girls to recognize their need to be loved and give love that will help them distinguish between healthy relationships and issues of the heart?

Statistics also revealed in an article written by Teresa Wiltz about teen pregnancy that 19 births per 1,000 among non–Hispanic teens is less than that compared to 39 births per 1,000 among African-American teens.[5] And the 42 births per 1,000 among Latina teens compared to the 31 births per 1,000 among Native-American teens. Other researchers from America's Promise found that teen pregnancy is the reason 30 percent of teenage girls drop out of high school.

Statistical data that draws conclusions based on ethnic identity is not as beneficial as understanding the differences between male and female behaviors in relationships. According to the Oxford dictionary, ethnic identity is defined as a category of people who identify with each other based on similarities such as common ancestry, language, history, society, culture, or nation. Ethnic identity, I believe should be the term used for describing people groups versus the word race. Because there is only one race of people who all have the same color of blood, that is—the human race.

Why and what is the purpose of all the comparisons based on skin color, race, or ethnic identity? These statistics imply my parents' teenage pregnancy and my mother dropping out of high school will become a trend with their children. What we should learn from statistics is what William Watt advises in his quote, *"Do not put your faith in what statistics say until you have carefully considered what they do not say."* What *are* the factors and what can be done to eliminate the probability of statistical data becoming a trend in any family or ethnic group?

Naturally, a girl's skin color has no bearing on how a girl's mind and heart responds to love or rejection. Therefore, what does statistics have to do with growing up and becoming the girl God purposed her to be? "Am I not more than a piece of data" and "how should I carefully consider what statistics do not say?" What are statistics inferring about me?

Because the Bible reminds us of the real issue. God shows no favoritism. God will accept every nation of people who fear Him and do what is right (Acts 10:34 NLT). Because *"the heart is deceitful above all things and beyond cure. Who can understand it?" (Jeremiah 17:9 NIV). "For from within, out of men's hearts, come evil thoughts, sexual immorality, theft, murder, adultery, greed, malice, deceit, lewdness, envy, slander, arrogance and folly" (Mark 7:21,22 NIV).* Therefore, creating statistics by ethnic group will not help the plight in America amongst our girls and boys. When feelings of love are mixed with their emotions, then the ability to reason is overpowered, especially during the puberty stages of their sexuality development. Understanding this fact will help boys and girls to heed the strong biblical instruction *"not to awaken love until the time is right." (Song of Solomon 2:7, 3:5, 8:4 NLT).* It is important for boys and girls to wait by being intentional about developing an intimate relationship because the feelings alone are not enough to have a lasting relationship of love and commitment.

Relationship Roles & The Impact on Self-Esteem

The key to healthy relationships is to become positive, courageous, and confident girls and women. It may seem difficult to achieve based on statistics, such as the ones identified in the article on "A Generation at Risk" conducted by the Step-family Association. The two types of families are traditional and non-traditional. In the twenty-first century, 68.7 percent of American children are living in non-traditional families, meaning not living with both birth mother and birth father but raised by a foster or adopted parents, grandparents, or guardians. Why? According to the Step-Family Association, about 23.3 percent of American youth are living with their biological mother, 4.4 percent of American youth are living with their biological father, and 30 percent are living in blended or stepfamilies.[6] And the U.S. Census Bureau reports 6.3 percent of American youth are living with grandparents, 1 percent are living in foster families, and 3.7 percent are living with non-relatives.[7]

On the other hand, none of these statistics include the traditional two-parent families. A traditional family is a group of people consisting of a father, a mother, and children living together in the same household.

Why may children end up repeating the same patterns and behaviors as their parents? How did the breakdown in their relationships occur? Relationships play a critical role in a child's formation and personal development, which has less to do with skin color. The quality of our relationships impacts the very core of our being. They affect our social development and how we feel about ourselves on into adulthood.[8]

By relationships, I mean a situation where two or more people are involved. A relationship develops based on the way those two or more people or things are connected and how they behave towards each other, which also includes the emotional association between them either by blood or marriage.

Relationships affect your self-esteem and ethnic identity, either negatively or positively. The relationship with yourself, with your parents and family (sisters and brothers), with peers, classmates, girlfriends, teachers, boyfriends, and those who come into your life for a season contribute to the way you feel about yourself. Your feelings, thoughts, and behaviors change according to the various relationships you are in and have been involved in. Therefore, positive influences are the key foundational ingredient to healthy self-esteem and ethnic identity.

Again, your first relationship is with your family. Family is pivotal to you understanding how you see yourself. Whether you are raised by both of your birth parents (traditional family) or raised by foster or adopted parents, grandparents, or guardians (non-traditional), the family is the first relationship you become aware of your identity. Are you adopted? The tagline for Troy Dunn's television show, *The Locator* is "you cannot find peace until you find all the pieces."

Family is the first place you decide that you are lovable and capable. When love is not in the family line, girls can be influenced by their peers and engage in behavior that may leave a lasting effect on their lives. This may spiral into low self-esteem. Low self-esteem affects growth and hinders dreams, especially if she feels rejected, unlovable, inadequate and incapable.

Family is where you receive your sense of belonging and connectedness. Family is where you are exposed to the first-hand knowledge about your Heavenly Father, who is God and the one who created you. Family is the process of where you become more aware of your identity as you think about who you are, decide who you are, and define who you are. By recognizing your own individual potential and qualities as an individual, even in a social context,[9] you understand your gender identity of being female and are comfortable in your ethnic identity as well, even if you are biracial or multiracial. This can be a good thing because you really have the best of both worlds, so to speak.

Parents teach how to choose the right way and make sound decisions with hopes you will remain on the right path. It is very important for you to develop a positive relationship with family and God first at home. In order, to grow up and become an adult woman, professional, wife, mother, and/or grandmother,[10] having positive self-esteem is the key to having healthy relationships. And healthy relationships are the key to positive self-esteem.

Your need to be loved is real because God designed you to have His nature. God is love. This is why getting to know who you are through the eyes of God, your family, and others are critical in your life. Love is a strong feeling of affection.[11] Children are born in purity and innocence to receive unconditional love from parents and family. This begins the journey of family love. Our whole being revolves around the love we experience in our own family, from God, and in other relationships. As we grow up, our personality and behavior begin taking form after one or the other parent or even another person in our family line.

Am I Just a Statistic–Self-Esteem

The alarm is sounded. There is a national self-esteem crisis in America. The Dove Self-Esteem Fund wrote a report called *Real Girls, Real Pressure: A National Report on the State of Self-Esteem*, exploring online data taken from 1,029 girls between eight and seventeen,[12] which revealed a number of interesting findings. What does it mean that 68 percent of teenage African-American girls feel they do not measure up in some way because of how they feel about their looks, performance in school, and relationships with family and friends? As a result, 50 percent of teenage Caucasian girl's report engaging in negative activities, such as disordered eating, cutting, bullying, smoking, or drinking, and only 41 percent of teenage African-American girls do. Then there is the 40 percent of teenage Caucasian girls who admit to talking badly about themselves when only 28 percent of teenage African-American girls do.

Also, according to researchers' pieces of data, the percentage rises remarkably higher to 95 percent among African-American teenage girls with low self-esteem. Because they want their parents to change their behavior toward them in at least one way, such as understanding them more, listening to them more, and spending more time with them. Even with the 42 percent who have mothers who criticize their own looks, 86 percent of girls in the age range of eight to twelve years old turn to their mothers as a resource when feeling bad compared to 53 percent in the age range of thirteen to seventeen. Does this data include the facts about how slavery and oppression affected a generation of minority females before the civil rights movement and its' subsequent effect on girls and their relationships with their mothers?

Yet only 22 percent of the girls in the age range of thirteen to seventeen will go to their fathers for help when feeling bad about themselves. But about 28 percent of the girls are more likely to go to their fathers in the age range of eight to twelve. By the time a girl turns sixteen years old, she is more likely to seek support from male peers, but not from her own father. Is it because the father no longer lived under the same roof as his daughter or was no longer in her life, which could possibly mean the father was not readily accessible to her to go to for that support?

According to researchers again, regardless of the age, teenage African-American girls are significantly less likely than their Caucasian counterparts to turn to their parents as a resource when feeling bad. This is perhaps related to why the increase in the numbers of African-American teenage girls who wish their parents would listen to them more.[13] Or could it be deeper than that? Does it depend on the generation your parents were born into? Or, as I believed, could it be the fear of what a parent might do to the other person so the parent is not told? Interestingly enough, girls may be living with negative side effects of their parents. As far back as slavery in this country or as recent as those migrating to this country from other nations, there are generations of negativity toward people of color. This affects our young girls because of what has been or not been instilled in them about their ethnic identity. Therefore, it may possibly become a factor in low or negative self-esteem.

What is the message from statistics?

In the twenty-first century, it is hard to understand the deeply rooted negativity about people of color. Statistics reveal a high percentage of girls with negative attitudes about themselves. In past generations the ethnic barriers our parents and grandparents endured may not include the love we all crave and were created to give. Love has no skin color. And girls do not have to repeat the cycle of their parents' past. The statistics only give a negative view of all the possibilities toward a positive you. Remember informed change and self-awareness is transforming.

What does the statistics not say? God loves everyone very much. He created us with no limitations, therefore, search for meaning to life and a desire to be in a relationship with Him. Girls raised with parents fully self-aware of the God who is love will learn to live a life in healthy relationships with others and no skin color limitations.

The Bible from the very first book of Genesis and continuing to the very last book of Revelation tells the story of God's love for us. He tells us the whole truth about our identity. Positive family relationships also consist of developing a relationship with God. The whole purpose for your life is to bring glory to God and to enjoy being in a relationship with Him forever. Your relationship with Him is just as critical and pivotal to your personal development and growth with your earthly family relationship. God created you to be in relationships because *"in the beginning God created the heavens and earth, and every creature and human being in His image. He created them, male and female, He created them"* (Genesis 1:26, 27). We will address in the next chapter what it means to be made in the image of God?

In conclusion, statistics about girls from the definition of "no more than a piece of data" suggests that if you come from a certain family, if you were raised a certain way, if you feel a certain way about yourself, if you are of a certain ethnic group, and if you live in a certain location, you are likely to do something negative versus something positive with your life. However, a girl's dream and subconscious desire is to be in relationships where she is loved and can freely give the love that Creator God intended her to give. It does not matter about the challenges my parents personally faced in society or the painful memories of my own past and wrong choices, I found out how to receive God's love and forgiveness. God's love has made me a better person. That is why William Watt's quote, *"Do not put your faith in what statistics say until you have carefully considered what they do not say."*

Statistics, in essence, are not the whole truth. Therefore, how would you answer the question "Who am I? Am I just a statistic?" A self-aware girl responds to the questions with "No, I am not! Is there more to me than a piece of data? Yes, there is!" Because ... I am created in the image and likeness of God (Genesis 1:26, 27). I am one of His image-bearers whom He is preparing to be a bride, beautifully dressed for her bridegroom (Revelation

21:2b). You are *special* to God. Yes, you are special regardless of what statistics reveal ... so carefully consider what they do not say!

- o   no matter what my family is or is not—adopted, foster, orphaned, married, divorced, separated, two-parent or single-parent
- o   no matter what my physical appearance may be ... color of skin, eye color, lip shape and size, body weight, hair type, and so on
- o   no matter how my parents, sisters, brothers, classmates, girlfriends, boyfriends, teachers, or anyone treats me
- o   no matter what is going on in the world or what it looks like—good and bad images
- o   no matter what past mistakes I have made ... wrong thoughts and insecurities about myself, running away from home and leaving my parents, attempted suicide, doubts, inabilities to do all I want, negative attitude, bad grades in school, sexual encounters, abortion, lashing out at school, fighting, stealing from parents or others
- o   no matter what others may do or say—by bullying, lying, maliciously talking about, gossiping, slandering, lashing out in anger
- o   no matter what my family's social status—poor, wealthy, or middle class.

The bottom line is no matter what ... I am a child of God, created in His image and likeness, God loves me, God values me, and it is God to whom I belong. What statistics reveal is of no significance. Why? Because as William Watt's quote reminds us to make our own affirmation that, *I will not put my faith in what statistics say (or what others say) until I have carefully considered what they do not say.* This is a good point of reference in finding our own identity, self-esteem, and ethnic identity.

A Love Letter from Your Heavenly Father

Dearest Daughter,

You are my love child! I am your Heavenly Father, the Creator of the entire universe and all its creation of African-, Asian-, and Caucasian-descent human beings. You were created the gift and reward that I gave to your parents, family, and the world to be loved and to be in a relationship with Me and others! I created you in love to feel, think, and be social as My chosen child to be in relationship with Me.

What the statistics do not say is so much more than what they do say. You were created a masterpiece. I made you in My image and likeness. Uniquely female you were created to be like Me in character and nature, to be safe in relationships, and to be loved with a pure innocence (Genesis 1:26, 27). To all who receive Me and believe in My Son, I named Jesus, I give them the right to become My children not born of natural descent, nor of human decision or a husband's will, but born of Me, your Heavenly Father (John 1:12, 13). That's how much I love you! I'd sell off the whole world to get you back, I'd trade the creation just for you (Isaiah 43:4 MSG). Your inner beauty will shine forth once you discover and understand the depth of the love I have for you. You are not a statistic even if you feel unsure about who loves you, whom you belong to, and how valued you are. You are My daughter by putting your faith in Christ Jesus (Galatians 3:26 NIV).

Now faith is being sure of what you hope for and certain of what you do not see (Hebrews 11:1 NIV). Others may look at your outward appearance and the circumstances which you may have come into this world and see you as a statistic, unloved, rejected, and unworthy, but I know and look at your heart (1 Samuel 16:7). You were created with mental (ability to reason, know right from wrong, thinking, intellect), moral values (love, righteousness, holiness, sanctification, loyalty), and social status (relationships with God and others, in fellowship with other humans). That's why I created you girl, female and boys, male. I, the Lord Your God and Father made male and female. My daughter, you are Mine. You are not a statistic! I love you!

Your Creator God, Amen!

Self-Discovery / Self-Reflection

Application

(1) Note: For all chapters, have a poster board (to use to create your vision), colorful pens, pencils, scissors, a ruler, glue/ tape, colorful construction paper, magazines, your photo album, and a Holy Bible.
(2) Note: For all chapters, invite your mother or a close adult female friend you admire to reflect and chat together about the questions, including the love letters.
(3) Find a photo of yourself as a newborn baby in a family photo, if you have one and put on the board
(4) Look up and write down on your vision board the Bible verses from this chapter that inspired you and use them to also answer the questions.

Thinking About Me: *Who Am I? Am I a Statistic?*

1. "Who Am I?" Write a list of ten character qualities focusing on how God created you in His image and likeness.
___
___

2. What have you learned about God and how He created you to love and be loved? What do you think about God and yourself after reading the love letter?
___
___

3. How do you feel about being born a girl? Do the way others treat you make you feel positive (hopeful) or negative (doubtful) about yourself?
___
___

4. Does statistics imply girls are failures? How will you act with other girls after learning about statistics and the way they may affect them?
___
___

Family is where life begins and love never ends.
—Unknown

Love makes your soul crawl out from its hiding place.
—Zora Neale Hurston

Love is the greatest attribute of God.
—Sunday Adelaja

We know it so well, we've embraced it heart and soul, this love that comes from God. God is love. When we take up permanent residence in a life of love, we live in God and God lives in us.
—1 John 4:16 (MSG)

CHAPTER 2

Who Am I? Growing Up Loved in a Traditional Family

Loved by God

God is love and He is the one who created all to love and to be loved. Love is what makes a girl's heart go pitter-patter. Love is the glue that holds everything together in relationships, until something breaks that bond and wreaks havoc in a girl's heart. The family is the first place you experience what love feels, sounds, and looks like. Every girl's desire is to be loved, be accepted and to love deeply. Love is impressive, beautiful, and just out-of-the-ordinary splendid, brilliant, and magnificent. Love is very good.[14]

Who am I?

This is a good question that we all ask ourselves at some point in time in our lives. First of all, you are loved. You were conceived in love when God made you in your mother's womb (Psalm 139:13). It is not too early for you to ask or even be thinking about it. Asking yourself now "Who am I?" will lessen the likelihood of you relying solely on statistics or what others say or believe about who you are. Being intentional about getting to know yourself means you are self-aware and mindful of your own character, strengths, and limitations. Tuning in to what you feel, think, say, and how you behave is self-awareness. These are reflected in your beliefs, values, moods, habits, dreams, personality traits, likes, and dislikes. It also helps you to recognize your behaviors and feelings toward others. With bullying running rampant in today's society, your own self-awareness will give it no power. You will be less likely to feel rejected and fearful.

Self-Awareness Benefits

Knowing yourself inside and outside is self-awareness. Self-awareness is not a one-time event. From a growing adolescent girl to becoming a healthy woman with positive self-esteem will depend upon you learning to love and live with yourself and being comfortable in your own skin. As your body goes through physical and emotional changes, it is good to tune in to what you are feeling, thinking, saying and how you are behaving. What you discover about yourself helps you to also tune in to the behaviors and the feelings of others.

Growing Up in Two-Parent Household

As we begin receiving love from both our parents, we also learn to give love. Love develops us emotionally and socially therefore developing positive self-esteem in us. To be loved and know we are capable of being loved,[15] this love produces in us our positive mental, physical, and spiritual health.

God purposed for every child to live with both parents in a marriage and family relationship (husband/wife and father/mother). Since the beginning of time, husband and wife, man and woman were expected to increase and multiply in birthing children into their family. Two-parent family relationships definitely have their advantages.[16] Through our parents or guardians, we learn to love and possess values of healthy self-esteem. Families in nurturing relationships live a well-rounded life.

Ethnic Identity- Who Am I?

Our ethnic identity is defined as the way we identify with a particular group and how it affects the thoughts and feelings we have about our membership in a specific ethnic group. Ethnic identity is how you think about who you are, how you perceive and define yourself. Adriana Umana-Taylor found that adolescence is a critical time for growing up in any ethnic group. She furthers emphasizes how in the formative years of adolescence, certain elements are needed for forming your identity[17] that builds positive or negative self-esteem.[18] The way you interact with peers at school, at work, and in the community is also indicative of how you associate with others outside your immediate family. The outcome may be negative or positive self-esteem.

I was yet too young to understand my ethnic identity and the negative perception by others, until one day, while working in an Alabama department store. The first words out of the mouth of a young kid, who came up to me from out of nowhere it seemed and he suddenly looked directly at me, and said, "Uuuugh, you are dirty. My dad said colored people are dirty." Up to that point, I had never heard negative words about myself as a person especially not about the color of my skin.

Having positive self-esteem is critical to reaching the greatness given to you by God. Being born a female of a certain ethnic group with brown skin, to specific parents, is an act of God. He created girls with the characteristics to love and to be loved and to be in relationships with Him and others. We were created with moral characteristics, such as empathy, honesty, integrity, courage, fortitude, loyalty, love, self-control, and others.

Positive or Negative Self-Esteem

Self-esteem is the confidence in your own worth or abilities—self-respect. Self-esteem is what you think and feel overall about yourself that will either result in positive or negative behavior trends.[19] Self-esteem is how you value yourself. Or a product of value we give ourselves as we believe ourselves to be blended with the value we assign to our abilities."[20] It is your sense of your own self-worth, your behavior, and how you relate to other people. Both self-esteem and ethnic identity affects your mental health.

Consequently, as a normal part of growing up is struggling with your own identity, which happens in stages, starting in the home with your family first. The questions we should ask ourselves are "How do I value myself?" or "What do I believe about my identity and my worth?"

The stages of growth development naturally run their course when both your mother and father are in your life. In two-parent families, girls tend to observe everything about both parents. The mother and father both play key roles in the positive development of their daughter from what she believes and how she feels about herself. Your self-esteem evolves from what you observe about how your father treats, responds, or reacts to your mother, his wife, and what you observe about your mother's response to her husband, your dad. By what she says, what she does, and how she attends to her appearance by the clothes and makeup she wears. We are constantly watching and subconsciously trying to figure out who we are and who we will be. While observing family members, we begin to practice how to be the way our parents and siblings are.[21] Can a girl trust her feelings and will she receive attention, be accepted, and affirmed or will she be rejected?

At the heart of our being is self-esteem, whether negative or positive, low or high. Every human being looks at him- or herself from one of two ways, either from a positive or negative viewpoint. Our self-esteem is healthy and positive when we have a sense of belonging, a feeling of individuality, and the ability to choose. All three are necessary, especially in our early personal development. My self-esteem evolved in cycles. The times I felt valued and happiest were with both my parents. All the attention was not on me, but each of us as a family unit. It did not bother me being in the midst of others without talking, but quietly listening and absorbing all that was being said.

Feeling Loved and Valued

God has created us with His spirit. While we traveled in our station wagon car with my parents across the United States, going to new military assignments, Dad made sure we took a detour to visit or be introduced to our relatives. He made sure we knew our extended family of relatives no matter where they lived in the USA. We were a close family. When I won the seat by the window more times than not, I tuned out what was going on around me and found myself daydreaming out the window. The clouds would form certain figures, and I would try to guess what they could be. Many times, I would be thinking about something and then get a peace about it.

We were loved, accepted, and had a sense of belonging, whether at meals, holidays, being tucked in at bedtime, and other special gestures or activities. Family time together was the norm, especially during the time we lived on a military base in Germany. At that time, our family had grown to two sisters (Teresa, Michele) and a brother (Buzzy). We were a family where love was present. According to psychologist Abraham Maslow in his hierarchy of needs theory, when the basic needs are met one feels protected, cared and provided for, then the sense of belongingness and attention is present.

While Dad was stationed in Germany, I was only about seven years old and the only one of school age who learned to speak the German language. Our stay in Germany was one of the most memorable times of my childhood. Positive vibes emanated with love and devotion from our parents. All our memories were about the family times together—watching Mom and Dad together, spending time with them, learning manners, and getting gifts. We were taught to be polite. I remember watching their expressions of joy. Our Christmas was a joyful time, decorating our first live Christmas tree with the fresh pine aroma throughout our home, sipping hot chocolate on Christmas Eve from Mom's handmade and personalized ceramic Santa Claus mugs, opening one gift before going to bed, and being taught how to set the dinner table for military friends visiting our home. During the holidays, or at any time that Mr. Brown, a special friend of the family would visit us, as a part of setting the table, a hand towel was draped over the back of his chair. When asked why a hand towel was on Mr. Brown's chair, Dad explained, that they both loved spicy food and hot sauce. In case Mr. Brown should sweat the hand towel is where he could reach it and wipe his forehead.

Early on Christmas morning, we jumped out of bed and ran to our parents' room to wake them up. It was Christmas morning and time to open our gifts. What happened to the fruit and nuts? None were left in the dish. Santa Claus had been there. Looking all through the living room, we found gifts everywhere and, of course, under the tree. The girls each received large baby dolls and strollers in different colors. The strollers were just like the ones the Germans used for their babies.

With the privilege of Mom being a stay-at-home Mom, she cooked well-balanced meals and tried new recipes despite us being typical kids who did not always like to eat the sweet peas or other vegetables she prepared. Not a day went by without us all sitting at the dinner table, saying our grace before meals and eating a full-course meal together as a family. We were not allowed to leave the dinner table until all our food was eaten from our plates, usually the vegetables, before we would sometimes fall asleep. Seeing that we were not eating it all, we were allowed to eventually leave the table without having eaten everything. We won out!

We enjoyed the winters. We had fun! Our base housing apartment complex had a fenced-in backyard with a hill steep enough for fun snow sledding. One day, my sisters, Teresa (four years old) and Michele (three years old), and me (seven years old at the time), with the help of both our parents, tried out our Christmas gift. We took our new snow sleigh out for a ride down the hill in the back of the base housing apartment building. Of course, I was in front, the oldest, Teresa was in the middle, and Michele was on the back. All bundled up in snow clothing and with a slight push from Dad, off we went down the hill. Wheeeee! Wheeeee! We were having fun until the sled picked up speed.

Oh no, going too fast we needed to slow down and stop. There was a fence and a street ahead. I could not slow down. What should I do? We barely slid right under the fence, but just enough to slow us down to a stop in the nick of time, right before going on the sidewalk into the street with oncoming cars. In haste, my parents rushed down the hill to make sure we were all right. We were fine. With the exception of Teresa (who was sitting in the middle). She got a very slight scratch across her forehead. We were all safe and unharmed, but a little shaken up by it all. Whether we were on or off the military base, the natives were friendly toward us Americans.

Two-Parents and their Children's Social Involvement

One day living in Michigan, all the snow was piled up outside our front door at least five feet high. Wow! Dad could barely open the door. But he managed to shovel us a way out. On another occasion, he made a man-made ice-skating rink for us by hosing down the yard with water to freeze on the side of the house. I cherished my first pair of ice skates. We learned to ice skate, took bowling lessons at the bowling alley on Saturdays and I learned to swim at the base pool. Although, I almost drowned in my swimming class. Once Dad took us to the ocean to swim, but as soon as I saw small guppy fish swimming in the water close to shore, I quickly jumped out. I was surprised to be in the same water with fish, when I had guppy fish for a pet in small fish bowl at home.

My parents signed me up for membership in the 4-H club,[22] where I got my first public debut on television. My parents enrolled us in Vacation Bible School (VBS) at the base chapel. It was so much fun. We learned to read the Bible, memorized verses, and watched Christian films at VBS about the life of Jesus Christ.

The most memorable scene in the film remains in my mind and heart to this day. With everything leading up to Jesus being whipped, punished, and nailed to the cross for our sins, I cried. Tears came streaming down my face, while I silently said, "Why? He did not do anything wrong." Then on the third day, Jesus arose from the dead. His death was not the end of the story. By the time I was ten years old, I had received my first Bible in the New American Standard (NAS) translation, while attending the chapel Vacation Bible School.

We were living the American dream. We were the traditional family with mother, father, and their five children. Dad was serious about providing for his family. Dad had a secure job with plans of one day retiring and owning our own home. Dad and Mom planned our future, which definitely included us graduating from high school and going to college. At the age of nine, Dad's Mom died. Growing up without his birth mom or living the American dream may have been the reason why my Mom was a stay-at-home mom. She was able to be at home and take care of us. *"If anyone does not provide for his relatives, and especially for members of his household, he has denied the faith and is worse than an unbeliever"* (1 Timothy 5:8 ESV).

Dad financially provided for and protected us, as the Bible commands. Mom was the perfect mother. She was skilled in being a great housekeeper, keeping everything clean and organized, an excellent cook, interior decorator, crocheter, and a thrifty and frugal seamstress/clothing maker, either making her own clothes and saving up to get us that nice outfit. Naturally, observing Mom's ability to use her hands and create anything from scratch, I learned to sew. She was a quick learner, and once she saw something she liked, she taught herself how to do it. It seemed that there was nothing she could not do. Mom was very outgoing, personable, fun, generous, well-put-together in her physical appearance, neat, and clean. She loved fashion and was known for being very well-dressed. She dressed us for school, cooked and fed us three meals a day, made sure our homework was done and kept the home clean. We ate breakfast and dinner meals together. It was not unusual to find in our school lunch boxes my favorite sandwich made with mustard, Teresa's with mayonnaise, and Michele's with ketchup with other goodies and a toothbrush and toothpaste to brush our teeth after lunch.

When I was about 10 years old, my Mom taught us to roller skate in an indoor roller-skating rink when we were living in Illinois. The packed rink full of adults and young people, Mom was having as much fun skating as she was teaching Teresa, Michele and me. Christmas gifts for Mom and her siblings growing up in the south were roller skates, jeans and a sweat shirt.

On Christmas Day, young people were outside on blocked off streets roller skating.

As a family, my sisters, brothers and me, also enjoyed the adventure of traveling in the car across country with our parents on trips to or from Alabama, Louisiana, Mississippi, Illinois, and Texas and California to either visit relatives or cultural sites, while on the way to Dad's next military assignments. We enjoyed our family outings. We were happy just being together with our Dad driving and Mom in the front seat listening to the radio. Mom and Dad alternated driving and we listened to age appropriate radio music selected by Dad. In our travels, we went to live baseball games in Georgia or to cultural sites in Texas or entertainment parks in California. such as Disneyland. We laughed, we played, and we fought with words as typical siblings do. Other than the normal sibling rivalry, our self-esteem was positive for the most part, it seemed. "It's my turn to sit next to the window. Mom, tell him/her to stop hitting so hard!" She would look back and remind us to play fair.

"Well," he/she would say, "I saw the Volkswagen Bug (car) first."

"Yes, do not hit so hard."

"Slug bug, you are it."

While on one of these driving trips, we were all enjoying ourselves, when out of my mouth came the words, "When I grow up, I'm going to join the military." My sisters and brothers started chiming in, expressing their desire to do so as well. However, as quickly as those words were spoken, Dad responded with, "No, you are not, you're going to college first; then you can join the military."

Family Basic Beliefs and Values

At an early age, Mom and Dad taught us basic beliefs and values. We first came to know of God by saying our grace or blessing of the food at mealtime. My Mom's grace is one I still remember: *"Blessed are the pure in heart for they shall see God" (Matthew 5:8 KJV)*, or sometimes she would say, *"Jesus wept" (John 11:35 KJV)*. Years later, I recall reading the Bible and making the connection that Mom's grace or prayers at mealtime were verses from the Bible, she had memorized. The Bible reminds us to put the Word in our hearts. *"I have hidden your word in my heart that I might not sin against you"* (Psalm 119:11 NIV). We also learned cute little rhymes to teach us manners while eating at the table together. When I was caught with my elbows on the table, they would all sing, "Sandra, Sandra, strong and able, this is not a horse stable, get your elbows off the table." Every night at bedtime, my parents knelt with us beside our beds and also taught us to pray the "Lord's Prayer," which is the prayer Jesus taught His disciples to pray (Matthew 6:9-13 KJV). All five of us would kneel beside our beds with each of our hands folded together in the prayer posture to pray the Lord's Prayer (unaware until later in life that these were the first verses we had memorized from the Bible). Matthew 6:9–10 (KJV) says,

> *Our Father which art in heaven,*
> *hallowed be thy name,*
> *thy kingdom come, thy will be done on earth*
> *as it is in heaven.*
> *Give us this day our daily bread.*
> *And forgive us our debts, as we forgive our debtors.*
> *And lead us not into temptation,*
> *but deliver us from evil.*
> *For thine is the kingdom,*
> *and the power, and the glory forever.*

And at the end of our prayer, we were taught to say, "God bless Mom, God bless Dad, God bless Sandra, God bless Teresa, God bless Michele, God Bless Buzzy, God bless Ken, God bless all the sick people, and God bless all the poor people … *Amen!*"

It is important to be trained and taught values and beliefs in the home by our parents or guardians, so when our relationships expand, we begin to recognize different patterns. Speaking of prayer, I remember one time when I was nine years old while living in Germany, my parents allowed me to spend the night at a German family's home with Adali, a daughter of friends of my parents. I said to her (after getting in bed and remembering) "we did not say our prayers on our knees." She said, "It is okay, we can pray in the bed." Although it felt strange to me, we both silently prayed and went off to sleep. This was a good example of recognizing how family relationships form self-awareness and self-esteem. I have preferred praying on my knees ever since and not in the bed because that was the way we were taught. The Bible informs us of the importance of children being taught in Deuteronomy chapter 6 and verse 7 (NIV) *"Impress them (commandments) on your children.*

Talk about them when you sit at home and when you walk along the road, when you lie down and when you get up.

Dad, the military man, was stern, very strict and our protector. There was no question of his authority. All I had to do was look at his face and I would obey. He monitored the places we went, the music we listened to on the radio, the friends we associated with, and the shows we watched on television. I enjoyed televisions shows such as cowboy movies, dramas, cartoons, and religious programs. On Saturday mornings, we watched Davey and Goliath, produced by the Lutheran Church. It was a valuable teaching tool on how to treat others and obey your parents, etc.

By the time we moved to California, my siblings and I would stay up late at night watching television. One night, we watched the Catholic Church's production of a Hollywood movie called the *Song of Bernadette*. I was mesmerized by it. A young poor teenage girl, Bernadette in Lourdes, France was chosen by God to experience a special visitation by the mother of Jesus, Mary, called the "Immaculate Conception."

When she shared her experience with others, no one in town believed her. It was a test, showing the importance of telling the truth to our parents and others without wavering. Bernadette told the truth no matter if others believed her or not. The government tried to suppress her claims and the church refused to get involved until one day the priest changed his mind and believed her. Something within me connected with Bernadette's special relationship with God. After she had experienced the divine presence of God, she later became what she always wanted to be … a nun. *"Train up a child in the way he (she) should go and when he (she) is old, he (she) will not depart from it"* (Proverbs 22:6 NIV).

Even after being mistreated and threatened, she did not succumb to the pressure to deny the truth. Bernadette stuck to her beliefs and did not let any human sway the facts and truth of what she saw. I was so impressed by young Bernadette's courage and the favor given her by God that I dreamed of one day becoming a nun devoted to God, too.

Daddy's Girl and His Temporary Absence

Children thrive off of affection, affirmation, acceptance. Dad was assigned to serve one year of a military tour of duty at Clark AB, Philippines without his family. Until Dad's return, Mom chose to live in Ohio with her firstborn sister, Ann, and her family. They welcomed us into their home until Mom found us our own home. It turned out my parents could only afford to live in public housing "the projects" until Dad returned to the United States to get us. This was our first time meeting my Mom's firstborn sister's family. As with most relationships, it took time for us to get to know each other. We were all close in age—eight, nine, and ten years old. Tension would arise on occasion among us. I felt uneasy around conflict, and I shied away from the interactions as best as I could.

Mom liked decorating, so her firstborn was there helping her move furniture. One time in particular, while moving furniture I was scared when Mom had to be rushed to the hospital for losing a lot of blood (hemorrhaging). Not knowing what it meant, it all turned out okay. She was back home with us.

My fifth-grade teacher, Mr. Harris, called Mom about my difficulty reading the chalkboard. My Mom took me to have an eye examination, and the doctor found no problems with my eyesight. During my middle school years, I had no close girlfriends (BFFs). However, from afar I admired two smart girls in my 4th and 5th grade class who got all the A's, Michelle and Esther. All excited the day I was named "good citizen" of the month. My photo with my name was displayed on the bulletin board for all to see. It felt really good and my self-esteem was boosted a notch.

Spring and summer were the least enjoyable times of the year. The doctors diagnosed me as being "allergic to grass" because the pollen in the air caused my eyes to itch and swell. I had to stay in the house. I cried and prayed on my knees a lot, not understanding why I was allergic to grass. Dad was absent and not with us. I rarely went outside to play because of it.

Psychologist Sigmund Freud is right on target when he discovered, *"I cannot think of any need in childhood as strong as the need for a father's protection."*[23] The crying may have also been due to me missing my Dad, too. I found myself in such distress and insecurity, that I prayed to God that I would wear glasses. Again, in class, Mr. Harris told my Mom that I was not concentrating on my class work and having difficulty reading the chalkboard. Mom took me to the eye doctor again. This time, the doctor prescribed the wearing of eyeglasses. This was an answer to prayer I would regret later, especially when appearance became important. In the meantime, the glasses became my security blanket, so to speak.

Birth Order and Self-Esteem

When a newborn child goes from the hospital to home, and then to church, usually the next question asked of the parents about their new bundle of joy (after hearing the name, weight, size, and if healthy) is "Who does she favor? Whose side of the family, mother or father, does she resemble the most?" I have heard some say I favored my father, and then others would say, "you are the splitting image of your mother." For the most part, people make comparisons by looking at the outward features, such as face, eyes, nose, lips, and hair and other features are recognized as we grow.

There is another question most times asked, "is this your first child or your second?" Yes, birth order also plays a significant role in a child's development. If you want to know why you feel, act, and behave the way you do whether with your parents, siblings, or others outside the home then consider your birth order.

Psychologist Kevin Leman[24] researched the topic with the question "Does birth order make any sense?" Yes, understanding the order you were born into your family will help you understand and sort through some of the reasons why you do what you do and how birth order forms your personality.

What is birth order? Birth order is the science of understanding your place in the family line. Were you born first? Second? Third? Or are you the only child?"[25] Your birth order in your family can affect how you decide who you are and how you feel about who are in your family.

Let's look at some characteristics of birth order and how it forms your personality.[26] The following are not concrete characteristics of who you are, but will give you an idea and may help you begin getting to know a little bit more about yourself. Does the birth order group mentioned come close to describing you?

a. firstborn child—perfectionist, reliable, conscientious, list maker, well-organized, hard driving, natural leader, critical, serious, compliant, scholarly, logical, doesn't like surprises, loves computers, wants to excel at everything, basks in parents' attention, structured, high achiever, creative, artistic (e.g. Beyoncé, Selena Gomez, Hillary Clinton, Oprah Winfrey, Taylor Swift, Lindsay Lohan, Paris Hilton, Malia Obama, Venus Williams)

b. *middle child*—mediator, compromising, diplomatic, avoids conflict, independent, loyal to peers, many friends, a maverick, unspoiled, people pleaser, rebellious tendencies, thrive in friendships, peacemaker (e.g. Barbara Walters, Jennifer Lopez, Cindy Crawford, Miley Cyrus, Julia Roberts, Princess Diana, Rev. Martin Luther King, Jr, John F. Kennedy, Diana Ross, Michael Jordan, Susan B. Anthony)

c. *youngest child*—manipulative, charming, blames others, attention seeker, tenacious, people person, natural salesperson, precocious, engaging, affectionate, loves surprises, uncomplicated, social, outgoing, fun loving (e.g. Goldie Hawn, Willow Smith, Sasha Obama, Hilary Duff, Solange Knowles, Sofia Richie, Zoe Saldana, Ariana Grande, Zoey Deschanel, Serena Williams)

d. *only child*—little adult by age seven, very thorough, deliberate, high achiever, self-motivated, fearful, cautious, voracious reader, black-and-white thinker, uses intensifiers ("very," "extremely," "exactly"), can't bear to fail, has very high expectations for self, more comfortable with people who are older or younger, natural-born leader, possesses a high level of self-control. (e.g. Alicia Keys, Chelsea Clinton, Condoleezza Rice, Eleanor Roosevelt, Elvis Pressley, Gloria Vanderbilt)

Birth Order & Receiving New Family Members

Since the family is where we decide who we are, a lot depends on our birth order, too. When we left Germany, we moved to our next assignment in Kincheloe Air Force Base (AFB) Michigan. I had fond memories of our family. Winters in Michigan were like no other place we had ever lived. In experiencing the joys of childhood, I was ten years old when the fifth child, my baby brother, Kenneth, was born. Dad gathered us all together in the hallway one day to give us ideas on names for us to choose for our new baby brother. We all voted and chose the name Kenneth E. With the help of Dad, we also enjoyed another naming ceremony of our first pet, a large beautiful furry white, brown, tan, and black collie dog. We named him Laddie because he looked just like the dog in the popular television series show *Lassie*.

Birth Order, Puberty and Siblings Paying Attention

Going through puberty brings about noticeable changes in your feelings, thinking, and behavior. This includes the normal rites of passage to womanhood, like experiencing your first period (menstruation) and the physical changes of growing breasts and hair in certain parts of the body.

It took me by surprise. I was in my 'tween years at twelve years old. Although my Mom had prepared me for the big anticipated day, it was the middle sister Teresa who was seemingly more prepared than I was when it happened. One day after school, still playing outside on Pearl Street in Illinois, I felt something different going on in my body. I did not think about it. It was not until Mom called us in to have dinner together. After dinner, I went to the restroom. Throughout the house, they all heard me scream. Immediately, Teresa ran in to see what was wrong with me. She said to me, "Go to your dresser drawer, and get the box Mom gave you." The little box had lots of feminine products. It was filled with dainty, girly items and books. I had already read them, especially the book on *Growing Up and Liking It* and others. Welcome to womanhood! From that point on, I changed physically, mentally, and emotionally.

That was a defining moment for me, while Teresa, the second born had obviously been paying attention to Mom's talks. Over the years, I can say Teresa seemed to pop up at the right time of decision for me. She was learning by observation from her first-born, which may be why she appeared to do the opposite of what I did by exploring things on her own. I observed her getting caught by my parents doing something she should not have done. She seemed to get the spankings more than the middle child, Michele or myself. We found ourselves crying a lot when Teresa got spankings. But the reality was Teresa was trying to find her identity, where she fit in as the second child and girl in the family.

In our identity development, birth order does play a role in forming our personality, worth, value, and identity. We are constantly watching and subconsciously trying to figure out who we will be or who we are. In Jean Illsely Clark's book *Self Esteem: A Family Affair*, teenagers practice how to be the way their parents and siblings are.

But I smile as I think about how Teresa, my first sister and my parents' second child, knew exactly what to do. I screamed with shock, and she remained calm, giving me instructions on what to do. How did she know the box was there in her firstborn sister's room and dresser drawers? Had she already been observing her big sister in a number of situations when I was clueless? Had she been paying attention to what was said or done with her firstborn sister?

It is normal to experience growing pains as you try to figure out where you fit in with your own family, parents and siblings.

Once Teresa asked me, if I would go to my parents and ask them for something that was for her. I said, you can ask for yourself. She said, when you ask you will get it. I remember how that struck me as odd that she noticed when I asked for something, I got positive results. I had not paid attention and never thought about it until she made that statement to me. On another occasion when in college, I was trying to make the right decision without disappointing my mother too much because I was naturally compliant, obedient, and a perfectionist always trying to please my parents. However, I asked Mom about moving out of the house into an apartment with a roommate, an active duty military nurse. Teresa jumped into the conversation saying, "If it were me, I would do it." My sister Teresa was a mediator. She was an independent thinker and a maverick. She was loyal to her peers, had many friends, and was unspoiled with rebellious tendencies. She thrived in friendships, whereas I did better in one-on-one and not in a group setting. In the midst of my conversations with our single-parent Mom and trying to make the right decisions, Teresa would be the one to quickly jump in and share her thoughts about the matter.

Fast forward years later, when I was out of the will of God in a wrong boyfriend relationship, it was Teresa who reminded me of the faith she had observed in me during my teenage years. She shared and testified about her newfound faith in God. She was attending a Bible-believing, faith-teaching non-denominational church, where she had received the baptism of the Holy Spirit. As I listened to her share, of course, I was convicted about getting my life right with God again and going back to church.

A Love Letter from Your Heavenly Father

Dearest Beloved Daughter,

I created you with *love*, an everlasting and unconditional love. I will never quit loving you. Expect love, love, and more love (Jeremiah 31:3 MSG)! You are one of my greatest miracles! Before your mother and father ever knew you, I "shaped you first inside, then out; I formed you in your mother's womb" (Psalm 139:13 MSG).

For nine months, all your mother and father knew was a baby taking form and growing in the womb. Your very well-thought-out physical body, mind, and soul was created by Me to consist of all the vital organs of a brain, heart, kidneys, liver, and lungs. Then with more tender loving care, you were made with eleven delicate systems, such as the circulatory, respiratory, digestive, excretory, nervous, endocrine, immune, integumentary, skeletal, muscular, and reproductive systems. All these systems work together in order for your body to function the way I intended. I breathed My breath of life into humans, making you living beings (Genesis 2:7).

Your parents had no idea if you would be a girl or boy, even if they requested the help of ultrasound equipment. I knew first you would be a girl. I set you apart as special to Me, your parents, and then to the world, in that order (Psalm 139:13, Jeremiah 1:5 NIV). They waited to hear the news when you finally made your grand entrance into their lives and the world. You were born-innocent, pure, gentle, cuddly, soft, and a trusting little baby girl—to specific parents. I made you in the birth order, I desire you to have my character and values of love, joy, peace, patience, kindness, gentleness, goodness, faithfulness, and self-control (Galatians 5:24,25, Genesis 1:26, 27). Your family is a people holy to Me. Out of all the peoples on the face of the earth I have chosen you and your family to be My treasured possession (Deuteronomy 14:2). In return, you must honor your father and mother that it may go well with you and that you may enjoy a long life on the earth. This is My first commandment with a promise (Ephesians 6:2).

Love, Your All-Knowing Creator

Self-Discovery / Self-Reflection

Application

(1) Find a baby photo of you with family, if you have one or draw one of you and put on your vision board.
(2) Chat and reflect on the questions below with your mother or a close adult female friend (mentor).
(3) Look up and write the Bible verses on your vision board that inspired you while reading this chapter and use them to answer the questions below.

Thinking About Me: Who Am I?

1. Are you living with both parents (traditional)? If not, is it your mother or father or foster parents or grandparents? What is your birth order?

_____
_____

2. Which one of your parents or family members do people say you look like or favor? What characteristics do you have similar to your mother and father or guardian?" Why do others say you look like or favor your parent?

_____
_____

3. How are the two types of self-esteem developed? List your strengths, limitations, values, beliefs.

_____
_____

4. Do you believe God created you a gift to your parents and family? Why or why not?

_____
_____

5. Do your parents and siblings make you feel loved, capable, and protected? In what ways?

_____
_____

A single Mom tries when things are hard. She never gives up. She believes in her family, even when things are tough. She knows that above all things ... a mother's love is more than enough.
—Deniece Williams

Being a single parent is twice the work, twice the stress, and twice the tears, but also twice the hugs, twice the love, and twice the pride.
—Unknown

You are all sons (daughters) of God through faith in Christ Jesus ...
—Galatians 3:26 (NIV)

CHAPTER 3

Who Am I? Growing up Loved in a Single-Parent Family

Loved by God with the love of a family

Family love is expressed in a variety of ways. Among the most needed ingredients for a child is to grow up in a healthy family relationship of affection, acceptance, and affirmation. Our family relationships influence what we believe about ourselves and how we think, feel, or behave when we are alone or with others. Love in a family is very beautiful. Love evolves in a family from infancy to adolescence to adulthood. There is nothing else like it in the whole wide world.

As in the beauty of nature in the early spring, when the flowers are in full bloom you will see an array of colorful butterflies floating in the air from flower to flower with bumblebees not too far from them. These beautiful and colorful butterflies were once caterpillars. Caterpillars that transformed into beautiful butterflies through four distinct stages. From the eggs laid on plants by the adult female butterfly to the caterpillar (larva) that carries out its job to eat, eat, and eat. The fully-grown caterpillar stops eating and transitions to the pupa protected inside a cocoon. It looks like nothing is happening until it emerges and continues to the adult reproductive stage, when it mates and lays eggs. This beautiful evolution is called the metamorphosis of the caterpillar to a beautiful butterfly. A similar metamorphosis occurs in the life of girls blossoming from an adolescent girl to an adult woman. Certain things must happen in the growth development cycle without hindrance.

We were one big happy family during the most formative stages of the first fifteen years of my life. And my siblings were 13, 12, 9, and 6 years of age when the significant life altering-change disrupted our natural cycle of growth developments. I had dreamed of marrying and raising a family like my parents until their marriage ended first with separation, then the divorce after 17 years of marriage.

A marriage union is when two people, a man and a woman are legally recognized as partners. Marriages may be terminated by annulment, divorce, or death. Divorce is the process of terminating a marriage union between a husband and wife. Marriages and families disrupted by divorce or separation takes a different course in an individual's life that affects the child's pattern of growth and development.

Mom for the last time packed our suitcases and with her five children left Dad in California. On a Greyhound bus, she headed back to her hometown— sweet home Alabama. Grandmother was her support system. Along with the normal teenage growing-up pains, I believe the breakup of our family was the most difficult time in the lives of their fifteen-, thirteen-, twelve-, nine-, and six-year-old children. Being uprooted near the end of my second semester of my junior year, I ended up going back to the same public school with the same classmates from middle school years. Despite the fact, we did not understand what happened that Mom had to leave Dad in California, I do know my growing-up years became more complicated.

Adjusting to the Transition

Over a period of time, the transition produced very low periods in my life where I felt inadequate and alone. Negative thoughts about my confidence crept in, I began to doubt and turned feelings inward. Based on research, the teens and 'tween years are the most crucial periods of our lives. Because of the changes going on in our bodies, physically, intellectually, emotionally, socially and behaviorally. My siblings and I were in the critical stages of adolescence. We were all affected differently by the sudden change. Mom no longer had the luxury of being a stay-at-home Mom. She began looking for a job.

With Mom's love of children, she applied and was hired as a teacher for the Montgomery Community Action Head-start program. She remained there until her retirement 27 years later.

Although, there was no major change in our weekly routine and responsibilities, I became Mom's primary assistant. During the week, my sisters and me shared the household responsibilities until our brothers were old enough. I tried to make sure daily chores were done, such as beds made, helping with homework and that it was finished before bed-time. On the weekend, we cleaned our rooms with clothes in closets or drawers and toys put back where they belonged. We each had specific assignments in the main areas, such as the living room, bathroom, and kitchen. They were cleaned, vacuumed, swept, and mopped by the three girls. My brothers took out the trash. I prepared and supervised my sisters in preparing basic easy and simple meals during the week, while Mom prepared the special big weekend meals. On Saturdays, Mom kept the practice of making sure we still did the fun things of swimming, bowling, or other events on the military base, at school, or in the local area. It was good we were still Dad's military dependents. We had access to the privileges of the local military base by using our identification cards to get access. Our outings included going to the base pool to swim, dive, and try imitating the butterfly techniques of the professionals. Butterfly strokes were pretty in form and looked easy but I never got pass just the trying phase.

I knew more was expected of me. Parents are stricter on first-borns. First-borns pave the path for their siblings to follow. Having been taught to live as an example for my sisters and brothers, our family without my Dad in the house was quite an adjustment. I became more distant and withdrawn. I was too young to understand why my siblings rejected me after helping them with homework. I may have been too impatient with them. The roles had changed with Mom being our sole provider. Occasionally, I ran into some resistance with my sisters and brothers with them doing their chores and homework, etc. It became a little confusing to me as well as them, was I their mother, father, or sister? How did they fit in the family structure now? Were they also sorting through their own identity by observing and measuring themselves around what big sister was saying or doing or the next sibling closest to them? Family is where we had learned the basics about our identity, values, and beliefs taught us by both parents, however, now there was only one parent we were living with.

Raised Up in the Church

On Sunday mornings, Mom continued grandma's legacy of raising her five children up in the church. She dropped us off to Sunday School and came back to the church service to hear sermons preached by our pastor from the pulpit. Sister Johnnie Calhoun was our Sunday School teacher who taught us from the Bible. Church was where I enjoyed music first by listening to the musical instruments, specifically the organ and the choirs singing soul-stirring songs. All the young people, including me would sing congregational hymns whether the deacons led us or the choir. Some of my favorites became "What A Friend We Have in Jesus, Pass Me Not Oh Gentle Savior, Amazing Grace, In the Garden," and others. Mom signed my two sisters and me up for the youth choir. Of course, she was behind the scenes encouraging the choir director to give us a chance to lead a song together. Yes, we were very nervous and shy, but we managed to do a good job for our ages singing as a trio "Give Me a Clean Heart." For some reason, we did not sing again.

Mom enrolled us girls in private piano classes with Mrs. Gibraltar, who taught lessons in her home. Practice was hard and boring. It took too long to finally feel I was learning. Oh yes, hit a key off note and I would feel the ruler across my knuckles. Mom noticed we began to lack motivation. The signs were our lack of daily practice on the piano. Mom stopped the lessons because she reminded us we did not have money to waste.

Yet, one day, out of the blue and no longer taking piano lessons, I felt the light come on for me. I said to Mom, "Can I play the organ?" Mom was the best. She did not scold me about not finishing the piano lessons. She started looking around to find opportunities for me to do what I wanted. However, while she was looking for an organ teacher, someone told her it would be best for me to start playing the piano first. She found the DeLoach piano studio, where group lessons were taught. The group was not as expensive as individual classes. I enjoyed the group sessions up to a point because I was writing my own songs. But, again I became bored and stopped practicing daily. Although, I did not realize it at the time, I believe it was because I was not hearing the sound of the organ. Instead of putting me at the organ and letting me play, I believe the adults saw what seemed difficult about playing the organ, therefore suggested I start with the piano. However, it was the sound of the church organ that inspired me and drew me to listening to how others played it. I do believe my dream of playing the organ would have come to pass. I really wanted to play the organ. And no one ever asked me why I wanted to play the organ. The sound and with the right teacher, I believe it would have motivated me to practice and I would be playing it today.

Praying for My Parents

The timing of my parents' divorce was a serious adjustment emotionally and spiritually. On the Sunday when I heard the Bible verse read aloud in my Sunday school class or church service, it stuck with me. In the gospel of Matthew chapter 6 and verse 6 in the King James Version (KJV), I received a revelation about prayer. *But thou, when thou prayest, enter into thy closet, and when thou hast shut thy door, pray to thy Father which is in secret, and thy Father which seeth in secret shall reward thee openly.* I remember thinking, "closet" I have a clothes closet. So, I made up my mind to take my Mom and Dad's divorce to the Heavenly Father and pray in secret believing that He will hear my prayers and reward me by bringing my parent's back together. I was so convinced by the verse that I literally took my favorite little red rocking chair to sit in my clothes closet, pulled the clothes back hanging on the rack, and slid the sliding wood doors closed to pray to my Heavenly Father God in private without anyone knowing. Their separation and subsequent divorce were very painful for me. I did not totally understand the depth of divorce at the time, but I know I was one sad daughter, who wanted her parents together.

I missed my Dad and our family being together. I cried a lot and often. Mom had to rely on me to help her with my siblings. Whenever Mom needed help with my siblings or assistance, I did what I could to the best of my ability. I kept my thoughts to myself, knowing my parents were divorced. When Dad was present, he was our security. I think I must have believed subconsciously deep down within me, the divorce may have been my fault because of the very intense incident which was the last scene the night we were leaving our home to never come back again. As the firstborn, a natural maternal closeness developed between Mom and me, which was probably why in the past Mom would let me know first on several occasions that she was leaving Dad. I begged her to stay. She did stay until the third and very last time.

One point of solace was, as the firstborn, I had the privilege of not having to share a bedroom with my four other siblings in Alabama. Therefore, I could secretly go into my "prayer clothes closet" and pray in private. From that point on, I found myself going to God in my clothes closet to pray before I would share with anyone. At that time, I did not believe I had anyone to talk to who would understand, certainly not my mother or father because they had other concerns on their mind and I did not want to be one of them. I tried to follow the rules they taught us. If I could not make it to the prayer closet fast enough, I would go into my room and hide by laying on the floor on the other side of the bed farthest from the bedroom door and no one could see me. I did not know any better. I took the Bible verse literally and I found comfort and joy in the quiet moments with the Lord.

Going to Sunday School and church was the beginning of me getting to know more about God as Father. *"Train a child in the way he should go, and when he is old he will not turn from it"* (Proverbs 22:6 NIV). What began as prayers of hope that my parents would get back together became an enjoyable time alone with God in my closet. When I needed to cry to someone, I found it easiest to go into my "prayer clothes closet" and tell God all about my troubles. I would walk out with a peace.

However, I do recall a brief on the spot out of the blue prayer I prayed one Sunday morning during worship service. While listening attentively to my pastor preaching about how Christians should live, I closed my eyes and silently prayed right there sitting on the pew "Lord, I want to know You like the pastor seems to know You." I wanted to obey God.

What is Confidence?

During the adolescent period of my life without my father present, again I struggled with having confidence in myself. Self-confidence is to trust oneself and in particular in one's ability or aptitude to engage successfully or at least adequately with the world according to Dr. Neel Burton. One day while walking through our living room I heard a clear message within me say, *"your confidence will come when you trust in Me."* Somehow, I understood in a childlike way the "Me" in that statement was God speaking to me and giving me the reassurance that only through trusting in Him could true confidence come. *But blessed is the man who trusts in the Lord, whose confidence is in him* (Jeremiah 17:7). In essence, God was telling me until I put my trust in Him alone, I would not be confident in feeling trust in my own abilities, qualities, and judgment. I needed to get to know and trust Him first.

Mom Single-Parenting

Although, Mom was no longer able to stay-home and had to work, she was resourceful and determined to make our stay at grandma's short. She acquired the skills needed to keep us from being on welfare and not having to live in government-assisted housing.

Single-parenting was not an easy task for Mom raising five children alone. Nancy Boyd-Franklin in her book "Black Families in Therapy" noted that single parenting did not make us dysfunctional as long as we clearly knew who was in charge and that we did.[27] Mom knew my dad meant well for her and the children, but they were young and naïve when they married. Dad was still family focused, therefore, he did keep in touch by phone, letter, and maybe a visit. However, it was not the same as both parents being in the same home. The distance made it hard for us to warm up to him since he was not around on a daily basis.

Remarriage and Blending Families

My parents had been divorced for six to eight years before they each decided to remarry. Mom and Dad both remarried when I no longer lived at home. I had embarked upon my own military career.

I remember hearing Mom say, she would not remarry until her girls were grown and no longer living at home. She kept her word. As my sibling brothers, Buzzy and Ken turned 15 and 12 years old, Mom flew with them to California keeping her promise with Dad. At some point during the divorce, they agreed to not separate the five of us and when the boys became teens, Dad would raise his sons.

Mom married once again to an Army man named Sandy Mushatt in December. Mom and Michele planned her wedding. She had a beautifully well-coordinated ceremony on the military base. About two years into the marriage and two months into my tour in Japan, I received a call from Mom with the news that I had a new baby sister, whom she affectionately called "Precious." But her birth name created by Michele began with the first few letters of each of the girl's names. Miles away from the joyous occasion, I shared the news with my surrogate military family, the Wellington's. In keeping the joy alive, they started fondly calling me "Sancheleresa's Sister." Michele, the peacemaker, shy, quiet, unassuming, thrifty, carpenter, artistic and the decorative one made the prayerful decision to return back to Montgomery to support Mom during Mushatt's later illness.

My Dad called one night from California while I was a year and a half into my first military career assignment in Texas. He said, "I want you to meet Mona." Mona was polite, friendly, and articulate with soft sweet voice. I enjoyed listening to her talk. At first, I was not sure why he had called at that hour to introduce her to me. Then when she gave the phone back to him, he told me he was going to marry her. Once they married in January, they took up residence in California. The concept of blended families was less of an adjustment for me than Teresa, Buzzy, and Ken who were living in the same household with Dad and Mona. Since Teresa was living with them by default she became the oldest child along with Buzzy becoming the oldest brother to two after him, Ken and Andre. So as far as I could tell, their new home life was an adjustment, yet they bonded quickly to 9 years old Andre and 7 years old Shawana.

Blended families may begin with some rivalry, jealousy, and awkwardness because two different families are merging their lives together. To refresh my memory, the question was recently asked Mona, "was it easy becoming a blended family?" As we shared our perspectives, we both agreed, "no, it was not." Mona shared that the girls were not nice to her. An example she gave is the time when I was visiting while on leave from an assignment. We finally met in person. My Dad asked me to ride with her to a job interview at McDonnell Douglas. She reminded me of a conversation we had on the way back to their home, I asked, "What do you and my Dad have in common?" She commented, "We both love each other, and we want the same things in life." And to put me at ease, she also shared these words, "…with me marrying your Dad, I am not trying to become your mother. I would hope we could become friends."

I believe I was subconsciously wrestling with the fact that both my parents are living. For a number of years, when I was missing my Dad and Mom being together I went into my "prayer clothes closet" to pray that God would bring my parents back together. New people were in my parent's lives, now. God was not answering my prayers. How am I to sort through what was going on within my heart and mind? How should I have understood why Mom shared with me on two occasions, she was leaving Dad. I begged her not to leave. She stayed until the last time. When you do not understand what went wrong, how do you make sense of new people coming into your life, as the husband marrying my mother and the wife marrying my Dad?

Researchers confirm that sometime children subconsciously believe they had something to do with their parents splitting up? All questions, a child does not know how to deal with or even address.

In new relationships and with different personalities, your identity and self-esteem will be tested. Where do I fit? Will I be able to be in a conversation with Dad and comfortably speak about Mom or will I have to be guarded because Mona is now his wife? Or vice versa will I be able to comfortably share and have a conversation with Mom when Mushatt is present? How should we be in relationship with the new wife, sister and brother or the new husband?

When I visited Dad and Mona over the weekend, it was usually not long enough to spend quality time getting to know my new siblings. Mona made me feel right at home. About seven years into their marriage, I was intentional about trying to establish a closer relationship with my new siblings' Andre and Shawana. Up to this point, my weekend visits during military business trips were nice, but too short to get to know our new family members. I finally asked Mona first could Shawana spend a summer with me. She said yes. I then asked Shawana if she wanted to spend a summer month with me. Shawana said yes. I think we both were excited. I planned a fun-filled month of local cultural events and activities for us to do together and get to know more about each other. We went to the zoo, shopping, movies, and church. This pretty, smart, adorable, inquisitive, playful, fun-loving and typical fourteen years old teenager, surprised me one day. She caused me to have an instant flashback to how Teresa would go through my things without asking my permission first. Shawana did the same thing catching me by surprise. All excited about finding jewelry and clothing from my closet that she modeled as one happy and content teenager.

It was an awkward moment. Being the first born, I had no older siblings to get into their clothing and jewelry. I never thought about going into my Mom's clothing, shoes, or things without asking her. Again, being the firstborn who is compliant, obedient and don't break the rules, quiet naturally I expected others to do the same. But hindsight is 20/20, I later learned and understand this is what siblings do go into sisters or mother's clothes, shoes, makeup and play grown up. The joy is in girls feeling loved and capable in their family. Positive or negative self-esteem is developed first in family relationships inside the home. This is a good example of birth order and how it plays a significant role in understanding sibling relationships and how siblings imitate one another. Siblings will be siblings looking to our parents first and each other, to feel loved and accepted. Siblings are trying to also understand who they are and where they fit in the family.

Birth order in blended families is another example of how self-esteem is developed in sibling relationships. Shawana's firstborn brother Andre was inquisitive, talkative, serious, fun loving, and somewhat of a jokester. His order in the family changed from firstborn with a baby sister, to younger of two older aged brothers and fourth child in the household. Andre was good about letting me know he appreciated my simple acts of kindness, such as sending cards especially on his birthday. Almost always, he would give me feedback to let me know how he appreciated me thinking of him. In our blended family with siblings having grown to seven with four sisters and three brothers, Dad tried to ensure we all knew, accepted, and loved each other as sisters and brothers should. Shawana, the baby child or last born was fun loving and precocious.

Teresa, the middle child of three girls, decided to ask Dad could she live with him in California. He and Mona agreed. For a number of years, she and my two brothers were raised by Dad and Mona. It was not an easy adjustment for Teresa (the second born who became the oldest in age in the blended household). Getting the father-daughter affirmation, attention, and acceptance was a challenge. Again, family is the first relationship for Buzzy becoming aware of his identity. Buzzy is the fourth child of Dad's and his firstborn son. Naturally in adolescent development, he was probably unaware of it but was trying to figure out his place in Dad's life in the blended family too. Is he loveable and capable? Boys tend to look to the male figure and their fathers as girls to their mothers. Buzzy became a star athlete on the track and football field. And since Ken was the lastborn of Dad's, he became the older brother to Andre and Shawana. All of us were trying to figure out where and how we fit into our new blended family, while also subconsciously seeking Dad's love.

A few years after graduating from high school, Teresa announced her plans to marry Kevin. Where would the wedding be held? Dad and Mona agreed to host her wedding at their home. Then after twenty plus years of marriage and her firstborn daughter Keisha graduating from college, Teresa decided to go back to college. This was a major milestone worth celebrating. The family flew to San Bernardino to celebrate. Cheering Teresa on as she walked on and off the stage with a bachelor's degree in Public Health in hand. The outdoor photo session took on another life and to everyone's surprise, Teresa had removed herself. Oblivious to me, someone had made a comment about which photos Mom or Dad should be in together. Teresa ended up off to the side in tears because this was her day, and everyone she wanted to be there was. In the midst of all the joy and excitement, a bombshell exploded, and Teresa voiced her displeasure at the unnecessary demand being made on her about who should be or not be in the photos. She explained how the photo session should have played out. I remained quiet, not getting involved because I was clueless.

While stationed in Denver, I remember receiving a call from married Teresa with the statement "Sandra, I want our family to be a family." I said, "I do to. Let's pray and fast about it once a month." She agreed and our sister Michele joined us over the telephone with them in California and me in Colorado. One month while Teresa and I took turns praying, the Spirit said, "when Dad comes to know the Lord your brothers will too." We prayed for the family and when I visited Mom or Dad and Mona, we went to church together. At some time after our monthly prayers, we learned that Dad had joined a church and was in training to become a deacon. We praised the Lord for the first step to answered prayers. You see, Dad was not one to be a regular "church goer."

Our blended family is a work in progress, but over the years we have come to understand one thing from that photo event and others that no one should be made to choose between one parent nor the other. We decided we will enjoy our celebrations of achievements and all will participate in the photo sessions. Through the difficult moments and prayers, I believe it has strengthened our blended family bond and with the help of the Holy Spirit we are encouraged to have open communications and friendships. We are a growing blended family emotionally and spiritually, both as individuals and collectively. Our many prayers about our divorced family and the affects it had on us all has given us hope as we witnessed my mom, dad, and Mona becoming friends. In those difficult times, God was there and He heard our prayers, He watched over us at all times, and He sheltered us from what could have devastating pain. *"The Lord is good to all, He has compassion on all He has made" (Psalm 145:9 NIV).*

A Love Letter from Your Heavenly Father

Dearest Precious Daughter,

I created you female. You are the gift I gave to your parents. Even when your mother or father failed you, I am a father to the fatherless. You were shaped by Me first on the inside and then out. I formed you in your mother's womb and I knew you, every bone in your body. I know exactly how you were made, bit-by-bit, sculpting you from nothing into something. Like an open book, I watched you grow from conception to birth; all the stages of your life were spread out before Me (Psalm 139:13–16 MSG). Body and soul, I marvelously made you to worship Me in adoration. Yes, I know you inside and out, you were created not only belonging to Me, but to your specific parents in a specific birth order. I set you apart to your parents and your blended siblings and the children after them that they may revere Me, the Lord their God. As long as you live keep all My decrees and commands to honor your mother and father whether blended family or not and you will enjoy a long life.

I decided to adopt you into My family through my first-born Son, Jesus Christ. What pleasure I took in planning this! I wanted you to enter into the celebration of My lavished gift-giving by the hand of My beloved Son, Jesus Christ (Ephesians 1:5,6 TMB). What great love I have lavished on you, that you should be called a child of Mine! And that is what you are (1 John 3:1 NIV)!

Your identity comes in knowing and loving Me. I saw all that I had made, and it was very good" (Genesis 1:31 NIV). In Me you live, move, and have your being (Acts 17:28 NIV). You are a spiritual and physical being with My character. I chose and set you apart female, holy, and a special treasure to me above all others (Deuteronomy 7:6 MSG). If your earthly father and mother is present or not in your life or blended or foster or adopted or no-parent family, I am your Heavenly Father, I see the trouble of the afflicted, I consider their grief and take it in hand, I am the helper of and a father to the fatherless (Psalm 10:14 NIV), and a defender of all am I in My holy dwelling (Psalm 68:5 NIV). You are loved by Me.

Love, Your Heavenly Father. Amen!

Self-Discovery / Self-Reflection

Application

(1) Find a family photo with you in and put on your vision board.
(2) Reflect and chat on the questions below with your mother or a close adult female friend (mentor).
(3) *Look up and write down on your vision board the Bible verses from this chapter that inspired you and use them to also answer the questions.*

Thinking of Me: Who Am I?

1. What is a family? Are you growing up in a single-family or blended family? Are you adjusting to different family dynamics?

_____
_____

2. What are your values and beliefs? How important are they in forming the person you will become?

_____
_____

3. What makes you upset or disappointed? How do you handle those situations?

_____
_____

4. Do you have a relationship with God? What do you believe about and how He loves and created you as a gift to your parents?

_____
_____

5. Do you attend classes and worship services at a Mass or church and read the Bible? Why or why not?

_____
_____

Part Two

You Belong to God, Our Relationship with God Based on Gender and Purpose Outside the Family

Girls can survive without a boyfriend but they can't survive without a best friend.
  —*Anonymous*

Friends come and friends go, but a true friend sticks by you like family.
  —*Proverbs 18:24 (The Message Bible)*

CHAPTER 4

What's Right with Me? Love and Girlfriend Relationships

You Belong to God in Girlfriend Relationships

Our family relationships also affect our relationships outside the home. Family relationships prepare us for interacting with peers, teachers, classmates, mentors, and girlfriends outside our homes. God created humans. He created us relational beings. In our DNA is the need to belong and be connected to others in relationships. So quite naturally, we will be drawn first to girls like ourselves.

As our world gets bigger, we start meeting new people at school and at church services. Our parents, sisters and brothers are no longer our only world. Thus, begins the process of trying to figure out where do we really fit in?

From infancy to pre-school age, the church and school is the new community for interacting with peoples. At church, the pastor or priest baptizes or christens or dedicates the baby at the request of our parents. We learn more about who God is. Our parents' commit to live and raise us according to the teachings of the Bible. We learn about how much God loves us. We get involved and experience worship by singing the congregational hymns, reading of the Holy Scriptures, and listening to the message from the Bible preached about God and His Son Jesus Christ. The church is the most important setting for learning and discovering our identity in Christ and meeting other like-minded individuals.

The other place for meeting new people is in either public, private, or charter schools, who may possibly become our girlfriends. A friend is a person you know well, someone you trust, commit to and like a lot. You have similar interests and mutual respect for each other. She is usually not a member of your family. A friendship is formed when two people are able to relate to each other. Once you enter into friendships, you are showing your ability to relate to other people, especially those of the same gender. As school begins, the test becomes how well you know yourself and your ability to choose the right type of friends to be in relationship with for a long time.

Best Friends Forever (BFFs)

Our girlfriend relationships are the first platform outside of the home, where we also begin to relate to others and ourselves in our own ethnic identity. A friend loves at all times (Proverbs 17:17a). There are three types of love in the Bible. *Agape* is divine love, *philos* is friendship love, and *eros is* romantic or desire and longing love. The one significant ingredient to healthy friendships is the philos love, usually between equals, expressed loyalty to friends, family, and community and requires virtue, equality, and familiarity. Ultimately, the character traits of "true friendships" you should look for and find in your BFF (best friend forever) are honesty, trust, commitment, availability, and loyalty.

No matter what state or country I have lived, it was not easy to make friends. The military moved Dad about every two years. I would end up becoming friends with at least one best girlfriend at a time from each assignment. The common denominator was usually our birthdays was the same date or our fathers served in the military.

California stands out as the most significant of all the places I have lived. I met my first BFF, Felicia in my freshman year of high school. Her stepdad was military. We discovered we were firstborns of two sisters, born in Alabama, same birthday month and year, and both attended the same Carousel Modeling School. We enjoyed modeling our hand-sewn creative designs in fashion shows. She was tall, vivacious, adventurous, outgoing and more talkative than me. We enjoyed each other's company. As we worked through our adolescent struggles of growing up, she inspired me because she openly expressed her feelings, which were my same thoughts. I became the listener and sounding board in our relationship.

In building healthy girlfriend relationships, be careful of the three deadly C's of *comparison, competition,* and *conformity.* Unless we are aware of the tendency that lurks within us to compare, compete, or conform, we will fall prey, be hindered, and lose the opportunity to soar in friendships with girls that stick closer than a sister (Proverbs 18:24 NIV).

Comparison

It is not wise to compare yourself with other girls and women. With comparison comes envy. Theodore Roosevelt said, "Comparison is the thief of joy." The Bible also addresses this issue in the book of Galatians chapter 6 verse 4 and 5 (NIV) ... *each one should test his own actions. Then he (her) can take pride in himself (herself), without comparing himself (herself) to somebody else, for each one should carry his (her) own load.*

You might ask, how can you escape comparisons with all the magazines, billboards, television, mass and social media portrayals of girls and women? How are you to know who you are? Marketing experts seem to do a good job at using their skills to display and distort images of imperfect girls and women, which suggests they want us to compare ourselves to the images and imitate them. These images are usually of people who look the opposite of who they really are. The images and photos are airbrushed to be picture perfect. It seems all too natural to have the tendency to compare our outward appearance by the way we look and dress with the way other girls look and dress or what we admire about them. Such as, their shoes or their ability to coordinate an outfit or makeup that looks good on them with what we have and wear.

As a matter of fact, a young teenager spoke up in 2012 when she was fourteen years old. Julia Bluhm, an eighth grader, challenged the popular teen magazine *Seventeen* to stop airbrushing the models.[28] Julia made what appeared a simple request by asking that they feature more real girls like themselves and do less warping, *meaning to distort or cause to distort from the truth, fact, or true meaning, biasing, falsifying,* of so many girls' self-esteem.[29]

Being satisfied or dissatisfied with our body and whether we are physically attractive, probably started when we entered into puberty. As the Internet, television, and media images become increasingly more prominent, we begin to learn how the influence of it all affects the way we feel, behave, and think about ourselves.

For example, there are seven in ten girls reported in "Real Girls, Real

Pressure: A National Report on the State of Self-Esteem" who believe they are not good enough or do not measure up in some way. It could be their looks, performance in school, or relationships with family and friends.[30] And about 53 percent of American girls at age thirteen are unhappy with their bodies. This percentage increases to 78 percent by the time they reach seventeen years old.[31] Another report suggests, a girl's self-esteem is more strongly related to how she negatively views her own body shape and body weight than how much she actually weighs. These girls are also four times more likely to take part in activities with boys that they've ended up regretting later.[32] Are there more deeply rooted issues among girls of color? Be careful not to put your faith in the data alone, but consider what it is not saying.

Another pearl of wisdom from the Bible also advises us to not compare ourselves with others. *Not that we dare to classify or compare ourselves with some of those who are commending themselves. But when they measure themselves by one another and compare themselves with one another, they are without understanding* (1 Corinthians 10:12 ESV). Your strength comes from God. This is one good reason to read the Bible for understanding and to learn how to apply it personally to our own lives.

Today, marketers are skillful in making girls subconsciously or consciously think and even daydream about their appearance and body shape. This may cause one to compare themselves with the images portrayed in the photos. The movie and music industry's subtle influences also draw us down a path of favoring a particular actress or music entertainer over another based on the way she looks; what she wears; how she looks in various hairstyles, clothing, and makeup; or what she owns. Their popularity heightens, their fan clubs grow, and girlfriend circles evolve around these celebrities on movie screens or videos or in live concerts and social media and Instagram.

Most obvious are the friendships built around iconic pop culture actresses or singers or athletes whom we admire, such as Miley Cyrus, Beyoncé, Taylor Swift, Selena Gomez, Emma Waters, Serena Williams, or Meghan Markle. They have the biggest impact on what we think about ourselves, therefore making it easier to compare ourselves to others by imitating their body and style.

On the other hand, when you are self-aware: *A person's gift makes room for him (her) and brings him (her) before great people (Proverbs 18:16 KJV)*. Therefore, remember famous people become talented in their own right. It is important to decide to never walk in anyone's shadow. The renowned, talented, and unforgettable Whitney Houston said it best when she wrote the revelation she received about her own life's journey in the song "The Greatest Love of All." The greatest love of all is inside of you.

At the start of the puberty phase, I began to become self-conscious about my physical body. The many military moves may have had a bearing on me spanning over eleven years from Alabama to Illinois back to Alabama to Ohio to Germany to Michigan to Illinois to Alabama again and to California before the last move when Mom brought us back permanently to Alabama. Mom moved her five children back to Alabama as a single parent to have a support system with her mother. The physical and emotional changes taking place within me affected how I interacted with other girls. Transitioning from the middle school to high school, the students did not seem the friendliest and it took some time to fit in with the girls. Did the students accept or reject me? Or was it just the dynamics of growing up and being a teenager? The move back to Alabama was only the second time I had attended a school where almost everyone was of the same ethnic identity. The first was in East St. Louis, Illinois. I believe the biggest hurdle in getting accepted and affirmed by my peers was figuring out where I fitted in. Who would be my girlfriend during this uncomfortable time? I was shy and did not have an idea how to connect with other girls. During gym classes, I would not change into my gym clothes while other girls were still in the locker room. It was nothing new because at home I was also private. Being alone without a girlfriend and doing things by myself was no big deal. I would wait until all the girls were out of the locker room either to change into gym clothes or wait to go into the shower and then into a bathroom stall to put on my clothes.

To avoid the temptation of comparing yourself, think about your own strengths, abilities, and likes and dislikes. What's right about me? God made us female with a different physical appearance than males. Yet, we are more than our physical appearance. When we look at others we tend to focus on looks first. Being born feminine and beautiful from exterior facial features to varying body shapes, facial features, hair color, nose, lips, eyes, and ear sizes are your specific qualities and attributes unique to you.

Therefore, knowing that you were created by God with so much right about you, then you should also be aware of what makes you feel comfortable in your own skin (regardless of your ethnic identity) without comparing yourself to others. God helps you to get to know more about who you are. He reveals His love to you through the right girlfriends He puts in your life.

Through the philo type love, you learn how to love and appreciate your girlfriend as God intended.

Bullying - Friends in Middle School: Another thought to consider is the phenomenon of bullying and how it is connected to envy and jealousy. It also affects the rise in suicides among young people. Is this possibly an outcome of people comparing themselves to others and lacking the sense of belonging when others reject them?

Did a middle school classmate, Avery, a native of East St Louis, Illinois, intentionally bully and pick a fight with me because she was comparing herself to me? I was in the hallway when the bell rung for a classroom change. Avery bumped into me in the hallway. I ignored it and kept walking. Once she saw the classroom I was going into, she stopped and stood in the middle of the classroom doorway, blocking me from getting clear and direct access into the room without touching her. I gently squeezed by her and went on into the room. My focus was to get in and out before the last bell rung to give a friend, Katie a pair of white shoes and be in my classroom seated.

I was coming out of the classroom heading to my class, Avery pushed me harder, saying that I bumped into her earlier. I had never been in a fight before. I refused to push her back. I just took it and kept on walking to my class. I was not going to fight her because I was afraid. I had not bumped into her intentionally. Why was she picking this fight with me?

There were not many people still in the hallway at the time. The bell rung, and everyone was seated in their classrooms. It was strange that out of nowhere it seems two young guys appeared, one standing on each side of Avery, holding up her arms and hands to keep her from swinging back at me, and encouraged me to go ahead and hit her back. It makes me wonder if anyone else saw the two guys. They held both her arms. Scared beyond belief and with hesitancy, I finally did what the guys said. I hit her back. "Again," they said. And I did.

See that you do not look down on one of these little ones (children). For I tell you that their (children) angels in heaven always see the face of my Father in heaven (Matthew 18:10 NIV). I did not know at the time that God dispatches His ministering angels to help defend those who belong to Him (Hebrews 1:14, Psalm 34:7). In my case, the guys must have been my protection sent by God.

Someone spread the rumor that there was going to be a fight after school. The school bus was crowded and packed to capacity with students anxious to see the fight continued. Teens were hanging off the overhead baggage rack. But, I was one very nervous seventh grader who had never been in a fight before in her life, not even with my siblings. When we got to my bus stop, I nervously got off the bus and began walking home. Only two other girls got off the bus with me. Avery did not get off the bus or was she even on the bus? The next day, when I arrived at school, my homeroom teacher instructed me to go to the principal's office. Nervous and afraid of the consequences, when asked I explained what happened. She had already heard Avery's side of the story. The principal then admonished me to not let it happen again. It was the first and last fight I had with a girl.

I'm not sure, but I believe I was one of the very few children of military parents who went to that middle school; the rest were local students. Usually, military families were provided housing on the base where the military parent worked, or they were given financial assistance to live in local cities near the base. Since my Dad was the sole provider for our family of seven and there was no base housing available, the realtor directed us to the urban community of minorities in East Saint Louis, Illinois, about twenty-five to thirty-eight miles from the military base. The majority of the students were natives of the city. I recall overhearing someone say that Avery was jealous of me. *Jealous? Why?* I thought. Jealous means hostile toward a rival or one believed to enjoy an advantage or feeling resentment against someone because of that person's rivalry, success, or advantages. It did not make sense. We were teenagers, so what did I possibly have for her to be driven to pick a fight with me. *"So in everything, do to others what you would have them do to you, for this sums up the Law and the Prophets"* (Matthew 7:12 NIV).

Avery's actions would be called bullying today. Her jealousy may have been because she was comparing herself to me. The fight made no sense to me.

Why not compare? Have you heard the story of the "Ugly Duckling" by Hans Christian Andersen? A fairy tale story usually told to children in elementary school about an ugly bird growing up among ducks who wanted to be accepted but was treated as an outcast because his outward appearance was not the same as theirs. As the bird grew up among the ducks, he one day discovered he was not a duck, but a beautiful swan. The theme of this story is about the search for our own identity rather than trying to be what we are not or trying to fit in.

Importance of Relationship with God and with Friends: Yet I do ask myself about the timing of other events in my life. Did this first-time fight happen before or after I responded to the pastor's call one day at church to pray for Jesus to wash my sins away. Was this God tugging at my heart for me to become a Christian by accepting His salvation gift, or had I already done that? Becoming a Christian meant acknowledging that you have sinned against God and disobeyed His commands in the Bible. When you admit that you have sinned and invite Jesus His Son to come into your heart to help you live in right relationship with God the Father and others, then your sins are forgiven and Jesus with the help of the Holy Spirit helps you do what is right and teaches you how to live loving others and yourself. Were those two boys sent by God to help me? In Hebrews 1:14 NIV, it is recorded, *are not all angels ministering spirits sent to serve those who will inherit salvation?*

During the church service one Sunday, there was a different feeling. In Paul's letter in 1 Corinthians 15:33 NIV, he reminds us, *do not be misled: 'Bad company corrupts good character.* Did the fight happen before or after I heard the preached words from the Bible when the preacher gave the invitation to everyone in attendance, "Do you want to have your sins washed away?" I believe it was the Holy Spirit of God tugging at my heart, speaking to me, and drawing me to naturally respond. You can get your sins washed away by praying, confessing your sins, and giving your heart to Jesus Christ. *And now what are you waiting for? Get up, be baptized and wash your sins away, calling on his name"* (Acts 22:16 MSG).

If you openly declare that Jesus is Lord and believe in your heart that God raised him from the dead, you will be saved. For it is by believing in your heart that you are made right with God, and it is by openly declaring your faith that you are saved (Romans 10:9–10 NLT). His gift is free. I had to acknowledge that I was a sinner (one who misses the mark, meaning failure to acknowledge God)[33] and believe in my heart Jesus Christ was God's Son and confess by faith I was saved. It was a step of faith that day to give my heart to Jesus: *"This is how much God loved the world: He gave his Son, his one and only Son. And this is why: so that no one need be destroyed; by believing in him, anyone can have a whole and lasting life"* (John 3:16 MSG). Then I was water baptized, which meant that I had made the decision in my heart to live in obedience to God according to the Bible and with the help of His Son, Jesus, and the Holy Spirit. Water baptism is a public expression of the decision you make in your heart that you are in the Christian family of God. When we choose to accept God's gift to live our life in a relationship with Him, *I tell you that in the same way there will be more rejoicing in heaven over one sinner who repents than over ninety-nine righteous persons who do not need to repent* (Luke 15:7 NIV). This life-changing experience was a miracle that occurred at Saint John Missionary Baptist Church in Illinois on March 17th.

Just like we get a birth certificate to remember our birthday, my baptism certificate is my remembrance of the first most important decision I made in my life—to ask for the forgiveness of my sins and to give my heart to Jesus Christ and be baptized into the Christian family. Amazingly enough, my parents had also been married twelve years on the exact same date. Only God orchestrates such events in our lives, and they are not coincidental. God inspired the psalmist to write in Psalms 139 to keep us focused on who He is and how important it is for us to know Him because God knows us. *Like an open book, you watched me grow from conception to birth; all the stages of my life were spread out before you, the days of my life all prepared before I'd even lived one day ...* (Psalm 139:16 MSG).

In reference to my 7th grade fight, I believe that God the Father knew ahead of time what my actions would be. *"And we know that all things work together for good to them that love God, to them who are called according to His purpose"* (Romans 8:28 KJV). God's ministering angels were on assignment, watching over my life and helping me at a difficult time. In the Old Testament text of the Bible in Psalm 91 verse 11 (NIV), *". . . for he will command his angels concerning you to guard you in all your ways."* And in the New Testament of the Bible, it is reemphasized by Jesus in the gospel of Luke chapter 4 verse 10 (MSG): *For it is written: 'He will command his angels concerning you to guard you careful.*

I prayed with my pastor, confessing I wanted to be saved and that I was a sinner, one who had transgressed against God. I can understand why I may have gone to the altar for prayer after the fight. My feelings within my heart and my conscience may have been teaching me right from wrong and about the sin of fighting. I believe the fight may have happened after I was baptized. What explains the two guys who may have been God's ministering angels sent to watch over me. The lesson I needed to learn about growing up is knowing when it is okay to fight back and not let anyone just walk all over me, to learn how to speak up for myself, to not be bullied. God knows each one of His children's hearts, and for me, this was the beginning of several life lessons about how and when it is acceptable to stand up for yourself and not let others be inconsiderate or take advantage of you. The two unknown guys giving me the courage to defend myself is an affirmation of God's Word. In the Message Bible, Romans 12:19 commands,*"Don't insist on getting even; that's not for you to do. 'I'll do the judging,' says God. 'I'll take care of it."*

Each girl is unique. A girl having at least one girlfriend is good. Was the fight because Avery may have not had any friends, and she chose to bully me by picking a fight? Maybe she had been rejected by others or not felt loveable or capable at home with her parents and family. I am not sure; however, I believe God allowed the incident for me to hear His message through the pastor.

Acceptance - Friends in Middle School: After being assigned to the seat right behind a girl in my 9th grade English class, one day I took the risk to start a conversation with her. Bonnie responded and the conversation began. I discovered she was a "military brat" whose father had served in the Army. We found we had common interests. She was a clothes designer too. She became my middle and high school best girlfriend in Alabama, and the relationship continued on into college until our circle of friends expanded. To this day, she thinks I tried to get her in trouble when we were both caught talking in Ms. Grove's English class. She did not realize how shy I was, how difficult it was for me to even initiate the conversation and how excited I was that she even talked to me. I was the shy new student at the school. She was the first to make me feel welcomed with her friendly, outgoing, beautiful, and positive attitude. Having doubt and insecurities, I was thankful she responded and was receptive to helping me feel comfortable in the new school setting.

As our friendship blossomed, I became a part of her family like a sister. Her family owned a local hair salon and boutique. Although, my mom was a beautician and did her daughters' hair, I was excited the day she allowed me to get my hair professionally styled. Of course, I went to Bonnie's family shop. We modeled in fashion shows together. On a limited budget when we started to college, we decided we would design our own outfits. One trait of a close girlfriend is when you dress alike. One night over the phone she talked me through what to do to create a pattern for a top we would make to wear to college the next day. Her mother, a Mary Kay Consultant introduced a group of teen girls to Mary Kay Cosmetics. She gave us facials and taught us basic skincare. One night over the phone, Bonnie and I decided we would make an outfit alike. We created and cut a pattern design for our outfit from newspaper. She described how we should blend our eye makeup colors to match our outfits. The next day, we celebrated the great job we did in designing and sewing our matching outfits. And looking at each other's face, we had also applied our makeup perfectly. Girlfriends have common interests and goals.

Competition

Competition can be a virtue or a vice. There are two types of competitiveness, which has an effect from the psychological and social well-being of a person. One side of competing to win is to dominate and outperform others. The other is to perform well and surpass your own personal goals. Competition among girls can be healthy once we are clear why we are competing.

For example: The two girls, we heard about on national television, who at the 2016 summer Olympics in Rio de Janeiro displayed good team sportsmanship. Abbey D'Agostino (twenty-four years old), a devout Catholic from Topsfield, Massachusetts, and Nikki Hamblin (twenty-eight years old) from New Zealand were running track when they stumbled and fell one over the other. When Abbey and Nikki fell on the track, Abbey encouraged Nikki to get up and keep running. Both girls got up to continue running when Abbey fell down again. Both girls picked themselves up and managed to finish the race. Both girls received the Fair Play awards by the Olympic Committee.

The Olympics is the leading international sports event, and these two girls visibly displayed two of God's attributes of kindness and unselfish ambition. *Don't push your way to the front; don't sweet-talk your way to the top. Put yourself aside, and help others get ahead. Don't be obsessed with getting your own advantage. Forget yourselves long enough to lend a helping hand (Philippians 2:3,4 TMB)*. Abbey had to have possessed the gift of unselfish ambition before the Olympics because when in competition the quality does not just show up out of the blue. Their self-worth was already a part of their nature. It was not based on what others thought. The gospel writer of Matthew 5:16 (NIV), *In the same way, let your light shine before men, that they may see your good deeds and praise your Father in heaven. And Love one another with brotherly affection. Outdo one another in showing honor (Romans 12:10, ESV). And two people are better off than one, for they can help each other succeed. If one person falls, the other can reach out and help. But someone who falls alone is in real trouble! (Ecclesiastes 4:9–12 NLT).*

What sports are you and your BFF active in? Bowling, swimming, basketball, volleyball, soccer, lacrosse, and jogging are all fun and can be team sports. I enjoyed sports; however, I was not a competitor, nor were my girlfriends. In high school, I enjoyed track and field. However, I did not pursue it. And I also enjoyed military drill and marching in formations.

When I finally decided to get pass my own fears, I tried out for a high school marching band position in the majorette corps with my BFF, but we were not selected. I had hoped to follow in my Mom's footsteps as a majorette at her Carver High School Wolverines, our alma mater. A few years later in my senior year, most of the girls I knew were being named the Most Beautiful or Most Talented or Most Likely to Succeed. I was happy for my BFF who was named the "Most Beautiful" because she was. She was also friendly, talented, outgoing, and kind. On another occasion, she entered a contest and was selected for the local Miss Beauty and Talent award. If it had not been for my BFF I do not know if I would have even tried out for the local teen contest, in which I did win the "Miss Congeniality Award."

Where did I fit in? What is right about me? I had good grades and was a member of the social clubs at school and in the city. However, I skeptically decided to take a bold step and let it be known I wanted to run for Miss Varsity. The past Miss Varsity's were beautiful girls. How could I compete if physical beauty is the sole criteria? I knew I was not the beauty queen type as defined by society at that time and to top it off, I wore eyeglasses. I beamed with joy upon hearing the news that I had been selected Miss Varsity, my senior year. I designed my two-piece outfit and modeled it with pride as I strolled down the football field arm in arm with the quarterback and his football teammate. My confidence was boosted another notch that day.

I grew comfortable in associating with girls of color. Because I was usually one of the only ones in my classes when moving from military base to base. I did not have time to connect and get to know the girls. By the time I graduated from high school my self-esteem was positive and helped me in college. The more I was around my ethnic group, the more comfortable I felt.

But the Bible admonishes us to be leery of a lot of friends. I became guarded, when I overheard girls talking about other girls. I took what I learned about gossiping from reading the Bible in Sunday school and church literally. *A gossip goes around telling secrets, but those who are trustworthy can keep a confidence* (Proverbs 11:13 NIV). *A troublemaker plants seeds of strife; gossip separates the best of friends* (Proverbs 16:28 NIV). I understood what it felt like after hearing girls talking negatively about other girls. I believe this was the other reason I shied away from girl conversations. Because I feared they would do the same and talk about me. I already knew my flaws. Think of your friends and assess your trust in and loyalty to them. I learned how to be a good listener and how to be the type of friend I wanted in a friend. *The godly give good advice to their friends; the wicked lead them astray (Proverbs 12:26*

NLT). *Don't be fooled by those who say such things, for "bad company corrupts good character" (First Corinthians 15:33 NLT).*

By the time I was a senior, I discovered that over the years the girls I enjoyed being one-on-one with were those considered outcasts or loners, like me. I was not one to compete, especially for another's friendship.

I do recall one day getting so upset that by the time I got home alone with no one there when for the first time I openly shouted at the top of my voice with anger and disappointment. Because that day I had decided for the first time to engage in a group conversation with some girls, which did not turn out like I hoped. I walked away feeling embarrassed and rejected. I shouted to myself when I got home, "One day, I will show them. Everyone will know who I am because I am going to get married on the capitol steps!" (thinking the Montgomery Alabama capital steps; a childish comment, I know.) Yes, what did one have to do with the other? I do not know but it was how I felt at the time.

The Bible teaches us about healthy self-esteem. *There are friends who destroy each other but a real friend sticks closer that a brother / sister* (Proverbs 18:24 NLT). It is difficult to get to know and trust more than one person at a time. Friendship takes time and energy and you have to know your own personality, strengths and talents first. In order to have quality friendships, you must become a friend first and you will know what you need in a friend. *Do nothing from rivalry or conceit, but in humility count others more significant than yourselves* (Philippians 2:3 ESV). In winning a race, a beauty contest, or anything that results in a reward or public recognition, it takes hard work, self-denial, and preparation. Our success and achievements should not be based on worldly standards. Put others first, consider their interests more important than our own by laying aside selfishness. Treat others with respect and common courtesy, which links us with Christ. Jesus Christ is a true example of humility. Our self-worth comes from who we are in Christ Jesus and His example of serving others without expecting anything in return. He loved and respected His Father, the oppressed, marginalized, and outcasts and was obedient all the way to the cross of Calvary.

Conformity

It may be easy and natural for 'tweens in middle school to feel the pressure to conform. By the time they are teens in high school, it is definitely challenging to be positive and confident. 'Tweens continue to struggle unless they know who they are and what is right about them. Do you understand what it means to be accepted and not rejected and to be self-aware and not bullied?

According to psychologist Abraham Maslow, our need to be loved and belong is crucial. And also self-esteem is achieved through confidence and achievement and the desire for reputation or the respect of others. Teens join girl clubs, sports, gangs, and cliques and select friends in an effort to feel a sense of belonging. One-way teens achieve this sense of belonging is to dress or act like or participate in activities and events with friends or members of the clique, club, gang, or team. Lee Grayson in his book "Conformity in Teenagers" suggests that in most teens' conformity may be a way of satisfying the belonging need.[34]

In order for your identity to be shaped according to the character traits given you by God, be true to your identity and be the kind of friend who shows herself friendly not conforming to the world's standards but to God's. As the Apostle Paul suggests to his reader in Romans 12:2 (NIV), *Do not conform any longer to the pattern of this world, but be transformed by the renewing of your mind. Then you will be able to test and approve what God's will is—his good, pleasing and perfect will.* The best way not to conform to what others are doing is to not be copy-cats or comply or behave according to socially acceptable conventions or standards. Let God transform you into a new person by changing the way you think about yourself and other girls. To no longer conform means to "fashion oneself "like another. By avoiding the worldly customs, fads, and trends, you preempt covetousness and arrogance from rearing its' ugly head. Let God change the way we think by praying and reading the Bible and ask the Holy Spirit to renew, reeducate, and redirect our minds to truly be transformed by the Holy Spirit (Romans 8:5). I would go into my "prayer clothes closet" to be with God when relationships seemed most difficult. I made up my mind I would not be like others. For example, when I got my first watch, I decided I'd do the opposite and wear it on the right arm versus the left, even though I was right-handed. I usually did the opposite of what others, making my style unique.

Love always protects, always trusts, always hopes, always perseveres (1 Corinthians 13:7 NIV). *A person of many companions may come to ruin, but there is a friend who sticks closer than a brother"* (Proverbs 18:24 NIV).

Girlfriends Destined by God

As I matured, I began noticing a pattern with the type girls coming into my life seemingly for a specific purpose and for a season. For example:

Girlfriends in College: During my sophomore year, I met and became friends with two peers who were classmates in the Business Administration program. Lois and MaeElla were from Tuscaloosa. Lois admired the way my BFF and I wore coordinated stylish outfits. And she thought of herself as a plain-Jane, she said. Although she was endowed with a beautiful head of long flowing hair, she simply took it and put it in a pony-tail. Once she discovered we were not as aloof, stuck up, and non-approachable, we all hung out with each other. These assumptions were made about each without all the information until the fear barriers were removed. Both Lois and MaeElla (an only child) were sharp and inquisitive in class. She articulated questions or statements well in class. They were friendly, outgoing, and became my friends. Since I was a local commuter student, they allowed me to use their dorm room to lay my head down or change of clothes between classes. They would also come by our house to eat and chill out. I met and befriended another local commuter classmate, Lillian. I met her in a class and learned she was also a member of the Belk-Hudson Teen Board. She was the fourth child of three sisters. Her sister and a guy I dated attended the same college in Huntsville. We became travelling buddies and study partners. We drove up to their annual classic football games and the Greek Show featuring her sister's sorority pledge line.

Girlfriends in our careers: People are in our lives for the specific purpose of God. When my active duty career began I met a sorority sister Ada through her military boyfriend Jimmy. They married and conceived their firstborn. I was honored to be asked to be the god-mother of my first adorable and precious god-daughter, Jamila. In my next assignment and frequent travels to Korea, I met and was impressed by the first female military lawyer, Theresa. Over the years, we fashionable, single, professional traveling partners. She invited me to attend annual national lawyers' conferences. In California and nearing the end of my assignment and boyfriend breakup, God sent me my second roommate, a single military woman, Jeanne. She was an animal lover from the Midwest, who grew up raising horses. When Jeanne realized the value of a pet companion for me, she persuaded me to get a pet cat. With her help and despite my fear of cats from childhood, I became the owner of a Himalayan kitten, the runt of the litter. I named him "Neko" (means cat in Japanese). Cats are low maintenance, however, she promised me if he does not work out for you, I will take him. Neko was a delight and kept me company. He was playful, loyal, non-judgmental, and unconditionally loved me. Yet, when I was travelling a lot, I had to leave him home alone. I decided to get him a female kitten companion and named her Joy.

God made a way in the midst of boyfriend troubles to send a Christian co-worker on my job, named Marsha to get me focused back on being in the community of other believers. As a female she sensed something troubling my spirit without me saying anything to her about it. She was sent by God to steer me back to Him. I had neglected going to Sunday School, church, and Bible Study as I was raised to do. Well, all her conversations were focused on God, His Son Jesus Christ, and the Holy Spirit. God was using her to get me going back to church on a regular basis. Marsha, along with two other women on different occasions had invited me to attend the same Bible-teaching church in Los Angeles. Because I listened to other people speak negatively about the mega church, regrettably, I never visited the church to find out for myself what God was guiding me to do. But, that did not deter Marsha's persistence in getting me to grow closer to God by reading my Bible and praying daily. After visiting several Baptist churches, I did not find the right one to join and subtly stopped going to church. She talked at length about the Scriptures and their application to our lives. We prayed together. She taught me how to pray God's promises in Scripture back to Him, how to pray aloud, and encourage me about how much God cared for me.

One day, out of urgency I called and asked Marsha to pray for me. She turned the request back on me by saying, "no, you pray." I said, No, I can't pray like you. Please pray for me. She still declined by saying, "no, you do it." She knew I was desperate and needed prayer. She chose the right time to make me pray aloud with her for myself. I am grateful for that day she taught me by trial and error how to pray with someone else, and how to pray for others and how to pray for myself according to verses from the Bible.

It later clicked why she also, spoke three words out of the blue once, "You are special! You need to see yourself the way God sees you." I had been focused on the boyfriend and not attending church or Bible Study like in past assignments. Boyfriends had taken the place of God. I use to go to church regularly, but I had stopped going to Calvary Baptist because it was hard to choose another church after the pastor retired and his successor having a very short stint as the pastor. Jesus answered them, *"Truly, truly, I say to you, everyone who practices sin is a slave to sin" (John 8:34 NLT SE). "And remember, if you were a slave when the Lord called you, you are now free in the Lord. And if you were free when the Lord called you, you are now a slave of Christ (1 Corinthians 7:22 NLT).*

Subsequently, by the time I got to my next assignment, I received on separate occasions, three God-sent sisters in Christ, three girls God chose to become my girlfriends. I praise God for —JoAnna, Bonnie, and Carolyn. His timing was perfect. We became, *"as iron sharpens iron, so one person sharpens another" (Proverbs 27:17 NIV)*. We were totally different in personality. But we possessed one common denominator, our desire to grow spiritually in the knowledge and relationship of God.

Carolyn, an active duty member and I met at the time God had called me back into a relationship with Him. I was starting fresh in Colorado, since God's divine intervention with me and co-worker, Marsha in California. While searching for churches to join in the local area, I also checked the base chapel to find out about their noon-time Bible Study. She was a commander of one of the units. I invited her to be involved in the Protestant Women of the Chapel (PWOC) Bible Study and she took me up on my offer. In our reflections of how our friendship evolved, she shared what she thought about me initially. To her I was a wimp and to me she was overbearing and seemingly too hardcore military. As she points out, we were like night and day. We often laugh about it. On another occasion I praise God for her obedience. I arrived home when the phone ranged. It was Carolyn who said, Sandra are you all right? Wondering why she was asking, she shared, in a quick moment she heard in her spirit to pray for Sandra, she immediately stopped what she was doing and dropped to her knees to pray in the nick of time. She asked what happened. I said, I was driving home alone on the freeway at the 55 or 60 speed limits, when I must have hit some black ice. My car made a 360-degree turn in the middle of the highway. Praise God, no other oncoming cars were nearby although I could see at a distance the headlights approaching. Your prayers were right on time as I was headed into what appeared an embankment from the center lane of the freeway, but the car spun right out of it back in the direction I was travelling and I kept going without having stopped. *"The earnest prayer of a righteous person is powerful and effective" (James 5:16b NIV).*

JoAnna was nearing the end of her military career as a nurse at the clinic. We spent time getting to know each other and I became intrigued by how God spoke through her intellect. As she was preparing to relocate out of the area with her two children, she invited me to lunch at a local Red Lobster restaurant. She was excited about sharing and us digging deeper into the meaning of the text she discovered in Ephesians chapter 3 verse 20 (NIV) *"Now to him who is able to do immeasurably more than all we ask or imagine, according to his power that is at work within us, to him be glory in the church and in Christ Jesus throughout all generations, for ever and ever! Amen."* We discussed it and prayed about it with expectancy of what God was doing in us.

Bonnie was the civilian I met while waiting to be interviewed for a Teacher's Training class at Happy Church. Our conversation started with me complimenting her perfectly manicured and polished nails and wearing a beautiful green gemstone ring. With a nice soft-spoken voice, she said my favorite color is green. She and her husband, William became my closest married friends. She taught me how to prepare a vision board for God to send me the right mate based on the Scripture *"Then the LORD replied: "Write down the revelation and make it plain on tablets so that a herald may run with it. For the revelation awaits an appointed time; it speaks of the end and will not prove false. Though it linger, wait for it; it will certainly come and will not delay"* (Habakkuk 2:2,3 NIV). Once I completed my vision board, she reassured me that God keeps his promises. In the waiting for Him to answer, she held me accountable in the waiting on God to bring me the mate He had for me. Bonnie and William counseled me and assessed the legitimacy of suitors to make sure they met the vision board and prayer list criteria. As counterfeits came, they helped me to ask myself the right questions and always directed me to Christ.

God sent for the first time I had ever seen, an ordained female Chaplain Craig to serve the Protestant community and be the Protestant Women of the Chapel (PWOC) Advisor. At the time of her arrival, I was serving as President of PWOC and very inquisitive about understanding the Bible. She volunteered to teach me how to read the Bible New Testament in Greek, the original language. I was thrilled about learning more about God and the fact that she would take the time to personally teach me. I started lessons with her, which was short-lived. I chickened out because of all the extra time needed and the intensity of the studies.

In order to stay knowledgeable and proficient in contracting, I attended annual National Contract Management Association (NCMA) conference. I observed a sharp military female in what seemed a sea of men. She was sharp and stood her ground. Mary was two ranks my senior. Our ethnic difference did not matter to us. We were females who became friends and a good support network for each other, she primarily for me.

By the time I moved to Ohio, God knew the support system I would need of women so He literally sent one from Texas a meticulous and brilliant professional human resources director and leader, who also became a friend and mentor, Carolyn, became affectionately known as "Sistah." God also positioned in my life, First Lady Noble of Shiloh Baptist Church, a retired female Air Force Colonel, a nurse trailblazer who distinguished herself by becoming the base commander. She was my prayer warrior, advisor, and mature friend. I became her and Pastor Noble's surrogate daughter. By the time I moved to Washington D.C., the Lord had already started working and building an opportunity for me to connect with an anointed retired couple to mentor me through a very emotional and mental hardship, whom I affectionately called "Mom V" and "Pop V. They became my eternal prayer warriors, friends, and surrogate parents' also. God knew the girls and women I needed in my life before I did. It was *"not without avail the prayers of the righteous were very powerful and effective"* (James 5:16b NLT).

I received a call from former college classmate Lois who was living in Boston at the time. She said, I am coming to Canton Ohio with my pastor and members of our church. How far are you she asked? I arrived in Canton, she introduced me to the pastor, his wife a sorority sister and other members. When from a short distance a young woman was walking towards her, I said she looks familiar. What is her name? Lois said, Esther. I did not recognize the last name but continued to think how familiar she looked. Lois introduced us. I said to Esther, you look so familiar. I asked a few other questions. But when she said she was from Warren Ohio I said I use to live there. Then it clicked, we were in the 4th and 5th grade together. She was the smart, straight A student I admired. Wow, I said to Lois who I met in college in Alabama and she was introducing me to a girl I was in elementary school with in Ohio many, many years prior. I eventually was able to show her the photos from our 4th and 5th grade classes with both of us in it. God divinely intervenes in our lives and He gets involved in every aspect from the womb until the end of life. Esther and I had the same birthday and year.

Girlfriends in our Sisterhood: During my career God predestined from our pledge line sister Gwen and me to reconnect after college about seven years into my career while assigned in Denver. Once she made sure I knew that her pastor, Reverend (Bishop now) Vashti McKenzie was coming to Denver to be the keynote speaker and preacher at our sorority Founder's

Day celebration. Her speech "Pressing for my Blessing" sustained me on my job with predominately all males and gave me hope that God will do the impossible, as He did for the Syrophoenician woman and her daughter (Matthew 15:21-28). Gwen and I bonded over the years as she kept me abreast of sorority events. And when I moved to the Washington D.C. area, our friendship grew closer. As God kept blessing and elevating her, she always remained approachable, generous, and humble.

Psychologist Abraham Maslow believes our behavior is motivated by love and belongingness, which includes friendship, family, intimacy, and sense of connection. I agree that by the end of my California tour and then both the Colorado and Ohio assignments, I grew spiritually by leaps and bounds. I was stretched to trust. Each girlfriend brought a unique gift of herself to our friendship. I learned more about myself and how to value what I brought to the friendship. More and more, I began to be comfortable in girlfriend relationships. I believe, I became less likely to stay in my comfort zone of what I perceived were better non-committal and non-judgmental friendships with guys. Maslow notes that self-esteem is built on confidence, achievement, and the desire for a good reputation. You must have the respect of others and respect by others.[35] He further emphasizes to self-actualize is the desire to become the most that one can be through morality, creativity, spontaneity, problem solving, lack of prejudice, acceptance of facts, vitality, creativity, self-sufficiency, authenticity, playfulness, and meaningfulness.

A Love Letter from Your Heavenly Father

Dearest Daughter,

I made you unique. Each girl is uniquely designed with a purpose. This also means you have a girlfriend made just for you and you for her. Therefore, trust Me from the bottom of your heart; and do not try to figure out everything on your own. Listen to My voice in everything you do, everywhere you go, I am the one who will keep you on track (Proverbs 3:5-6 MSG). You will not have to compare, compete, or conform to the standards of others, but I will provide you with sincere friends who will not draw you away from Me. Watch what I do, and then you do it, like children who learn proper behavior from their parents. Mostly what I do is love you. Keep company with Me and learn what love is. Observe My Son and how His love was not cautious, but courageous. He did not love in order to get something from you but to give everything of Himself to you. Love like that (Ephesians 5:1-2 MSG). For I know you and those who will be your best friends. I chose you and them to be in the same image and identity as My Son Jesus, the firstborn among many. And having chosen you, I called you to come to Me. And having called you, I gave you right standing with Myself and I give you My Glory (Romans 8:28-30 ESV).

    I created girls to be friends, you to her and she to you with the same godly beliefs. There is a friend who sticks closer than a brother (Proverbs 18:24 NIV). Two are better than one, because they have a good return for their work: if one falls down, her friend can help her up. But pity the person who falls and has no one to help her! (Ecclesiastes 4:9,10 NIV). Motivate your girlfriend(s) to acts of love and good works. Therefore, do not avoid worshiping Me together but spur each other in the faith (Hebrews 10:24 NLT). Don't be selfish or try to impress others. Be humble, consider others better than yourself (Philippians 2:3 NLT). Do not become friends with those who reject Me. How can you make a friendship out of right and wrong? That's not partnership; that's war. Is light best-friends with dark? (2 Corinthians 6:14 MSG). It weakens your commitment to Me. Darkness is the temptations that keeps you from doing what is right and good in My sight. A righteous person will do what is right and what pleases Me first. Therefore, be friends with those who revere Me and committed to living by my instructions and being trained to live obeying My counsel. My love fills the earth! (Psalm 119:63,64 MSG).

    Do not run when you face conflict with peers. Love them. Let them bring out the best in you, not the worst. When they give you a hard time, respond with the energies of prayer. You will be acting as a true child of Mine giving your best (Matthew 5:44, 45 MSG). My angels help and guard your life in difficult times (Psalm 91:11). Love unconditionally with a friendship love. My love is patient and kind. Not jealous or boastful or proud or rude. Love doesn't demand its own way, is not irritable, and it keeps no record of being wronged. It does not rejoice about injustice but rejoices whenever the truth wins out. Love never gives up, never loses faith, is always hopeful, and endures through every circumstance (1 Corinthians 13: 4 NIV). There is no greater love than for someone to lay down their life for their friend (John 15:13 MSG). AMEN!

With love, Your Friend, God

Self-Discovery / Self-Reflection

Application

(1) *Find a photo of you and your girlfriends, and add it to your vision board.*
(2) *Reflect and chat about the questions below with your mother or a close adult female friend (mentor).*
(3) *Look up and write down on your vision board the Bible verses from this chapter that inspired you and use them to also answer the questions.*

Thinking about Me: What's Right With Me? Love & Girlfriend Relationships

1. How will you start imitating God and be careful not to imitate other girls?
_____
_____

2. What are 5-10 memories or qualities you most admire about your girlfriends / BFFs at school or church?
_____
_____

3. Is it easy or difficult to make friends? Do you compare, compete, or conform to what you think about your classmates, their families, and homes?
_____
_____

4. How do you and your girlfriends resolve arguments or disagreements? Or have you ever been bullied or in a fight? How does rejection make you feel?
_____
_____

*Your heart is precious to God; so guard it and wait
for the man who will treasure it.*
—*Author Unknown*

*You are the daughter of the King: so walk like it, talk like it, dress
like it, and wait for the godly man who treats you like it.*
—*Author Unknown*

*Imagine a man so focused on God that the only reason he looked
up to see you is because he heard God say, "That's her."*
—*Author Unknown*

CHAPTER 5

What's Right with Me? Love and Right Relationship with Boys

You Belong to God

Belonging to God is not easily understood when boys enter center stage of your life. When you hear the word *love*, what comes to mind? It is a word so often used to describe a variety of feelings and emotions about people and things. I love ice cream. Girl, I love those shoes you have on. I love my pet cat, Neko. I love to dance. But is this the same type love meant when it comes to girls and boys in relationship with each other.

Love makes a girl's heart go pitter-patter. Love is the glue that holds everything together in relationships, until something breaks that bond and wreaks havoc in her heart.

Solid relationships are essential in your social development. Do you daydream about falling in love? Do you have thoughts of being a wife and a mother and having a career? Usually, without saying it, a girl naturally thinks of one day marrying her Prince Charming. Yes, hearing those three little words, "I love you," usually get a girl's heart beating faster than normal when a guy she admires finally rolls them right off his tongue onto his lips and into her ears. It is a deep love that makes you dream of one day being a beautiful bride, having a Princess wedding, and becoming the wife of the man who loves you and showers you with his unconditional love.

Hopes of a Fairy-Tale Life

As you may know for yourself, the average girl enjoys reading or watching a good fairytale movie about the romance of girl meets boy Prince Charming—*Snow White*, *Alice in Wonderland*, *Beauty and the Beast*, *Hansel and Gretel*, *Sleeping Beauty*, *The Princess Bride*, *The Princess and the Frog*, *Frozen*, and many others. When she grows up she enjoys seeing her fairytale dreams come alive on screen from romance novels, such as *I Believe in a Thing Called Love*, *Just Friends*, and *My First Love*, or movies, such as *Sleepless in Seattle*, *Breakfast at Tiffany's*, *Pretty Woman*, *The Wedding Planner*, *How Stella Got Her Groove Back*, *Grease*, *Coming to America*, or even reality shows like *Real Housewives of Orange County / New York City / Atlanta / Beverly Hills / New Jersey*, and many others. Yes, it's in our DNA to love and to be loved.

Will your Prince Charming show up in your life as in the fairy-tale? He could show up in a similar way as in one of my all-time favorites, *Cinderella*. Cinderella is a beautiful love story about a kind-hearted and thoughtful girl whose mother died. Her father remarried, and his new wife became the evil stepmother with two daughters who all mistreated Cinderella. When Cinderella's father died, the treatment got worse. Cinderella became a servant in her own home by cooking the meals, cleaning the house, and having to sleep by the fireplace with the hot coals. Her step-sisters turned a beggar away. But, Cinderella offered him food and for her kindness, he spoke a blessing of good fortune to her in return. Soon after she was invited to the prince's ball. He was in search of a wife. The two step-sisters intercepted her invitation and totally ignored Cinderella's request to go with them. In despair and disappointment her fairy godmother showed up and transformed Cinderella into a beautiful Princess.

At the ball, Cinderella won the heart of the prince and it was love at first sight. At midnight she rushes from the ball to catch her pumpkin carriage after dancing with him. The prince runs to stop her when he noticed one of her glass slippers was left behind. The prince searches and finds Cinderella. He reveals himself to her. The moral to the story is Cinderella was kind, unselfish in serving others, had an inner beauty of the heart, compassionate, loving others without expecting anything in return, and good came back to her. She got her wish and Prince Charming asked her to marry him.

A girl's idea of marriage and the role of a wife usually comes from these type of fairy tales, or from the pages of magazines, reality TV shows, the

Internet, social media, or maybe her own parents' marriage. The constant images of girls imitating their mothers in their high-heeled shoes, makeup, and clothing, sitting and sipping tea with her Barbie and Ken dolls. Barbie says goodbye (at the door) to her make-believe husband Ken, as he leaves home for work. Although, this may be a girl's idea of love and marriage, there is still more to it!

Moral Character~A Girl of Virtue Obedient to God's Law

Two of the key ingredients to growing in your identity in Christ is living and loving yourself and others by possessing moral character and virtues. This is true of every human being. Moral character is the standard you set for right and wrong behavior. A moral person builds right character by their actions. A moral person follows the rules of conduct and has the character made up of positive virtues, like Cinderella. What is virtue? In the *Oxford Dictionary*, virtue is the behavior showing high moral standards or a quality considered morally good or desirable in a person, which includes virginity (chastity), integrity, honesty, loyalty, humility, compassion, forgiveness, authenticity, generosity, perseverance, politeness, kindness, optimism, reliability, conscientiousness, self-discipline, courage, fortitude, trustworthiness, respect, responsibility, fairness, caring, and citizenship, to name a few. That is simply, doing what is right and avoiding what is wrong. What is character? The *Webster Dictionary* definition of character is the mental and moral qualities distinctive of an individual, a person's good reputation, strength and originality in their nature.

Boy & Girl Relationships

Girlfriend-and-boyfriend relationships are inevitable. The fact is girls naturally relate to love, affection, kind treatment, and admiration from guys. Therefore, the boy and girl should discuss at the outset what they expect from the relationship. Yet, the most difficult task is to understand and recognize the purpose he is in your life. Is he just a platonic (philos, non-sexual) friend? Or is he a marriage prospect?

The Role of Boys in a Girls' Life: A significant milestone in your life is the stages of development from puberty to adulthood, where physical, mental, and social changes, trigger your thinking about boys in a different way. Because you were created to be in relationship, God planned for one male and one female to be attracted to each other, to marry, birth children, and build healthy families in admiration of Him first. God knew it was not good for man to be alone. That is why He created the female for her to be his equal helper and companion in marriage. For both male and female to be fruitful and multiply by marrying, having children and together having dominion over His creation.

> *In the beginning, the Lord God said, "It is not good for the man to be alone. I will make a helper suitable for him. So the Lord God caused the man to fall into a deep sleep; and while he was sleeping, he took one of the man's ribs and closed up the place with flesh. Then the Lord God made a woman from the rib he had taken out of the man, and he brought her to the man. The man said, "This is now bone of my bones and flesh of my flesh; she shall be called 'woman,' for she was taken out of man." For this reason a man will leave his father and mother and be united to his wife, and they will become one flesh (Genesis 2:18–24 NIV).*

For this reason, it is imperative for you to understand two critical things before entering into a relationship with boys. As a female, first you should know your likes and dislikes, strengths and weaknesses and second know your personality and character traits and values. This will be your thermometer for making the right choices about the role boys will be in your life, either purely for friendship or solely for marriage.

One of several good biblical examples about female friendships and marriage is found in one of the two books in the Bible named after a woman. Ruth, the Moabite, the daughter-in-law of Naomi was known to *"all the fellow townspeople as a woman of noble character" (Ruth 3:11 NIV)*. When Ruth's husband died, she pleaded with Naomi, her mother-in-law. *"Don't urge me to leave you or to turn back from you. Where you go I will go, and where you stay I will stay. Your people will be my people and your God my God. Where you die I will die, and there I will be buried. May the Lord deal with me, be it ever so severely, if anything but death separates you and me" (Ruth 1:16,17 NIV)*. Ruth was capable, efficient, and possessed the quality of sterling character, great ability, and had an industrious nature. She later married Boaz. Boaz and Ruth were the grandparents of King David and ultimately from their family tree and lineage was born Jesus, the Messiah and Savior of all humankind.

God made the woman for the man to be united in one spirit and with noble character, *"The wife who of noble character is her husband's crown, but a disgraceful wife is like decay in his bones" (Proverbs 12:4 NIV).* And *"a wife of noble character who can find? She is worth far more than rubies"* (Proverbs 31:30 NIV). These verses give us insight into how God was very intentional and purposeful about how He made girls to interact with boys and be accountable in relationships such as Ruth's with mature Christian women. He created male and female specifically for a committed and covenant relationship of marriage and reproduction. Since a girls' sense of belonging is rooted in and grows out of how she is loved, treated, and responded to by the men or boys in her life starting with family, then she must understand and behave knowing the difference between the two types of relationships with boys.

In becoming girls to women, the Bible teaches us that *"Charm can mislead and beauty soon fades. The woman to be admired and praised is the woman who lives in the Fear-of-GOD" (Proverbs 31:30 TMB).* Being of strong character, great wisdom, compassion, and possessing many skills improves our self-esteem, self-respect, confidence and self-worth.

Boys as Friends (philos). A girls' sense of belonging is also based on how she is loved, treated, and responded to by the men or boys in her life. A girl might choose to hang out with boys as friends for a number of reasons. Boys are usually easier to talk to than girls. Because girls are less likely to compare themselves to or compete with boys, they become more of an older brother to hang out with, confide in, learn sports from, and trust to protect and look out for them.

When my parents split up, I wanted a big brother. I found myself enjoying hanging out with my male cousins and popular athletes on mom's side of the family, Paul, Clarence and his brothers. They did not mind me occasionally tagging along with them at sport events or other activities.

However, I befriended one classmate, Robbie Henry, who appeared to be too religious or a bit "nerdy" to others. Every morning in our homeroom class, his voice came over the intercom. He read a verse from the Bible, gave a meditation followed by a prayer. When he finished, he'd come back to our homeroom class. Sometimes, I might ask a question about something I read in my Sunday school class, in the Bible, or heard in a sermon since he seemed knowledgeable of the Bible. He would do his best to explain. From those conversations a friendship began. He did not profess to know all the answers, but I enjoyed the conversations.

Boys as Boyfriends and Dates: Sixteen is usually the age most parents set for their daughters to start receiving boys at their home or going on dates. What exactly is dating? There is a difference between dating someone or being in a relationship. *Depending on the person and their culture,* dating may mean going on dates to events or activities with a person of the opposite gender with the purpose of getting to know and spending more time with each other. Or dating may mean a man and a woman are trying to figure out whether they are right for each other and ready for a long-term marriage relationship or commitment. Dating can mean a girl and a boy have made a commitment to each other, they are exclusively boyfriend and girlfriend together and not dating anyone else. Each one is committed to the other and officially agrees to the terms of the relationship. Some girl and boy relationships may naturally start out as a friendship of common interests, but later becomes romantic primarily out of curiosity.

Father Daughter Relationships & Influence on Boyfriends

The first person of the opposite gender in a girl's life is her father. He is most likely her first parental love… a healthy father–daughter love. Elizabeth Weiss McGolerick in "The Importance of the Father-Daughter Relationship" writes girls who have a healthy parental relationship with their Dad from infant to toddler, 'tween to teen, and into young adulthood more than likely will mature into strong and confident women.[38] It is said that girls usually end up with husbands like their fathers or another male role model who has most influenced their lives. Her relationship with her father influences the type of man she will date and eventually the husband she will marry.

Girls and women may struggle with male relationships on into womanhood, if they experienced a painful childhood event and did not grow up with their fathers in their lives. Usually for these girls, Iyanla Vanzant[39] observes, they will experience difficulty in forming a healthy bond in dating and relating to boys and men in their adult lives. When strong male role models are in a girl's life, she will have positive interaction with other males. And boys need a healthy relationship with their fathers as well to know how to treat girls.

Having my father in my life up to the initial fifteen years of adolescent was a blessing. I looked up to my Dad. He was handsome and a distinguished looking man with pre-mature salt-and-pepper hair. I admired him so much that I grew up hoping I'd one day have salt-and-pepper hair like him. He showed us love by what he did for us as a family, although pretty strict on his children. But at 15 years old and at a critical time in my growth cycle, he was absent. My dream of a marriage like my parents was shattered. I was clueless about how to interact with boys. How should you be in or not be in a boyfriend and girlfriend relationship?

During the required health and sex education course, I took the first year of high school in California, Dad used my homework as an opportunity to counsel me about what I was being taught. Dad successfully discouraged me from wanting to interact with boys, while he was present in our lives. We discussed what I should do and not do. As boys attempted to talk with me, I am sure dad knew he had one less worry about the city boys having access to his daughters because entry on a military base is only allowed with specific adult authorization. For the boys of families who lived on base, Dad's intimidating demeanor discouraged them from even looking our way. When we wanted to participate in fun base activities and events, like shopping, bowling, skating, swimming, or activities at the base youth center, Dad was somewhat lax especially once he confirmed the names of the adult chaperones, when needed. In most cases, we reassured Dad that boys were not the reason we were going to the youth center, theater, base exchange, bowling alley, and so on. His do and don't principles were ingrained within me.

The divorce took some time getting used to. With the puberty changes in my body and mind, the divorce, and single-parent lifestyle resulted in me having self-confidence issues, as I called it. I believe sleep was my way of escape. I slept a lot, taking naps in order for time to go by fast. Mom did not understand why I was sleeping so much and neither did I. I came home from school, did my homework, made sure my sisters and brothers were taken care of and that was it. There were nights Mom would get us out of bed with pajamas on to rush Buzzy to the emergency room at the military base because he had another asthma attack. Mom tried to figure out why I was sleeping so much. She would get upset with me. One day, seeing me sleeping after school again, she asked if I was pregnant. I was shocked because I did not understand why that question. "Mom, I am not doing anything," I said.

Not understanding why so much sleeping, she made my first gynecology appointment, just in case.

Boys Showing Interests ~ What does it mean?

When boys start showing interest in girls beyond friendship, then her moral character is tested. And when she fails to stick with her virtues, the guy succeeds in finding her weak spot and wins her heart and gets access to her body.

While in high school, I noticed classmates who had boyfriends. I would hear girls bragging about getting promise rings. They committed themselves to one boy and no one else. It all seemed normal and what was expected of girls and boys our ages. But Dad had set the rules for his daughters about boys. In his absence, obeying his rules did not seem like a big deal at first. Until my heart and mind began to respond to the guy who showed interest in me with harmless conversation. We were friends first.

Dad was not physically present to enforce his strict dating rules. Despite the fact he taught us morals of what to not do, how does a girl protect her heart? This was a difficult time of dealing with boys without Dad. Even with his long-distance telephone calls and letters, discussion about our boy relationships never came up during my teen years. We did not call to ask him about what to do or not do. Although, he called us, he did not seem discouraged by our lack of response to his calls. It was challenging for all of us.

But one year ahead of me in high school was a boy named Yearnell. He began paying attention to me and showing interest beyond the usual. After school he started waiting for me to walk and talk on my way home. He reached for my books to carry mine on one arm and his own in the other. When we reached a point near my home, he turned around and headed back in the direction of the school to get back to his home across town. By giving me attention with his well-versed youthful conversations, acts of kindness, friendly and playful nature, he slowly opened the door of my heart. Now what? What do you do with your heart when the words of affirmation and acts of kindness come from a boy?

Is this the guy I will marry? Now the big day finally arrived. Yearnell, the firstborn of his parents took me home to meet his mother. An immediate bond seemed to take place with me and his mother. He and his two brothers had the fortune of having both their parents raising them. Our relationship was sealed the day he told me he loved me and gave me a promise ring. We committed our love to one another. We will get married, have children, and live happily ever after. It was official.

We were boyfriend and girlfriend talking on the phone every chance we could in our free time. He was a frequent at our house, but absolutely not allowed while mom was absent. We did a lot of fun things together and on special holidays, I received special cards and stuffed animals. All our classmates knew our status with each other. Other boys knew to stay away from me. I was taken. He was also the first to teach me how to drive a standard shift car.

I cared a lot for him. I loved him. Then he began gently convincing me to do what we should not do. Based on what I was taught in the health education class and after having had the "talk" from Dad and Mom. Mom's focus was about girls entering womanhood and the "facts of life." Dad had talked to me before their split, so in my head, I knew what not to do.

Did Yearnell know better? *"The heart's deceitful above all things and beyond cure. Who can understand it?* "(Jeremiah 17:9 NIV) How then do you find balance in what the head says, yet on the other hand, what the heart seems to be feeling? Do you respond by rationalizing we are going to get married? Do you convince yourself, we are committed to each other? Or his mom likes me. And my mom likes him. What about all the times Mom invited him to family outings, such as to the beach or other places? How does a girl know how to sort through all the emotions and feelings? Where was Dad to keep this boy away from his daughter's heart?

I knew not to get pregnant, but not how to control the feelings stirring up in me. Because a boy was giving me attention, saying all the right words, buying me nice things, writing me love letters, introduced me to his parents, and telling me he loves me. Because a girl's DNA is about the need for love and giving love, what do you do?

Interestingly one day out of the blue, I ran across a book with a pink cover about you, love, and God called *The Sex Thing by Branse Burbridge*. In reading it, the principles were what my parents basically taught me. However, the one question still remained: How did a girl keep her heart from feeling and resist the temptation based on words she was hearing? When the Bible also commands girls and boys to *"Run from sexual sin! No other sin so clearly affects the body as this one does. For sexual immorality is a sin against your own body" (1 Corinthians 6:18 NLT)*. The scholars of the Life Application

Study Bible note that God created sex and it is intended for marriage.[40] Sexual sin outside marriage always hurts someone. Because it violates the commitment necessary to a relationship, it deeply affects the personality of a person, which responds in anguish when we harm ourselves physically and spiritually. It also often brings pregnancy or disease.[41] It hurts God immensely because the human body is where He dwells in and lives with Christians by His Holy Spirit.

In also reading the Bible many times and recognizing the command not to fornicate, how does one obey? Excited about my discovery and knowing that Yearnell also attended church, I decided to share what I found in Scriptures with him. Thinking that because the Bible said not to do something, then he will choose to obey too. He did not respond as I thought he would. If Dad were in our lives, would he have suspected Yearnell and I were going through the manhood and womanhood stages of puberty? Which may have been why Yearnell thought he was in love with me and also the same for me thinking I was in love with him. My heart did not know how to distinguish and handle the difference enough to resist the temptation.

The Relationship Shift

Once we disobeyed God's command, bad things started happening between us. Our fun and playful times together became few and far between. Situations arose and my commitment was being questioned which led to us arguing. He thought guys were either coming on to me and me letting them. I was his girlfriend only. The arguing turned into him hitting me. At first, I did not hit back nor say anything. I tried to prove him wrong by defending myself with words. He did not believe me. Until one day, I got mad enough that I began hitting him back.

Our relationship was not fun anymore. It became mentally and emotionally draining. We managed to makeup with his nice words or a gesture of gifts. He loved me and I loved him. But why did we have to fight. He was jealous. Of what? Did he think hitting me was the right way to be in a relationship with a girl? I was committed and not thinking of going anywhere else. We were going to get married. We had gone all the way in the relationship to prove we loved each other by doing so.

Dad was miles away. Another pivotal moment in our relationship was during the time joy came upon my sisters and me when we received a package from Dad. We did not always answer his phone calls or talk very long, nor did we freely call him. But Dad still managed to let us know he was thinking about us. All three girls received beautiful rings in the mail. Mine was a beautiful fourteen-karat gold sapphire ring. My boyfriend noticed it and asked me where I got it from. I told him. He asked if he could wear it. Thinking nothing of it, I let him with the promise he'd give it back in a few days. Days and weeks went by and he had not returned it to me. When asked, he said without apology he accidently lost it. Now that was the other worst decision I made. Letting him wear a ring from my Dad. I forgave him and moved on in our relationship. I let feelings for my boyfriend cause me to take Dad's gesture lightly. He had never met my Dad. Dad was not a topic of discussion nor did he know how important that ring was to me. Even though, it did not visibly affect how I felt about him, subconsciously my feelings were hurt. It was my fault.

As he was approaching high school graduation one year ahead of me, we were still arguing, fighting for no apparent reason, and making up. I was suffering silently, until I went to my Heavenly Father teary-eyed, I shut my clothes "prayer closet" doors calling out to God and I prayed. I recalled the last argument and fight Mom and Dad had before we came back to Montgomery. What would they do to me when they found out I had participated in the forbidden act? What would they do to him? I feared if I told Mom he was hitting me, then not only would my sisters, brothers and me not have our Dad living with us, but we could lose our Mom too. I could not tell them. Who could I go to? God my Father will hear me when I go to Him in private and shut the door. He will answer. *But Jesus said, "Let the little children come to me. Don't stop them! For the kingdom of Heaven belongs to those who are like these children"* (Matthew 19:14 NLT). I prayed and cried and cried until I heard the words in my spirit *"go tell his mother."* My first thought was she would never believe me over her son. I wrestled with those words with questions going back and forth until I was desperate enough to obey. Why would she believe me?

As I continued to wrestle with it, I finally got up enough courage to go to her. I shared with her what he was doing to me. She looked at me and said, *"you don't deserve to be treated that way."* I had no clue what response I'd get, but this one was liberating. I was not her daughter. She did not take sides with her son nor me. She did not reject me or judge me because I was not her daughter. She simply said eight words and I was truly happy to have listened to my inner voice to go to her. I needed to hear from a woman, I was of value and did not deserve to be treated as if I was not. I received the strength needed to help myself break loose from the stronghold of negativity and help me see myself in a way opposite of the negativity I would hear him say to me. I was liberated and eventually with no change in his behavior, I had enough mental and emotional strength to say I quit you and mean it. I left to never look back.

Of course, I had feelings for him and it was not easy, but I had to go on with my life without him. It took some time to heal, but I was glad to have obeyed the voice of the Holy Spirit within me. Amazing how God gives us the warning continued in verse 19 of First Corinthians chapter 6 *"Don't you realize that your body is the temple of the Holy Spirit, who lives in you and was given to you by God? You do not <u>belong</u> to yourself, for God bought you with a high price. So you must honor God with your body"* (NLT).

His mother did not use words to blame me, she simply made a statement of fact, *you do not deserve to be treated that way*. To this day, I appreciate those affirming words from another woman. Her surprise response gave me the courage and strength to no longer take the emotional, verbal, accusatory, and physical abuse.

Dating and Staying Pure for Marriage ~ Sexual Purity

Your mind, heart, and body belong to God. But how not to commit sexual sins with boys is a challenge, while the entire body is going through adolescent and puberty changes. How and what should girls be doing to maintain sexual purity and keep their virtue and moral character in tact? Sexual purity according to Bible instructions is simply this, *"God wants you to live a pure life. Keep yourselves from sexual promiscuity. Learn how to appreciate and give dignity to your body. Not abusing it, as is so common among those who know nothing of God. . . if you disregard this advice you're not offending your neighbors; you're rejecting God, who is making you a gift of his Holy Spirit"* (1 Thessalonians 4:3-5,8 MSG).

Some girls have commented, "I wish I had waited." *"God does not call us to be impure, but to live a holy life. Therefore, anyone who rejects this instruction does not reject a human being but God, the very God who give you His Holy Spirit"* (1 Thessalonians 4:7,8 MSG). You can wait until marriage. Yes, I found out it can be done. It is not widely known because all too often it is easy to assume other girls have given into the temptation of romance and sexual immorality and not wait until marriage. Yes, I am so glad there are men and women in the 21st century who waited! To name a few girls and boys who waited until marriage are singer/actress Carrie Underwood, athlete Tim Tebow, hurdler/bobsledder Lolo Jones, sitcom Sisters actress Tamera Mowry-Housley, former professional football athlete Kevin Jonas, singer/actress Jordin Sparks,[36] author/screenwriter/ Christian Cheryl McKay, athlete/football coach Colin Kelin, producer/author/ preacher DeVon Franklin, professional surfer Bethany Hamilton, actress Lisa Kudrow, Christian singer/musician Colton Dixon, actress & Christian Sarah Drew, and Christian musician / singer Jamie Grace.[37]

Role Models-Fatherly Figures

Girls need strong male role models to look to. How should a girl form a healthy bond with fatherly figures or face challenges in dating and relating to boys when her father is absent in her life, especially during her teenage years? Because girls who grow up without the love, nurturing, and protection of a father usually manifests in different negative ways in her adult life. The need for a sense of belonging becomes greater and more evident. It is as much a human need as food and water. She needs to know she is valued.

The lack of belonging becomes loneliness. Possible signs of the belongingness needs are first revealed in how we perceive how our father and family accepts us. Then outside of the family, positive or negative self-esteem may stem from how we are accepted by classmates, neighbors, members of sports teams and in the church and houses of faith. Without this sense of belonging in a positive way, one can feel rejected, abandoned, and lonely, like a loner without a home, family, or group association.[42]

During my senior year of high school, although I was not involved in any sports, I heard about and observed the fatherly demeanor of one of the football team coaches. And one day, as other times, a voice within me said to go to him and ask the question, *"Would you be my godfather?"*

He invited me over to his nice home to meet his wife and family. They agreed to be my godparents. His wife was a librarian and the mother of two boys. As I now look back, this was the transforming work of God in me to know His Holy Spirit and obey Him leading me to this mature two-parent family household. For our God is *"a father to the fatherless, a defender of widows, this God whose dwelling is holy" (Psalm 68:5 NLT)*. Although, a child without their father is significant, the Lord God provided me with the gift of a surrogate four-member family to receive protection, love, and acceptance in the present during the high school and college years.

Although our relationship had ended, there were still days Yearnell tried to makeup with me. He wanted me back. But if I were to be alone with him anywhere, I was afraid I would go back with him. He probably knew that too. I called my male cousins and their friends, one time in particular about 5 to 6 of them came to my rescue. On another occasion after the breakup, I asked my godfather to get him to leave me alone. Coach, who was well respected by all the students, met with Yearnell, and his attempts to be near me stopped. I don't believe Yearnell knew that Coach was the fatherly figure in my life and my godfather. But, like my Dad used to be when we lived together, Coach became my fatherly protection. The interventions worked and I moved on with my life.

Dating and Breaking Up Beyond Teenage Years

Psychologists suggest that girls tend to admire characteristics of the key men in their lives, such as fathers, uncles, and brothers. And girls become young adult women, they may subconsciously be drawn to a specific type of man. It is hard to understand the motives of the heart. Typically, a girl lets her guard down and the goal of the pursuer is achieved. Acceptance, affirmation, and affection draws girls to guys, especially when she never received verbal affirmation before.

With no textbook or seminar training on how to protect the heart created to love and be loved, how does one discern right from wrong and resist the temptation to let the guy lead her on when he has no solid plan or intention of marrying her?

Mom and grandma warned me about another guy, Filos who they believed was not the right one for me. He was nice, smart, witty, intelligent and ambitious. After dating for about two years, I was his girlfriend. We were in love. When he took me home to meet his parents and family what a surprise and warm fuzzy feeling it was. His parents were accepting and welcoming of me in the family. They liked me and I liked them. We spent a lot of time together at their family home. I fitted right in with his two-parent family. At every opportunity I spent time with him at their family gatherings, holiday events, celebrations, movie time, and major events, etc. I really enjoyed being with them.

While Filos was pursuing his dreams, he also encouraged me to dream and pursue mine. He was resourceful by investing in real estate property. He tried encouraging me to do the same. When he purchased his first home, I found myself hoping he would commit to our future marriage together. We talked about it. I did not get a solid no or disagreement. I still maintained my own address, paid my own rent, but found myself gradually moving some of my things in his home. I stayed in the relationship as long as I did. I was drawn to the possibility of us getting marry. Deep within me was the hope we would likely model his two-parent family.

When Filos shared with me that his dream assignment application had been approved and he would be relocating, I then took the initiative to search for jobs in the area too. I found a job, applied for it, and was selected for a teaching position. No, he did not ask me to. We had been dating, living, and acting as if we had a future together. Based on his actions, which seemed to be all the typical signs of a pending marriage proposal, I rationalized an assignment near him would make it easier.

Interesting, how I feared getting a teaching degree in college because I was fearful of public speaking. However, I forgot all about those fears, I applied for a teaching position to be close to my boyfriend. My hope was he'd propose and we would get married soon thereafter.

Less than a year in the teaching job, I found out on my own, Filos had another girlfriend. Seeing the remnants of evidence that she had been visiting him from out-of-state, as difficult as it was, I adamantly asked him to choose. He chose her.

The break up happened about the same time as a scheduled temporary duty (TDY) to teach in Oklahoma. Alone in the visiting lodging quarters, I fell in the middle of the floor cried my heart out uncontrollably to God. I searched for verses in the Bible to help me get through it. What was I doing wrong? What did I need to learn? This was very painful. *"Guard your heart above all else, for it determines the course of your life"* (Proverbs 4:23 NLT).

Through it all, I discovered how guys end up defining love for you. Some try to get away with all they can because they do not know what they want. Some may even lie or avoid specific topics or change the subject until you realize it has become a guessing and waiting game. Some, not in all relationships, when they believe their career is on track, then they decide they are ready for marriage. He goes back home to marry his childhood sweetheart or another acquaintance from the past. But what I did learn, although a bit too late, to pay more attention to the warning signs, leave the relationship sooner, and not let it linger in hopes of his proposal. Yet, the most valuable lesson was to be intentional about spending regular quiet time with God seeking His guidance and wisdom about the mate He has for me and not wait until after my heart was broken.

Boy Relationships with a Blind-Side

The reality is that not all girls think about relationships or love the same way. The varying degrees of what love looks like to individuals depends on the types of positive or negative experiences they have had in their upbringing and families. Or maybe she had some wrongs done to her and she cannot distinguish between what was right or wrong. Maybe she did not have an example or model of what a true love relationship should look and feel like. Or she may have the "la-la land" concept when everything goes well. One may have both parents in her life to show and teach her the beauty of marriage between a man and woman, or maybe there are no role models in her life.

Friends with Benefits: But is the "friends with benefits" (FWB) arrangement an alternative relationship life-style that God intended for girls of character and virtue? The answer is no. However, FWB is becoming more and more of a temptation for girls who may believe they have no other option. Where did the idea come from? It is so important that before becoming a part of a fad, a girl knows herself, her values, her beliefs, and have moral character. What is right from wrong? It is critical for her to decide first to investigate how and where the origination of an idea, fad, event, or activity before accepting and agreeing to engage in it. In 2011, *FWB* became a popular televised romantic sitcom based on a line in the song "Head over Feet" released in 1995. It appears that the original song was meant to be about a "committed relationship" between a man and woman rather than a casual one.

God and the Bible are clear about how we are to live in relationship with boys. On the Christian Broadcasting Network (CBN), Dannah Gresh tells the "Myth of Friends with Benefits."[43] The urban dictionary defines *friends with benefits* (FWB, a euphemism) as "two friends who have a sexual relationship without being emotionally involved." FWB relationships are unrealistic expectations of a girl and boy only having sex with each other and for one not to want a commitment or become romantically interested. Friends with benefits are a myth. It is scientifically impossible to be in a sexual relationship without a girl becoming emotionally involved. Why is this? FWB stifles a girl's true feelings of love. FWB distorts the feelings of genuine love and her hopes of eventually falling in love and committing to a partner for life.[44] God originally created her to love and be truly loved in marriage. When girls consent to an FWB arrangement, they are rarely able to ignore the feelings or emotions of bonds and attachment that a sexual union with their partners conjures up. God's original plan was—and it still remains His plan, a male and female relationship is to ultimately be a marriage covenant between a husband and wife before God.

It is God's will that His creation be sanctified (set apart as or declare holy; free from sin), that humans should avoid sexual immorality, that each of us should learn to control our own body in a way that is holy and honorable, not in passionate lust like the heathen, who do not know God; and that in this matter no one should wrong his brother or take advantage of him. The Lord will punish those who commit such sins, as we told you and warned you before. For God did not call us to be impure, but to live a holy (dedicated or consecrated to God; devoted to the service of God; morally and spiritually excellent) life. (1 Thessalonians 4:3–7 NIV)

Rejection: Once a girls' heart has been opened to love and later crushed by rejection from the boy she once trusted her heart to, how can she avoid being rejected again and again? It is usually not easy to surrender your heart to a guy again after the first devastating heart break when the hope was to get married. When marriage doesn't happen, the feelings of rejection hurt to the core. All types of questions come to mind, including doubt about misreading or misinterpreting or misunderstanding what was communicated to you by him. Or overlooking the fact he had been non-committal from the outset of your relationship. Does the rejection mean you are a failure? How should handling rejection and the matters of the heart be taught within and outside of the family? All good questions causing one to stop and think about where the source of rejection comes from. I found myself often saying to a boyfriend, I quit you before he could say it to me!

Non-consensual Encounters or Intimate Partner Violence: Clear boundaries must be established in relationships with past, present, and future boyfriends. Why, because what if a past boyfriend you clearly broke up with comes back into your life and you are cordial and polite to him, but he knows your weakness and forces himself on you against your will, without your consent? What do you do when the non-consensual encounter with him happens?

Who will believe you? Do you stuff it and move on? You should pray! And go to a mature Christian woman, you trust. Do not keep it in. *"Give your burdens to the Lord and He will take care of you. He would not permit the godly to fall"* (Psalm 55:22, 1 Peter 5:7 NLT). God never intended for His daughters to be violated by another in any way against her will.

Wrong Relationships: Being young and naïve, I remember being subtly drawn into a relationship under the wrong premise, such as with an older man. He noticed my abilities and talents. He was friendly and observant. One project led to another. He began exposing me to lots of fun and adventure. I was growing and maturing beyond my vices, gaining confidence in myself such as no longer biting my nails. Yet it became a relationship of regret and had to be broken off. For some reason many years gone by and no pending marriage, then another reason to rationalize and accept a man's word even his friends over my own intuition and conviction that something was not right in his efforts of persuading me to be in a relationship with him. After not heeding the warning signs and the truth finally exposed, embarrassed and paralyzed with shame and guilt, I feared God would never forgive me. So I contemplated ways I would take my life. But I heard God's voice . . . not to do it. He gave me the strength to leave the relationship. *"The gatekeeper opens the gate for him, and the sheep recognize his voice and come to him. He calls his own sheep by name and leads them out. After he has gathered his own flock, he walks ahead of them, and they follow him because they know his voice"* (John 10:3,4 NLT). Thank You, Lord Jesus!

Trauma, Sexual Violence, #MeToo Movement: Transitioning from childhood to young adult life can be rocky, especially when girls experience childhood trauma, such as rape, death in the family, witnessing a crime or gun violence, death or suicide of a close friend, domestic violence, natural disaster, or chronic bullying, etc. Therefore, it is easy to succumb to temptation and be lured into human and sex trafficking when your self-esteem is low and you are vulnerable. Also, according to the "Dating Abuse Statistics," nearly 1.5 million high school students have been physically, sexually, emotionally, or verbally abused from a dating partner in a single year.[45] One in 10 high school students have been purposefully hit, slapped or physically hurt by a boyfriend or girlfriend.[46] With the #MeToo movement on the rise, girls should no longer suffer in silence and *abolish the* identity crisis affecting youth across the nation and around the world. *"A thief is only there to steal and kill and destroy, I (Jesus) came so they can have real and eternal life, more and better life than they ever dreamed"* (John 10:10 NLT).

Seek Counsel from Mature Women

Where do you go? Who could I trust to guide me so this would not happen again? Where are the mature Christian women to confide in, to trust, to give godly counsel, not judge, but yet hold me accountable? After building up the courage to confide in someone, a senior military woman came to my mind. Out of desperation for help and prayers to God in my distress and shame, I invited her over for dinner. I confessed I was in a wrong relationship hoping to be counseled and receive sound advice. I wanted to and always have loved God but how to obey God's biblical instructions about male and female relationships, I was clueless. She listened, but was unable to give any sage advice. I was desperate for practical guidance and direction.

Where are the Christian women who are living the Word of God? And successful Christian career women who are living the single life with hopes and dreams of falling in love and someday marrying? *"Similarly, teach the older women to live in a way that honors God so they can teach the younger women" (Titus 2:3 NLT).* It is so important for girls and women to have mature Christ-like mentors of the same gender in our lives. Who will be open and honest about sharing their experiences and journey of coming to the saving knowledge and love of Jesus Christ? Girls need mature and pastoral women of faith to teach us how to live obeying God by knowing His Son, our Savior Jesus Christ.

Strayed Away from God

Every time I opened my heart to love, I allowed temptation of the flesh to subtly draw me away from God. I did not understand fully the concept of temptation. Temptation defined in the Greek dictionary is putting someone to the test or is the trial of a person's fidelity, integrity, virtue, constancy, etc.[47] Temptation also defined in the Oxford Dictionary is the desire to do something, especially something wrong or unwise. How does one not let her heart be drawn to what appears to be love from a man? *The temptations in your life are no different from what others experience. And God is faithful. He will not allow the temptation to be more than you can stand. When you are tempted, he will show you a way out so that you can endure (First Corinthians 10:13 TMB).*

At times, I sensed God calling me back to Him by drawing me to go to the chapel because I had not successfully found a convenient church off base. I needed to be in worship service and at church programs to hear God convicting me in my spirit to return to Him. *"...how from infancy you have known the Holy Scriptures, which are able to make you wise for salvation through faith in Christ Jesus. All Scripture is God-breathed and is useful for teaching, rebuking, correcting, and training in righteousness, so that the man (person) of God may be thoroughly equipped for every good work"* (1 Timothy 3:15, 16–17 NIV).

With sorrow and remorse, my broken heart felt the blow. I acknowledged my sins against God, my Heavenly Father and with a repentant heart prayed for forgiveness as I found written in Psalms 51:1, 2,4, 7,9, 13 (NIV)

"Have mercy on me, O God, because of your unfailing love. Because of your great compassion, blot out the stain of my sins. Wash me clean from my guilt. Purify me from my sin. Against you and you alone, have I sinned; I have done what is evil in your sight...Purify me from my sins, and I will be clean; wash me, and I will be whiter than snow. Oh, give me back my joy again; you have broken me—now let me rejoice. Don't keep looking at my sins. Remove the stain of my guilt. Create in me a clean heart, O God. Renew a loyal spirit within me...Then I will teach your ways to rebels/transgressors, and they will return to you..."

Our Heavenly Father knows all about us and draws us to come to Him in prayer. He hears and comes to our rescue and saves us from harm when we surrender to Him and call on His name.

The Power of Forgiveness

In the midst of feeling rejected and disappointed with myself about each boyfriend breakup, I asked myself "what was I doing wrong?" Will anyone ever love and marry me? Yet, the Lord God never left me alone. From reading the Bible and praying, I learned the importance of getting my heart right with God. In looking back over past relationships, seeking God with a repentant heart of forgiveness I began falling in love with God. He gave me a sincere heart by running to Him and not away from Him. I learned how and began trusting in Him more and not only when I had a devastating break-up. As I experienced God's unconditional love, I began to understand what real forgiveness feels like because of all the times He had forgiven me. Therefore, I had to also forgive those who I believed hurt or rejected me. I learned how to not carry a grudge or bitterness in my heart. I made peace with God first by admitting where I was wrong. The Bible reminds us when we pray *"Hear my cry for help, my King and my God to You I pray"* (Psalm 52 NIV). *"In my distress*

I called to you, I cried to my God for help. From His temple He heard my voice, my cry came down before him, into His ears" (Psalm 18:6 NIV).

I was also led to contact past boyfriends to ask their forgiveness and let them know that I also forgive them. It is written in the words of Jesus, *"to open their eyes, so they may turn from darkness to light and from the power of Satan to God. Then they will receive forgiveness for their sins and be given a place among God's people, who are set apart by faith in Me" (Acts 26:18 NLT).*

The Bible goes on to tell us in the New Testament, *"And when you stand praying, if you hold anything against anyone, forgive him/her, so that your Father in heaven may forgive you your sins" (Mark 11:25 NIV). "If we claim to be without sin, we deceive ourselves and the Truth is not in us. If we confess our sins, he is faithful and just and will forgive us our sins, and purify us from all unrighteousness. If we claim we have not sinned, we make Him (God) out to be a liar, and His word is not in us" (1 John 1:8–10 NIV).*

It took time and lots of prayers to understand that a broken heart does matter to God. I found myself taking all my tears and pain to the Lord in my "prayer clothes closet." *"Feel my pain and see my trouble. Forgive all my sins" (Psalm 25:18 NLT). "Cast your cares on the Lord and he will sustain you; he will never let the righteous fall" (Psalm 55:22 NIV).* Yes, I found myself giving all my worries and cares to God, learning how to lean and depend on God. I discovered that if no one else cared about me, God did.

The Bible is a book of *love* and reminds us of God's love towards us. He guides all humans to love and to live. *"You must love the Lord your God with all your heart and with all your soul and with all your strength and with all your mind,"* and *'Love your neighbor as yourself" (Deuteronomy 6:5, Luke 10:27 NIV).* Treat others like you would like to be treated. *"So in everything, do to others what you would have them do to you, for this sums up the Law and the Prophets" (Matthew 7:12 NIV).*

Therefore, developing and nurturing positive and healthy relationships with God, your parents, girls, boys, motherly and fatherly mentors is critical. Until Prince Charming prayerfully comes into your life and pops the question, will you marry me, trust God entirely and wait. Do all you can to live a life of moral character! Remember wait on the Lord because it can be done!

My Prayer: Dear Heavenly Father, I love you. As Jesus taught the disciples to pray in Matthew chapter 6, I ask you to forgive me of all my sins as I forgive those who have sinned against me, especially in all of my male and female relationships. Please *"Search me, O God, and know my heart; test me and know my anxious thoughts. Point out anything in me that offends You, and lead me along the path of everlasting life" (Psalm 139:23,24 NLT).*

I confess, I gave my heart, mind, and body to those I should not have given myself too, all in the name of love. My heart belongs to You. My mind belongs to You. My body belongs to You. All of me belongs to You. I realize how temptation drew me away from You into a life of sin against You and also from the plans You intended for my life. I forgive all those who hurt me and also those I may have hurt. I speak their names to you and acknowledge and repent for disobeying Your Word. I thank you for never abandoning me and sanctifying me in Your truth to patiently wait for me to return back to You. Thank You for cleansing us all of unrighteousness (1 John 1:9). Make us brand new in our relationship with You, a new creation, that we become ambassadors of Jesus Christ (2 Corinthians 5:17,20 NIV). Have mercy upon us, Oh Lord, I pray in the name of our Savior Jesus Christ (Luke 11:4 NIV). *Amen!*

A Love Letter from Your Heavenly Father

My Precious Daughter,

How priceless you are to Me. Worth more than rubies (Proverbs 31:10). I took special care in creating you female, feminine, and a girl having the capacity to look inward to feel, to sense, and to know. You possess the energy uniquely directed towards relationships, nurturing, helping, and loving others. While on the other hand, I created boys, male and masculine oriented toward things, to explore, and to achieve with the physical energy to measure, move, build, and conquer.[48]

Both girls and boys were created with biological and psycho-social differences, with unique roles, and the ability to love deeply only in the bonds of a marriage covenant, though. I know it is difficult understanding the significance of the changes going on in your body physically, mentally, and emotionally. But it is the natural part of growing up for every girl to have a heart that experiences those "funny" feelings? However, be careful to not awaken love until the time is right (Solomon 2:7, 3:5, 8:4 NLT). Your virginity virtue is yours until I present you to the right mate to marry you. He will be a man who has the same values and beliefs as you do. My promise is that the man who finds a wife finds what is good and receives favor from Me (Proverbs 18:22 NIV). The right mate is the one I have chosen for you. However, if a boy asks you to engage your body for sexual reasons to him before marriage, then he does not respect you and he definitely is not the husband I chose for you. Don't allow friendship type of love turn into lust, setting off a downhill slide into sexual promiscuity, filthy practices, bullying, or greed (Ephesians 5:3 TMB). Have nothing, not even a hint to do with sexual immorality, impurity, lust, and evil desires. Don't be greedy, for a greedy person is an idolater, worshiping the things of this world (Colossians 3:5 NLT). Do you realize that your body is actually part of Christ's body? Should a man or woman take his body, which is part of Christ, and join it to a prostitute? Never! And don't you realize that if a man joins himself to a prostitute, he becomes one body with her? The two are united into one. But the person who is joined to the Lord is one spirit with Him (1 Corinthians 6:15 NLT). Flee from sexual immorality (fornication). Sexual sins are different from all others because it violates the sacredness of your own body, where the Holy Spirit dwells. I made the body for My God-given and God-modeled love for you to become one with your husband (1 Corinthians 6:18 MSG). All other sins a person commits are outside their body, but he/she who sexually sins against his/her own body (1 Corinthians 6:18).

Become spiritually one with Me first. Do not pursue sex. Sex avoids commitment and intimacy, leaving you lonely. Model my love, for "becoming one" with another. You cannot live how you please by squandering what I paid such a high price for. The physical part of you is not a piece of property belonging to the spiritual part of you. Since you belong to Me and I own all of you, let people see Me in and through your body. (1 Corinthians 6:17-20 MSG). Don't team up with those who are unbelievers. How can righteousness be a partner with wickedness? How can light live with darkness? What harmony can there be between Christ and the devil? How can a believer be a partner with an unbeliever? And what union can there be between My temple, your body and idols? I am the living God and you are My temple where I dwell: I will live in them and walk among them. I will be your God, and you will be my people. (2 Corinthians 6:14-16 NLT).

Know the instructions given you by the authority of the Lord Jesus. It is My will that you should be sanctified *(set apart as or declare holy; free from sin)*: that you should avoid sexual immorality; that you should learn to control your own body in a way that is holy and honorable, not in passionate lust like the pagans, who do not know Me (1 Thessalonians 4:2-5 NIV).

Just as I created Mary the mother of Jesus for a divine purpose, so I have also done for you. Mary was a virgin engaged to be married, when I summoned my angel Gabriel to appear to her saying, "Greetings, favored woman! The Lord is with you!" Confused and disturbed, Mary tried to think what the angel could mean. "Don't be afraid, Mary," the angel told her, "for you have found favor with God! You will conceive and give birth to a son, and you will name him Jesus...Mary asked the angel, "But how can this happen? I am a virgin (Luke 1:28-31, 34 MSG).

Marriage, My daughter is designed for a male and female couple who are created in My image to "Prosper! Reproduce! Fill the Earth! Take charge! Be responsible together for fish in the sea and birds in the air, for every living thing that moves on the face of Earth" (Genesis 1:28 MSG). I am the Lord your God who oversees every aspect of your life until I will join you with the right mate made especially for you. I will never leave or abandon you (Deuteronomy 31:6,8). I will always guide you in the path of righteousness. I do not have favorites, but accept people from every nation who fear Me and do what is right (Acts 10:34–35).

I have a beautiful and wonderful surprise awaiting you, dear daughter. For I am the Lord your God, the Holy One of Israel your Savior, since you are precious and honored in my sight and because I love you, I will give people in exchange for you (Isaiah 43:4 NIV). I, the Lord will fulfill My purpose for you; My love endures forever— I do not abandon the works of My hands" (Psalm 138:8 NLT). Therefore, put on the virtues of integrity, loyalty, compassion, kindness, gentleness, and patience, and over all these virtues, put on love, which binds them all together in perfect unity (Colossians 3:1, 14 NIV).

    You will be a good woman who is hard to find, and you will be worth far more than diamonds. Your future husband will trust you without reserve, and will never have reason to regret it. I want you to desire growing up and becoming a woman who does excellently and surpasses all others. Beware charm is deceitful, and beauty is vain, but be the woman who reveres (*fear, admires, honors, hold in high esteem*) Me, you are to be praised and the fruit of your hands and your works will be your praise in My gates and in My courts (Proverbs 31:10, 30, 31 MSG). Amen!

Your Everlasting First Love, God

Self-Discovery / Self-Reflection

Application

(1) *Find a family photo of your father or a male fatherly figure and add it to your vision board*
(2) *Reflect and chat about the questions below with your mother or a close adult female friend (mentor).*
(3) *Look up and write down on your vision board the Bible verses from this chapter that inspired you and use them to also answer the questions.*

Thinking About Me: What's Right with Me? Love & Right Relationships with Boys

1. Is your father in your life? What do you enjoy doing with your father? Is it positive or painful, happy or sad?
_____
_____

2. Have your parents talked with you about the facts of life? Is it being taught in classes at your school in a health and sex education?
_____
_____

3. What is the difference between dating boys and being in a "philos" friendship? Is it easy or difficult for you to interact with boys?
_____
_____

4. What is moral character? What do you know about being in a boyfriend relationship? Do you understand what the Bible teaches about sexual immorality? Explain.
_____
_____

5. Do you daydream about getting married one day to be a wife, a mother, and having a career? Explain
_____
_____

Part Three

You Are Valued by God, Our Relationship with God in Our Callings and Decisions

The future belongs to those who believe in the beauty of their dreams.
—Eleanor Roosevelt

"Little girls with dreams become women with vision"
—Unknown

"The biggest adventure you can ever take is to live the life of your dreams"
—Oprah Winfrey

Be not afraid of greatness, some are born great, some achieve greatness and others have greatness thrust upon them.
—William Shakespeare

CHAPTER 6

What's Right with Me? Born with Dreams, Gifts, and Talents

Your values come from God and He values you

In the earlier chapters, we noted how important your relationships with God, family, and others are in knowing who you are and building positive self-esteem, self-identity, and ethnic identity. Yet, there is still more to getting to know who you are. Within each person's psyche are also dreams, gifts, and talents uniquely given to you by God. Positive self-esteem is not only developed through positive family and peer relationships, but also in how you use your God-given gifts and talents to achieve your dreams. Dreams are a cherished aspiration, ambition, or ideal. The glass-ceiling has been broken in most career opportunities. Girls can dream of becoming CEOs, President of their country, lawyers, doctors, nurses, world leaders, scientists, explorers, astronauts, scientist, architects, professional athletes, mothers, wives, and many others, in essence the sky is the limit.

We were born and raised to dream. My parents had dreams and they instilled them in us. First and foremost, they dreamed of their children finishing high school and going to college. And quite naturally, being in my parents' presence, it was just right to also dream of following their example of one day falling in love, getting married, having a beautiful wedding, being the perfect wife and mother of lots of children, and living happily ever after just like they were doing. Yes, I was loved in my two-parent traditional family because of all the positive opportunities we experienced having both of our parents' love, nurture, provision, and protection.

Knowing you are loved helps you to learn to love yourself, to dream and strive to become all you can be above and beyond your highest expectations of yourself. An unknown author makes an important observation about dreams: *"Never let it be said that to dream is a waste of one's time, for dreams are our realities in waiting. In dreams, we plant the seeds of our future."*

Growing up and developing into a beautiful person is a unique transformation of inner and outer beauty, such as the visible transformation of the monarch butterfly. During that process, you begin to understand why mysteriously out of nowhere it seems people have entered your life. According to the plan God has for you, those people are strategically placed in your life to help you achieve your dreams using the gifts and talents unique to you.

His dream for me, my parents' dream for me, and finally my dream for myself all unfolds as God intended when I was in Mom's womb. God knew it (Psalm 139:1,13).

In Pursuit of God-given Gifts and Talents

God created and equipped us to be a success since the beginning of time. Genesis chapter 2 verse 15 (NIV) records, *"The Lord God took the man (woman) and put him (them) in the Garden of Eden to work it and take care of it."* God is with you all the way, and He reassures you of that fact. The Lord God declares in His Word in Jeremiah 29:11 (NIV), *"For I know the plans I have for you, plans to prosper you and not to harm you, plans to give you hope and a future."* The journey may be challenging, difficult, and painful, but certainly God has the final say, and He knows what is best for you. That is why He continues with the words from verses 12 and 13 in Jeremiah chapter 29 (NIV), saying, *"then you will call upon Me and come and pray to Me, and I will listen to you. You will seek Me and find Me when you seek Me with all your heart. I will be found by you,' declares the Lord ..."*

Career Decision: What is my talent? Talent is a natural aptitude or skill you are born with. With high school graduation fast approaching and no finances for college. Dad's words to his firstborn were about to come to pass. Remember what he said to his five children years before he and mom divorced. In the moment, enjoying the travels and all the possibilities, we dreamed of a future in the military by saying, "when I grow up I'm going to join the military?" Dad quickly chimed in and said emphatically, "No, you will go to college first."

The dynamics of our family structure had changed by the time I was in high school. Mom was a 33 years-old single-parent head of household adjusting to a new lifestyle with her five children. Now, the question, "Can we afford to pay for my college tuition?" I was in a peculiar position to make the right choice because my parents believed I would pave the path for my siblings to come after me or "follow suit." What decision would this firstborn make, knowing the expectations of her parents? Was I about to be tested? Would I go to college or choose marriage? Would my younger siblings follow in my footsteps, whatever the decision may be?

The decision was challenging. At the time, I did not know exactly what I was interested in doing for the rest of my life. One thing for sure, by receiving my high school diploma I was well on my way to a college education.

But, where do I start? I had not originally factored in my grades, passing SAT scores, or involvement in national and local community service projects, such as Xinos Club, Elite Club, 4-H Club, and Girl Scouts, which were all good to apply for college. But, where was the money going to come from to pay for my college tuition? Mom, who was on a very tight budget, provided for us, cared for us, and ensured all our basic needs were met with no extra money left over for college.

At the time of my high school graduation and struggling with the decision about what would be a happy medium in pleasing Dad by going to college and pleasing Mom by attending college close to home? What would be my major or degree program and where should I go? I knew I was not interested in getting a teaching degree offered by the college in my hometown and grandmother had planted the seed for me to consider becoming a nurse like her. As much as, I wanted to be close by to help Mom with my siblings, I could not stomach the idea of working in a hospital. At that point, I had hoped my second dream would come true. I wanted to get married to the man who loved me and who I loved in return. I would be his perfect wife and mother of lots of his children.

What Am I Good at Doing? Oh, what about fashion designing? I am creative, artistic, and enjoyed designing clothes, sewing, and modeling. I got the sewing talent from Mom. She was good at it. She had an eye for fashion and interior decorating. Yes, I could imitate her skills and talents. I accredit the gift of modeling to the training I received at the Carousel School of Modeling. I grew out of my bashfulness with positive self-esteem when it came to designing and modeling my own fashions. Not only was I able to design women's clothing, I designed men's fashions too. The day I walked into one of the stores in the mall and discovered my faux fur coat hanging on the rack of a popular retail store chain with the label of a famous designer. My coat I say, because I had designed and wore my own identical coat about a year or so prior to it coming out on the market and sold in stores. My self-esteem was boosted another notch in a positive direction. Another notch of confidence came the day I received the news my application was accepted and I was selected to be one of the teenagers on the local Belk-Hudson department store Teen Board. Whether modeling or designing my own creative fashions, these were great career options.

Will My Career be in Fashion Designing? I began narrowing the possibilities of a career vocation to schools where a major in fashion designing was offered. The quote by W. Clement Stone gives some perspective about deciding on a major, *"aim for the moon, if you miss, you may hit a star."*

In reviewing the American Fashion College of Switzerland catalogue and magazine advertisements, I was drawn to the magnificent and natural beauty of the country. This one just felt like a right fit and a wonderful opportunity for me to perfect my fashion designing skills. The distance did not deter me from pursuing my dream despite the fact the college was in a country with four distinct seasons. I had lived and grew up in very cold climates before in Germany and Michigan. I applied. Maybe I had subliminal reasons as the firstborn with burdens who wanted to get away from home to 4,822 miles over the Atlantic Ocean to the tranquil and serene country in Lucerne Switzerland.

My second college application was to Massey School of Fashion Design in Atlanta, Georgia, which was only about a three-hour drive from home. Thrilled about receiving their letter of acceptance, I called my Dad in California with the good news. I had been accepted to go to college. At that time, I had not heard back from the American Fashion College of Switzerland. I needed the money for college tuition. Dad asked me a few questions about the school and then said, "You can do that later. You need to go to college." My bubble burst. I went silent to Dad's stern and determined response. With his direction given over the telephone, I hung up disappointed. But once I got over his response, I started searching for colleges in the local area.

As I was torn between what Dad was mandating and Mom's preference of me attending college closer to home, I called my BFF who was also deciding on a college. Since Bonnie was already a highly sought-after model in Alabama and Georgia, I shared my news and encouraged her to apply to the Massey School of Fashion Design, that also offered a modeling component. I only applied for the fashion designing degree program. However, her Mom was not convinced Massey College was for her daughter. It was too far away from home. Turns out our mothers just wanted us to be closer to home.

Looking for Local Colleges in the area: Don't give up. In a quote from Jesse Owens, world record-setting Olympic athlete *"We all have dreams. In order to make dreams come into reality, it takes an awful lot of determination, dedication, self-discipline and effort."* Okay, what about the local college? We took a chance and just showed up on the college campus one day. Their key major degree programs were education related. Being fearful of public speaking, I was not interested in becoming a teacher. And no way was I going to pursue a teaching degree. Since, both of our parents did not have the finances for us to attend college, she and I took a big step of faith. In the Admissions Office, we met Mr. Hill, an older, fatherly, and wise gentleman. He listened and advised us in a father-daughter manner and answered all our enrollment questions. Then we both asked, "What about the money needed to pay for college?" He pointed us to the financial aid office. We did as he instructed. The financial aid officer laid out various possibilities. The best option was the Basic Educational Opportunity Grant (BEOG) for commuter students who were from low- to middle-income families and seeking higher education.

College and AFROTC: Our first day of college she and I registered for our first-semester freshman courses in the gymnasium. It was packed with lines of other students doing the same. As we finished registering and came to the end of the line, we noticed at the last table a man in a military uniform. We approached him to listen to what he had to say. He piqued our interest as we listened attentively about the Air Force Reserve Officer Corps (AFROTC) program. When he finished and before answering his question I asked, "can we think about it and get back with you tomorrow?" He said, you sure can. The next day, I reminded Bonnie of our promise we made to get back with him. She was not interested. I decided to follow suit. We did not get back to him with an answer.

Freshman year behind me and now the sophomore year rolled in with the same registration process. This time I was with another high school classmate, Ruby. Approaching the end of the line, the AFROTC recruiters boasted of a brand-new program called the "Buddy Program." Interestingly enough, the previous year, when Bonnie and I registered for class, the Buddy Program did not exist. Ruby was fascinated and enticed by all the opportunities and benefits. I believe none of her immediate family had ever served in the military. The Buddy Program was intended to get friends to join the military and embark on an adventurous journey together. With the promise of also being assigned to a military base together, Ruby was very excited about the possibilities. It energized me enough to do it again! I naturally became the spokesperson for the two of us. I asked the recruiter, "Can we get back with you tomorrow?" He said, "Sure."

When tomorrow came, I said to Ruby, "We have to get back with the recruiter with our answer. Do you want to still join the AFROTC under the Buddy Program?" She hesitated and changed her mind by saying no. We did not get back with the recruiter.

Approaching the end of spring term my junior year, I was driving home from my part-time salesperson job on the same route as I always take home when suddenly on Glen Grattan Drive, I heard the words within me say "Check out the ROTC program." That was one of those moments like the excitement of preparing for your first day of school. I could not wait to get home, take a bath, go to bed, get up the next morning, get dressed, and rush off to the campus to speak with someone in the AFROTC Detachment. It was very clear that I must follow through to take this action. I did not have an appointment so I asked the assistant, if I could meet with the professor. She let him know he had a walk-in who wanted to speak with him. I introduced myself to Lieutenant Colonel Clarence, U.S. Air Force Detachment Commandant. He politely and professionally received me as I shared I was here to "Check out the ROTC program." He answered my questions the same as a seasoned, stern and wise father would do. He explained the commitment and what was involved. "Oh, one last question, is it true what they say about women in the military?" His response was profound. "Look outside this window," he said. "It is just like when you came on this college campus. If you did not come here that way, it will not make you that way." He added, "So by joining the military, if you are not already that way, the military will not make you that way." I understood. I thanked him, and as I was leaving his office, I reminded him, "I am only here to check it out."

I followed his instructions on where to pick up my military issued uniforms. Thus, began my pursuit of the AFROTC on my own and without friends. Excited about my decision, I could not wait to tell Mom. She tried to discourage me the first time I mentioned it. But that was before I heard the words, "check out the ROTC program." My aunt and grandmother both also tried to discourage me. They believed the military was for boys. Their beliefs about girls in the military conflicted with what I often heard people saying "they would send their sons to the military to make men out of them."

Summer Camp Training: Timing is God's perfect timing. WOW! I received notification of my selection to attend the AFROTC summer field training "boot camp" at one of the local bases. We would be evaluated during the six- to eight-week-long field cadet training camp for our leadership potential and readiness for more intense training in our junior year of college. Once we passed all prerequisites, we would be commissioned in the U.S. Air Force upon graduation.

On the first day of my arrival, everyone was checked-in and assigned a roommate. After so many hours, my roommate never showed up. For me, it was a blessing in disguise. My prayers were answered. No roommate because at home I had a bedroom to myself. Fortunately, I was the only girl in the whole camp who did not have a roommate. Thank you, Lord, for answering my prayer. *"But when you pray, go into your room (closet), close the door and pray to your Father, who is unseen. Then your Father, who sees what is done in secret, will reward you"* (Matthew 6:6 NIV).

One of my deep-rooted fears surfaced during the summer camp experience and leadership training. In the midst of learning a lot, I was bashful in groups. The whole experience was around team activities, whether in sports flickerball, war game exercises, or public speaking and team briefings. During a war game exercise, I listened and observed team members speaking strategies aloud attempting to get us out of enemy territory. I whispered to our team leader an idea I had. When he did not use it, I took it as not the right solution.

At the end of the exercise, each group debriefed about the strategies used and what was learned from the experience. Our team leader asked me why didn't I put my suggestion out for the entire group to hear? It was a group exercise where everyone needed to hear and decide together on the strategy best for all. Apparently, I had the right solution. If I had spoken up we would have successfully accomplished the task. After listening to all the groups, the teacher reinforced the importance of fast thinkers speaking up in a crisis so everyone can hear and decide. Everyone's input is important. He turned to me: "Sandra, next time speak up, even if it means standing on the top of a table to get others attention and for them to listen … do whatever it takes, share your ideas. Do not be afraid." I learned a valuable lesson from that experience.

At the end of summer camp, I was paid a total of $484.00 for the training. With this unexpected blessing, I used it to buy my own car. When my parents were together, they promised my siblings and me for our high school graduation we would get a car. We held on to that promise. However, under the circumstances of their divorce, they forgot the promise. Not being able to contain my excitement, I went to Mom with the news. And she went to grandma since she knew some people at a Buick car dealership. I was going to buy myself a car with the money I earned.

After Grandma asked me a series of questions checking to see how responsible I would be in making the monthly payments, she agreed to co-sign. She also made it clear, I was not to come to her if I missed a payment. It was my full responsibility to pay for it. The salesman showed me a like-new used Buick four-door sedan car with a white top and mustard-colored body, I could afford. I liked it. He wrote up the contract, took my $484.00 down payment, and calculated a monthly payment of $94.00, which would be covered by my monthly ROTC check of $100.00. I was thinking about Mom and my siblings, when I chose the four-door sedan. As the firstborn, I could help Mom transport them to places they needed to go. I became the proud owner of my very own first new (used) car.

Overcoming the Fear of Rejection

Former President Theodore Roosevelt once quoted, *"keep your eyes on the star, and your feet on the ground."* My junior year of college was a landmark one for me. I begin the process of tackling fears. After successfully completing the challenging summer boot camp training, I believed I could tackle anything. With boldness, I stepped out to face the possibility of rejection in becoming a member of the sorority of my dreams, a member of the marching band, and getting my own apartment.

The Sorority: My travelling buddy, Lillian and I on one particular occasion drove up in her orange Volkswagen car to Huntsville for their annual classic football game and Greek Step Show. The Step Show showcased fraternities and sororities about to end their pledge season. Her sister Sandra and her sorority pledge line were very impressive. The crowd was roaring with excitement as the girls uniformly dressed and looking good came onto the stage. Then a series of choreographed rhythm and sounds to foot movement, hand clapping and singing began. It was an unforgettable and impressionable experience for me. To my surprise, during a visit to my favorite uncle Charles and aunt Bettye's home in Texas, I discovered that my aunt was also a member of that same sorority. I had always admired her and enjoyed being in her company. She was a woman of academic, civic, and social achievements. There was just something about the women of this sorority that resonated with me. I wanted to become a part of it.

When the date, time, and place of the "RUSH party" was announced, it was time to put away my doubts and fears. Despite what I heard about the intense initiation and pledging process, I made up my mind it could not be any different than what I experienced in the ROTC field training a month prior. I had discovered the secret to facing my fears. I submitted my application. To my surprise and overwhelming joy, I was accepted along with twenty-one other girls. About half of them were graduates of local Montgomery public schools and the surrounding area. We pledged, we bonded, and we, the "Tantalizing 22" crossed over into a sisterhood that promotes academic excellence and public service, Delta Sigma Theta, Inc. *"Now faith is being sure of what we hope for and certain of what we do not see"* (Hebrews 11:1 NIV).

The Marching Band: During the same fall season, for the first time ever the all-male marching band was no longer off limits to girls. College life exposed me to opportunities that I did not know existed. Going to at-home and away football games, I was astonished by the performances of the all-male marching bands during the half-time shows led by four drum majors with high-energy, choreographed performances, and showmanship. Being a lover of music and dance, I wanted to be in the marching band too. The traditionally distinctive marching band style was now opened to girls. I had successfully completed the ROTC military summer field training, been accepted to pledge my favorite sorority, so why not try out for the marching band. Although I did not play an instrument, this was another joyful event, I was one of twenty-three girls selected to be the first ever ASU marching band flag corps.

The Apartment: My third act of boldness in my junior year after completing the summer camp training, I reasoned that since ROTC was preparing me for a military career that would take me away from family, I needed to start weaning myself early from family attachments. I knew once I was on active duty I would not be able to come home any and every time I wanted to or when things did not go my way. I asked my Mom about moving out. With apprehension and getting up enough nerves, I stood in the middle of the hallway at home, I said Mom I met an officer nurse at the base-exchange (BX) store, First Lieutenant (1Lt) Samuelita, who is looking for a roommate. She is a sorority sister from Virginia. When she heard I was a ROTC student, we discussed the possibility of us renting an apartment together. "Mom, this is a good opportunity for me to prepare for my military career. I will still be living nearby. However, having my own apartment will help me get acclimated to living on my own and adjust to a military career without family." Mom's reaction was like comparing it to someone who just heard the news of the death of a loved one, but she agreed.

About one year later Samuelita met a military man, fell in love, and they got married at the base chapel. Three became a crowd. With the money I was making from my part time job, I could afford to share rent with her. However, since I had become accustomed to living on my own and it did not make sense to move back home, I called Dad who came to my rescue. I found a one-bedroom apartment that I could afford. Dad agreed to help pay a portion of the rent so I could complete the remainder of my college senior year.

Staying Stylish While Avoiding Unnecessary Attention

Although I ended up in a four-year college not majoring in fashion designing, I was enjoying college life. I was making new friends in my classes. I believe no one really knew of my dad's military background other than Bonnie. By the time I was in my junior year, taking the ROTC classes it meant having to wear the military uniform. Since my first career choice was fashion designing and with limited spending money, I continued using my talent to design, sew, and wear my own stylish outfits. Therefore, I chose not to bring attention to myself about the decision I made to "check out the ROTC program." With none of my friends in the program, I secretly changed into the military uniform right before class and immediately after changed back into my stylish college outfits.

At first, I was leery about joining the military because I thought it would make me become too independent. I did not want that to happen because I wanted to marry someday. But as I became comfortable in my AFROTC studies, I began contemplating my major again. How would I be able to use a business education degree in the military? There were no teaching jobs, I assumed. I thought I should change my major. I did the research to find my first- and second-year courses were the same ones required for a business administration degree. That would be a better option for an equivalent military specialty. I wanted to be able to still graduate on time and not lose any course credits I had already completed. I was able to successfully change my major to Business Administration making both Business Education and AFROTC my minors. I was commissioned in the U.S. Air Force with about five other young women and twelve young men.

Entering My Career & God Chosen Mentors and Fatherly Figures

Two months after my commissioning ceremony and being named surprisingly the AFROTC "Most Improved Cadet," I reported to my active duty assignment in July. Although, the assignment I received was not one of my top three choice locations on the AFROTC "dream sheet," California being the first, I did get the state of Texas my other choice. Thus, began my military career in one of the specialties I chose, Procurement. I called Dad with the news. He was happy for me and gave a simple example of what I would be doing in Procurement. You will be purchasing supplies that the Air Force needs, such as pencils and toilet paper, etc. However, I came to find out, it was much more than like preparing contracts for construction of buildings and services such as custodial, laundry and purchasing supplies and equipment for different base organizations. Dad also said I know some military nurses in the area, so he gave me Annie's number to contact her once I arrived. I did call her and she invited me over to her home. We maintained contact throughout my career.

My first active duty boss, Captain James was knowledgeable, welcoming, and intentional about me getting acclimated to my new job and career, along with the non-commissioned officer-in-charge (NCOIC), Master Sergeant (MSgt) John and the most efficient & personable secretary, Mrs. Karen. The entire office staff, mostly civil service civilians and a few military personnel, welcomed me with open arms. After settling me at a desk, I was given several large binders of the Federal Acquisition Regulations (FARs), jokingly referred to as the "bible" of procurement, and volumes of supplements to read—regulations filled with difficult-to-read and not enjoyable legalese. While waiting for a procurement school training slot, I received immediate on-the-job training (OJT). New to the military protocol, one day while walking from the office parking lot, crossing the street and going into the procurement office building, some airmen driving by spotted this girl in her military uniform. With their heads hanging out the window, they spoke words as guys do when making advances to a girl. The girl was me. I played it off, ignored them and walked right on into the building. The professional, sharp and astute, MSgt John respectfully invited me to his office. He informed me that he had just witnessed the entire scene with the airmen. He reminded me of the military protocol and the respect due me as a female and an officer. They were in violation of military protocol by disrespecting an officer. He informed me he knew where to find them. He would take the necessary action.

Career Training & Establishing Networks

About six months later, during the cold, wintery months, I received news a training slot opened up for me to attend the Basic Procurement Course in Denver, Colorado. The course was very intense. I had to discipline myself and make studying a priority. I had to be careful not to get too distracted by the beautiful sunny Rocky Mountain state in the mile high city. Some peers from the basic and advanced procurement courses decided not to be "the all study and no play" class. They organized social activities for all who would come. I learned how to have fun while studying hard. When invited to go skiing with the group at first, I said no. I had never skied a day in my life. One of them said, "You can do it. We will enroll you in a ski class, while we ski." I did not want to interfere with their fun or from them having a good time or slow them down in any way. It was hard for me to resist after their convincing rebuttals.

Upon our arrival at one of the breathtaking ski resorts, I was first instructed by the group how to put on the ski gear and boots. Then, it was off to the ski classes. The classes are full. *Oh no, now what am I to do?* I felt bad. Now they were going to be stuck with me. I could not go sit in the car. With my insistence to not get in their way, they stopped to take the time to teach me a few basics, how to ride the ski lift, how to fall down, and how to get up. Not to hold them back from a beautiful day of skiing, I encouraged them to go ahead without me and enjoy themselves. "I will be fine." Off they went, and there I was left to be adventurous on my own. Young five-year-old children were speeding in and out on skis, including elderly seniors skiing too. If they were able to do this, I should also be able to. Wow, discoveries about another sport I could grow to enjoy.

My second military boss in this assignment, Major Dennis, introduced me to home Bible Study with his wife and other young military members. Their two well-mannered, polite, and cute children Sean and Shannon became my private vow of what I would one day name my children.

The course network had opened up doors for my next duty assignment. Back at the home base in Texas, my career advisors notified me from San Antonio that they were looking at my records for reassignment in one year. Some overseas assignments were open in Japan and Germany. When I heard the position was in airlift contract administration, I remembered meeting a Major in the advanced procurement course in Denver, whom I believed was in a similar job so I called him. He informed me that since our meeting, he had been promoted and was the new headquarters selecting official for all airlift contract jobs. He explained what the job entailed and encouraged me to think about it. *"The Lord directs the steps of the godly, He delights in every detail of their lives"* (Psalm 37:23 NLT).

Surprising Adventures and Challenges Overseas

With only two years on active duty, I accepted the position and arrived a second lieutenant to Japan to then pin on my next rank of first lieutenant. Entrusted with immense responsibilities for a junior officer serving overseas, it was one of the best and most well-kept secrets in the Air Force procurement career-field. Up to that point in my career, there were very few female role models in positions other than nursing. I learned that my predecessor was a military woman but I had just missed the opportunity by one month for her to give me on-the-job-training (OJT).

My overseas home away from home was filled with camaraderie among peers, senior officers, and their families at base functions and social gatherings. Those relationships also evolved into a network of mentoring opportunities. Having a big united family and support system abroad made the world of difference. I cherished the newness of it all. Being in a land of few English-speaking natives and street signs, cars built for driving on the opposite side of the road, cultural uniqueness, annual traditional festivals, and varieties of food delicacies was a challenge, but very rewarding. Some military members did not survive the tour of duty.

Oh, what about church? While settling into my new base living quarters and work area, the church was the next community of people I needed to connect with. Since I was raised in the church, it was a must, especially living in a foreign land. Recommendations were given for local off-base churches. It was difficult navigating my way off the base. I did not start attending church until near the end of the assignment. I realized too late what the benefits of being in a community of believers would have been.

But God intervened. I finally made my way to the chapel. The chaplain introduced a new Bible Study series about God's creation from Genesis to Revelation. After becoming more consistent in attendance, the chaplain asked me if I was interested in directing the chapel's first gospel choir. Although, I was member of our church choir back home, I did not have a trained voice to sing, let alone direct a choir. So why was my faith not stronger than my fears? Feeling insecure and afraid, I declined. In my opinion, I did not have the needed skills to be a choir director. I did not pray. I should have prayed and asked if this was God's will for me. Would there be training I could go to? Where was my faith to go in my prayer closet and ask? *"[A]sk and it will be given to you; seek and you will find; knock and the door will be opened to you"* (Matthew 7:7 NIV). Some twenty years later, I discovered that it was God's timing. The military had put into place an initiative for all base chapels to provide a "gospel service" for diversity in accommodating the religious life of all people.

A Relationship with God Means Ask & Receive

After the devastating blow in my personal life and heart, God granted me what I asked for. I was selected to attend the competitive Squadron Officers School (SOS) training course back home in Alabama, a detour en-route to my new assignment in California. The junior officer's professional military education course was required for career progression. Being back in the United States and in "Sweet Home Alabama," I needed time to spend with my Mom and family, again.

When I successfully completed SOS, my new position required thorough and intense examination by senior leadership before I would be certified a warranted administrative contracting officer. Although it took months to prepare, it was a bit intimidating. Some study techniques shared by others who had already blazed the trail were to write on index cards possible questions and the answers and quiz myself. It was well-known by all I would have to be verbally examined by a board led by a tough, no-nonsense Procuring Contracting Officer (PCO) examiner, Mr. Trevidor. The first time I nervously failed. However, after successfully completing the second interview examination, the Air Force credited me with good sound business acumen. My lesson learned, if at first you don't succeed, never give up.

Since Dad did not live too far away in southern California, he and Mona welcomed me to stay with them and commute into Los Angeles until I found my own apartment and settled in my new job. His first words of advice were "all that glitters is not gold." In essence, Dad was saying to me beware, "not everything that looks precious or true turns out to be so."[49]

I found a two-bedroom apartment in Torrance. I drove into Los Angeles (LA) to worship at Calvary Baptist Church, similar to my church back home. Every Sunday, the hour between Sunday school and worship services, immediately children and adults rushed downstairs finding their way to the kitchen and to the sweet aroma of food cooking, especially the fried chicken. Enjoying the fellowship and with one another. Not only did I attend worship, I also attended Bible Study until the senior pastor later retired. In many of the LA churches, it was not unusual to find yourself sitting on the same pew with celebrities. Ray Parker Jr., the singer-songwriter, record producer, and actor in the movie *Ghostbusters* is one example, I can give.

With the government's system of checks and balances in place, I succeeded and was ready to move on to more increased job responsibilities in my career.

Growing in the Knowledge and Relationship with God & His Intervention

Upon my arrival to my next assignment, another prayer was answered. Where will I go to church? Before leaving California, my sister Teresa planted a seed into my life by giving me the name of a faith-based church and Bible teacher in Denver. The timing was good because I was also entering a season of desiring to know God better. When listening to the car radio, I heard a teaching that piqued my interest. The person speaking on the radio was the female teacher, Marilyn Hickey who happened to be the name my sister gave to me. Listening to the Denver radio broadcast, I heard her teaching from the Bible. I did not hesitate to call the church to find out the time and place of their weekly Bible Study. The pastor of Happy Church answered the phone and gave me the directions and times of the services. Pastor Wally's wife, the acclaimed teacher of the Word of God, she taught the congregants the basics of how to apply God's Word to our lives and live out our faith on a daily basis. She made the Bible a joy to read and study. From that time on, I became a member of the church.

On a regular basis, renowned Christian artists visited our church and ministered to us in song, drama, teaching, and preaching. My thirst and hunger for a relationship with the Lord Jesus grew by leaps and bounds. I attended just about every worship service, Sunday school class, drama play, concert, workshops, seminars, and other events offered at the church. In describing the experience, I like to say I was inspired by the teachings on how to live by faith, putting the Word of God into practice. I could not wait to get to the church every week for the doors to be unlocked and opened so I could go in. Being taught the Word of God book-by-book, verse-by-verse, and page-by-page was a first for me. Something within my soul was connecting me to God and my desire to go deeper in knowing Him. My childhood prayer in Alabama was coming true, "Lord, I want to know you like the Pastor seems to know you," as I listened to them preach.

The ministries available and the worship experience were amazingly rewarding. Even singing with the deaf ministry, while they signed and sung worship songs was joyful. Pastor Wally, an older and stately gentleman was a true worshipper whose example inspired me to freely enter into worship. He often sung with such sincerity of heart, it seemed. I found myself being freely drawn by the Spirit and actually experiencing true worship on another whole level. He expressed his love and worship of God through singing what I believe was one of his favorites "As the Deer Panteth" (based on Psalm 42:1).

> [50]Chorus: You alone are my strength and my shield
> To You alone may my spirit yield
> You alone are my heart's desire
> And I long to worship you

I grew by leaps and bounds during this assignment too through both my local church and the programs offered through the military base chapel. I desired something not found in earthly relationships. I realized I needed a deeper, more personal relationship with the Lord Christ. It was a long hard journey to the discovery that my boyfriend could not fill the void that

I was lacking. It made sense that I was becoming more spiritual in how I was connecting to God versus being religious and ritualistic. Yes, it meant reading and studying the Word of God and putting into practice what I was reading and desiring to live by. I was falling in love with the Lord.

Discovering My Spiritual Gifts

Every person came to church with their Bible, and in every service, we studied what the Bible had to say about specific topics, such as faith, prayer, relationships, trust, grace, salvation, and finances. As a single woman, I was an active member in the Singles Ministry. One sermon in particular preached by the Associate Pastor Howie called "Sold Out for Jesus" stirred up the desire to know and love Him. He also taught us that we had gifts from God. I was intrigued. I approached him right after service, pleading to find out more about what gifts were mine. He recommended I read a specific book about all the spiritual gifts. While reading, I was to highlight all that I identified with. I completed my assignment, made an appointment, and went back to speak with him. He looked at the marked-up book. I waited to hear what my gifts were. He responded with the words that my strongest spiritual gift was teaching. He said, the Sunday school department would be a good start. I could begin teaching second graders. I hesitated because in my mind, I thought I would be teaching adults. I commented, "I am single and do not have children. I do not know how to teach children."

He smiled and said, "If you can teach children, you can teach adults." He gave me the name and asked that I contact the superintendent of the Sunday School department to get further instructions.

This was a great opportunity. Now that I knew my gift, I wanted to use it for the Lord. In order to prepare me to teach, the church provided mandatory teachers' training. I learned to two key points. First how "subconscious vows" play out in our lives. These vows are past events that happened in our lives that we either subconsciously chose to forget them or decided we will never experience again. Second, there is no bad child. Pray for discernment as you observe a child's behavior and wait then for God to reveal what action you should take. Most of what I learned from the training, I applied it to my own personal life and subsequently, in the classroom I was assigned to teach second graders.

One Sunday morning, the superintendent called me an hour or so before the Sunday School class to ask if I would lead the class that morning. I was shocked that they would ask me to do that so soon. She said the primary teacher was unable to be there. She reassured me of the format and said I would have everything I needed when I arrived. Oh no, I would miss morning worship service that I so thoroughly enjoyed because Sunday school met at the same time. I lived about thirty minutes from the church. This was a last-minute crisis. I had to rush to get ready and make the drive in the snow and be on time. A miracle happened that morning. Time on the clock literally stopped. I was on time. I met with the Superintendent and taught the class.

Without a teacher's aide or anyone to assist me in class that day. Recalling what I learned in teacher's training, I looked for the least likely students to engage. In the seat to my left, in the last row in the back of the room, was a young boy with glasses whom I asked his name. He said, Slade. I asked if he would read the text from the Bible? Slade responded, "I cannot read." I am not sure where it came from, but without hesitation, I said, "That is okay. I will help you."

As he tried to read, almost word for word, I helped him, and then I moved to the next person to continue reading. At the end of class, I asked all the students to come forward to let us close in prayer. We all got in a circle with Slade standing next to me, and we held hands. When I asked, "Who will pray?"

Slade raised his hand and asked if he could pray. While I do not remember the other prayers, I do remember a key part of Slade's prayer. I believe God was speaking through him to confirm with me He had gifted me to teach. Slade prayed, thanking God for his teacher. Tears welled up in my eyes.

Even with my hesitancy about teaching and leading the class, God showed me that when I trust Him, He will take care of my needs, desires, and fears. At the end of class, to my surprise, I was presented with audiotapes of the worship service. I found out this was the bonus they provided to teachers, so they would not feel they missed out on the worship service. I could still listen to the preached Word on cassette tapes while using my God-given gifts and talents to serve in ministry.

When the superintendent informed me that the primary teacher would not be returning, she asked if I would be the primary teacher for that class. Of course, I accepted after the confirmation from God in Slade's prayer. I believed I could do it. From that point on, every Sunday, I was expecting to see Slade again. The other students were regulars. I decided to ask the

Sunday school superintendent about the missing student Slade. She said she had no record of him ever coming before that day or after. From that moment, I believed that Slade may have been an angel sent by God to confirm that He had chosen and gifted me to teach. *"Do not forget to entertain strangers, for by so doing some people have entertained angels without knowing it"* (Hebrews 13:2 NIV). I was to be a teacher despite my fears and changing my major in college. The spiritual gifts characteristics for teaching is one's love of in-depth study of the Scriptures with the desire to know God, teach others, and who get excited about putting into practice what was learned.

Facing Peer Pressure and Teaching Fears with Prayer

With my fears of public speaking and after a brief introduction to Toastmasters International in Los Angeles, California, for the first time I got serious about getting over the notion what I had to say was not important enough that others would listen to me. I joined a Toastmasters International chapter to improve my public speaking skills. I used the opportunity to talk about topics of a soul-searching nature and anything related to "purpose." I had to stop thinking others did not want to hear what I had to say. I was an instructor now and a supervisor of men, the peer pressure almost paralyzed me. I had prayed for this assignment to be closer to my boyfriend.

In searching the Bible, I looked for ways to get God's help out of the mess I was in with my boyfriend, overcoming my classroom fears, and dealing with the co-worker relationships. *"Thou therefore gird up thy loins, and arise, and speak unto them all that I command thee: be not dismayed at their faces, lest I confound thee before them" (Jeremiah 1:17 KJV).* When the preacher used this as a text in a sermon, I believed it was God speaking to me. Just as He spoke to Jeremiah, I was to do the same in the classroom. Do not look at their faces in fear of what may look like they are frowning upon your teaching skills or making expressions like you are not getting across to them. You cannot determine from the expressions on their faces what they are learning or not learning or whether they are listening or not listening. That verse came into my life at the right time. I hung on to it every time I stood up in the classroom to teach. I had to have faith that although under the wrong circumstances I applied for the job, God still took care of my fears. Having broken up with a boyfriend, I could not quit the job. I needed God to continue helping me be successful despite my dilemmas.

I was being tested not only in overcoming my fears in the classroom, standing before the students but dealing with male co-workers who challenged my authority as their supervisor. One day, I went into the office real early in the morning to pray a heartfelt and genuine prayer to the Lord. Heavenly Father, I trust in you. You know the plans for my life and if I am in your will at all, would You please let me know by the guys coming into the office this morning at least today saying, "good morning" to me? As they arrived each one had to walk by my cubicle so they could not miss seeing me. First captain, who was not comfortable with women in the workplace believed we should be homemakers and at home raising children. He quickly whisked by me saying, good morning. I responded with "good morning." Not really paying attention and having forgotten the prayer that quickly, I continued reading and preparing the lesson plans for the day. A few moments later, the other Captain colleague also walked in saying, "good morning." Again, looking down at my work I heard him and just said good morning back. The next thing I knew he was standing still at my door way bouncing back and forth, I did not look up until he said, "I do not know why I am standing here." I looked up at him and the light went on. And I said with excitement in my voice, *oh, good morning!*

On another occasion, I walked into Captain Dan's office to get him to take an action on a task. Although, he was the least of my co-workers I expected an adversarial response from, he caught me off guard. He refused to do it by adamantly saying, "No." I instinctively and verbally reacted with very harsh words back to him. I could not believe the words that came off my tongue and out of my mouth. I had never said those words before. I was so convicted to the core of my wrongdoing that I ran swiftly from his office down the hall to the office of a Christian civilian man and minister, Mr. Owens. I shut the door so fast and tried to calm myself down, panting and talking. I told him I just said in anger the wrong words to my co-worker, you've got to pray for me. He stopped what he was doing and prayed. I had to obey what the Bible teaches about seeking forgiveness from God and from others. *"...and forgive us our sins, as we have forgiven those who sin against us...If you forgive those who sin against you, your heavenly Father will forgive you. But if you refuse to forgive others, your Father will not forgive your sins"* (Matthew 5:12, 15, 16 NLT).

As I left Mr. Owens office to head back to Captain Dan's office to ask for his forgiveness for my words spoken in anger, he was walking out of his office toward me in the hallway. As soon as I opened my mouth, he said, "I am sorry about what just happened. I am obviously the problem because that was not you. I know you are a Christian." I was shocked at how God immediately turned the situation around. It was mind blowing to hear him admit he was the problem. From that time until the end of my duty there, he and I became friends. God used him to get me to attend my first Company Grade Officers' Association (CGOA) meeting where the new center commander Major General Larry would be speaking and conducting the elections of new officers. Captain Dan convincingly encouraged me to run for President. This was my first meeting I reluctantly did not decline the nomination from the floor to run for the office of President. Oh my goodness, I won.

Be Happy Affirmations

At the tail end of my previous assignment, I created a list and continued to add to it from that time on to encourage myself with self-talk. I titled it "Be Happy!" For the first time, I discovered my creative side by writing poems out of my brokenness (see Appendix). My joy of writing evolved during my Quiet Time with God as I journaled my prayers. It became habit-forming and very helpful.

1. Establish stronger faith in Jesus
2. Attend regular worship services
3. Nurture family ties and friendships
4. Total commitment to completion of MBA program
5. Study and pass ACO exam; be full-fledged ACO and a competent one
6. Read Bible, *LA Times*, *DARS*, Earl Nightingale, *Business Week*, weekly *Wall Street Journal*
7. Pray without ceasing; give thanks unto God
8. Study GMAT and pass exam
9. Think positively and have self-confidence
10. Try to understand boyfriend and not get upset with his tone of voice and commands
11. Attend the Bible Studies (Divine Institute)
12. Watch weight and exercise
13. Write and strengthen vocabulary

14. Practice makes perfect—speak out, communicate whatever it is, reiterate, reinterpret articles read
15. Tithes
16. Stay on a budget
17. Don't be so sensitive
18. Do not rely on others for your happiness!
19. God is the answer, acknowledge Him in all ways, lean not on my own understanding (Proverbs 3:5,6)
20. Boyfriend and I can be best friends
21. Boyfriend is your friend, although he's always so critical; it's for my benefit
22. I've got to succeed for myself not *anyone* else; stop basing my actions on someone else
23. I can do it! I've got to do it through Christ who strengthens me
24. Give me strength, Dear Lord!

Growing in My Relationship God

Not only was I a local church member, I also got involved in the base chapel. Some may say it was coincidence but I say it was God's providence when I showed up at the chapel as the same time the Chaplain was looking for someone to lead the Protestant Women of the Chapel (PWOC) program. I had stopped by the chapel one day to find out if they offered Bible Study or prayer during the weekday lunch hour. He expressed his excitement about me showing up. After a few questions, he offered me the position of President to reactivate their PWOC program. I accepted.

It turned out to be another remarkable experience of spiritual growth for me. I found myself witnessing to other female officers, wives, students, office mates, and others about the Lord Jesus Christ. During the day in the workplace on breaks or at noon lunch-hour breaks, I'd go to the chapel to get inspiration through Bible Study. Also, in the evenings, I attended weekly Bible Study at the church. Sundays, I attended worship services at Happy Church where I received the baptism of the Holy Spirit.

In order to go deeper in my study of the Bible, I took a big leap of faith and enrolled in the church Bible College. This was a significant milestone for me because what I was receiving on Sunday mornings and in Bible Study made me thirstier for the knowledge of God. Despite the difficulty of the course, I stuck with it, completed it, and passed, although barely.

As I continued to grow in my relationship with Jesus, my confidence on the job evolved. For quick accessibility and ready reference, when the opportunity permitted, I kept copies of the Bible from the chapel in my office credenza to give copies to those who were receptive. There was no doubt about my faith and those who observed me. I was overjoyed the day one of my peers and office mates decided to share with me what he knew about God. Captain Chris said that while growing up as a child, he was taught we all had guardian angels. No matter where he went he made sure his angel had room on his chair or a seat to sit right beside him. On another occasion he shared a passage in the Bible about Philemon that reminded him of me and how I was an accepting and forgiving person. Another instance, when his arm was injured and he returned back to work he joyfully shared with me another Bible scripture he found that helped him heal. He read it to me *"Come, let us return to the LORD. He has torn us to pieces but he will heal us; he has injured us but he will bind up our wound" (Hosea 6:1 NIV).* Although I had difficulty initially working with him because he was an excellent instructor full of knowledge and wit. But, I do recall these special moments God used to encourage me despite the circumstances. *"In the same way, let your light shine before men, that they may see your good deeds and praise your Father in heaven" (Matthew 5:16).*

I believe one Bible verse in particular that I learned in the Bible study class at Happy Church stuck with me as I sensed the Lord playing it out in my own life: *"For I know the plans I have for you,' declares the Lord, 'plans to prosper you and not to harm you, plans to give you hope and a future. Then you will call on me and come and prayer to me, and I will listen to you. You will seek me when you seek me with all your heart. I will be found by you, declares the Lord..."* (Jeremiah 29:11-14 NIV).

My testimony as I look back at my time in Denver, Colorado is how God opened so many doors for me. *"The LORD directs the steps of the godly. He delights in every detail of their lives. Though they stumble, they will never fall, for the LORD holds them by the hand" (Psalm 37:23 NLT).* Even as I faced some serious challenges, obstacles, and temptations of the heart, God still never failed me or rejected me. How would I know who should be my boyfriend and future husband? Just as God's chosen people were commanded to set stones as a memorial forever after crossing over the river into the land promised them (Joshua 4:7), the same was my assignment in Denver because of how I grew exponentially in getting to know Jesus personally, relationally, biblically, and spiritually. Denver is my "memorial experience."

What God Has for You is for You, Boyfriend or Not

I was fascinated by how events in my life were positively unfolding. It was through the amazing intervention of God that the fear I had after graduating from high school was no longer haunting me. I ended up being a teacher in my military job and a volunteer teacher at my church. What the enemy of doubt tried to do to me in college keeping me from discovering who I was and my true identity in Christ Jesus was being revealed. *"For God did not give you a spirit of timidity (fear), but a spirit of power, of love, and of self-discipline (a sound mind)"* (2 Timothy 1:7 NIV).

About thirteen years prior, upon graduating from high school, I refused to get a teaching degree because of the fear of failure, ridicule, or rejection. Yet here I was with two teaching ventures because I fell in love with a guy. When I applied for a teaching job to follow Filos, I succumbed to my fears with hopes he'd marry me. I was in love, or so I thought. He broke my heart.

Yet as Joseph, the son of Jacob and Rachel, discovered after God came to him in a dream about his future that no matter what obstacles come in my life, the Sovereign God knows and cares. Joseph learned that the harm intended for him *"But God intended it for good to accomplish what is now being done, the saving of many lives"* (Genesis 50:20 NIV). In my case, God got me back on the righteous path that He knew all along was for me.

Don't Stop Praying

After being in Denver for a while, maybe not even a year, my boyfriend, Filos, and I finally broke up. On July 4th, in my brokenness and unable to go out of the house to celebrate with friends the Independence Day of our nation, I stayed at home. Discouraged about not knowing whom to believe or who was or was not the man to be my husband. I gathered the Holy Bible, a red poster board, scissors, and markers and placed them in the middle of my bed. I learned about a Bible verse and decided to apply it to my heartfelt need for God to intervene in my life about relationships. *"Write the vision; make it plain on tablets, so he may run who reads it. For still the vision awaits its' appointed time; it hastens to the end—it will not lie. If it seems slow, wait for it; it will surely come; it will not delay ...*" (Habakkuk 2:2,3 ESV). I searched the Bible to find all the biblical references to relationships and marriage. I was asking God to find me the mate He has for me because obviously I was doing something wrong. Who do You have for me?

In the Happy Church Singles Ministry at my church, I was taught what the Bible tells us about singleness based on the text in First Corinthians chapter 7. Was I to be single for the rest of my life or does God have a mate for me? I want to live as You command us to. On the vision board, I wrote the scriptures pertaining to marriage and relationships. The board consisted of images from magazine clippings about my "dream" wedding day, my dream wedding gown, our dream honeymoon to the Holy Land Israel, and three children (two boys and a girl).

July 4th turned out to be a very special day for me. I believe God heard my sincere prayers that day because of the sign of the rainbow He gave me the days to follow. I do not recall seeing rainbows in the sky prior to this significant time in my life of seeking a deeper relationship with God. "*Whenever I bring clouds over the earth and the rainbow appears in the clouds, I will remember my covenant between me and you.*" (Genesis 9:14,15a NIV). What God promises, He is faithful to ensure it will come to pass.

As my tour in Denver was coming to an end, I was given a book to read by a young adult military female I happened to meet at Happy Church. This was my first time, I believe, ever reading an allegory (a story, poem, or picture that can be interpreted to reveal a hidden meaning). I thoroughly enjoyed the reading from beginning to end. *Hind's Feet in High Places* by Hannah Hurnard was a relatable story I could relate to about the yearning of God's children to reach new heights of love, joy, and victory without fear. Reading the book was a climatic and inspirational end to my Denver assignment, my "memorial experience." Denver is where, I like the character "Much-Afraid" in the book was taken from being fearful to becoming a spiritually connected young woman who had a divine encounter with God Almighty.

Yes, in the midst of my relational inadequacies, I met the living Word of God, my Lord and Savior, Jesus Christ in a new way. Denver was my place of new beginnings, of stepping out on faith to accomplish symbolic firsts, such as facing challenges and blessings of overcoming teaching fears on the job and at the church, purchasing my first home, being elevated to a Master Instructor, enduring a broken relationship, reactivating, leading and becoming the President of the Protestant Women of the Chapel (PWOC), becoming the President of Company Grade Officers Association (CGOA) on a fluke after only attending one meeting and the support of Captain Dan, asking for and getting the first time ever CGOA seat at the Center Commander Major General Larry's weekly staff meeting table, and other blessings. Yes, ever since I heard his first speech to "Go Make a Difference," I did all I could to try my best to live it. His speech was like I had heard from God, Himself telling how to succeed in life and my career making a difference from that point on.

I also experienced a lot of spiritual first, such as reading the Bible in one-year from Genesis to Revelation, exercising the spiritual disciplines of meditating, studying, fasting, memorizing scriptures, witnessing to others, praying more with a group, journaling, and being taught biblical financial principles of money management, accepting speaking engagements, teaching biblical seminars on the Ephesians chapter 6 spiritual armor of God, and fasting for five days on my first ever private retreat using the Daniel fast model.

First Spiritual Fast and Private Retreat

I took leave from work. I did not know how to make it work by going away to the mountains so I decided to make it a stay-at-home spiritual retreat. I called my sister Teresa to let her know I would not be available for a week, but not to worry. If Mom or Dad should call you looking for me because they are unable to reach me, please let them know I am okay. I will be unplugging all my phones, no television, and tuned off to the outside world spending the five days alone reading the Bible and praying. I drunk plenty of water and every day at 12:00 noon, I ate steamed spinach. By the end of the five days, I had learned how to listen and trust the Spirit of God to overcome my fears.

On Saturday coming out of the fast and off the retreat, I called Mrs. Mary, the mother of my pastor's wife, Marilyn. As one of the Sunday School department leaders, she befriended me with spiritually wise and motherly counsel. I just had to share with another spiritual mentor about what I had experienced on my five-day retreat with God. She met me for lunch. I shared, while she listened attentively. I was encouraged by her prayer of thanksgiving to God for my divine encounter. Later I was invited to her home for a meal. She surprised me with a wonderful gift. My very own felt storyboard, like what we used in the Happy Church Sunday School Department to teach the children. She had it designed specifically for me to visually teach the text on the whole armor of God from Ephesians chapter 6 verses 10 through 19. She knew I was serving on active duty in the military. Therefore, the main character piece was a military soldier, that also included all the soldier's pieces of whole armor of God, i.e. the belt of truth, breastplate of righteousness, shoes of the gospel of peace, shield of faith, helmet of salvation and sword of the Spirit.

The Detour Assignment

Military assignments are usually three to four years. In my third year in Colorado, I put on my "dream sheet" where I would like to go next. My sights were on Washington, D.C. for two reasons. It was where I believed God revealed my mate would be and a woman at my church had also prophetically confirmed what God had already revealed to me. And quite naturally I wanted to go where my future husband would be right away. Also, I just wanted the opportunity to live and work in the nation's capital.

> *And we know that in all things God works for the good of those who love him, who have been called according to his purpose. For those God foreknew he also predestined to be conformed to the likeness of his Son, that he might be the firstborn among many brothers. And those he predestined, he also called; those he called, he also justified; those he justified, he also glorified* (Romans 8:28–30 NIV).

It was time for my next move. My military career advisor at Randolph AFB, Texas advised me the only opening in my specialty was in Ohio. I was not interested after hearing about the personnel issues and their repeated failure to pass the command level Inspector General (IG) inspections. The job just was not appealing. I declined the position and kept waiting to hear of other job openings. My question to myself: why was I not given an option of a choice assignment with good growth potential and to go to Washington D.C.?

The General Officer at the Headquarter (HQs) had his Executive Officer call me after I declined the Ohio job, to pass on to me what the general said, "You will go to Newark AFB." With that command, I no longer had a choice. I was going to another assignment that began with a fear of failure. My predecessors had not been successful. On the airplane to a house-hunting trip, I looked out the window at the land and green pastures below when a sense of peace came over me as the pilot was making his descend into the Ohio airfield. I was reminded of God's words to Joshua the military leader whom He called to succeed Moses about taking the children of Israel into the Promised land, *"I will give you every place where you set your foot, as I promised Moses. . . be strong and courageous, because you will lead these people to inherit the land I swore to their ancestors to give them"* (Joshua 1:3,6 NIV). This was significant.

Reaching Back to My Youngest Brother

A new study shows that a relationship with both parents is crucial. A father's love is as important to a child's emotional development as a mother's, a large-scale study has confirmed. After the house-hunting visit, I called my youngest brother Ken in California to ask if he would like to move to Ohio with me. There was about a ten-year difference in age between he and I. It will be a new start for both of us. I was in a financial position to reach back and help him achieve his fullest potential. He said yes because he was also going to call me with the same request. It was a confirmation.

He flew to Denver and we drove to our new beginnings in Ohio. We moved into a two-bedroom townhouse. After getting acclimated to my job and the area, we visited the local community college for him to apply. He was accepted. My 6 feet tall, good-looking, athletically inclined and clean-cut baby brother tried out for the basketball team and made it. We were on the path of new beginnings prepared for us by God.

After a number of visits to churches in the immediate and surrounding area, we decided on the local Shiloh Baptist Church. I was torn between going to a non-denominational church similar to Happy Church. The World Harvest Church in Columbus was the closest one, but a commute. However, one Sunday in particular while I was sitting in the second row of the pews in the local Shiloh Baptist church a few seats over from the First Lady, I saw a vision from the cross in the pulpit. From the cross two arms and hands starting at the elbows down were reaching out to me as if giving me a gift-wrapped in brown gift paper and a large ribbon and bow tied around it. Not understanding what was going on, I did not instantly reach out to accept or even reach forward to get it. In my mind while gazing at it, I was thinking no to the color of the wrapping paper or how the bow was tied. I was trying to decide what to do? Should I accept it? Was the gift being given to me? It was strange and for superficial reasons, I was about to reject it. Then it occurred to me this was a gift from God for me. I reached up and received the gift. When I opened it, a huge ten-karat diamond ring was sparkling with brilliance. Oh my, I almost refused this beautiful gift. The unspoken message given I was about to miss a very special blessing. Do not go by what you see. *"Trust in the Lord with all your heart and do not lean to your own understanding. In all your ways acknowledge Him and He will make your paths straight"* (Proverbs 3:5,6). God was telling me this assignment to Newark, Ohio was His gift to me from Him and this was the church. I was to not be afraid of the bad report about the job nor compare myself with my predecessors for whatever their limitations may have been for the repeat IG findings and the personnel issues. *"I became a servant of this gospel by the gift of God's grace given me through the working of his power"* (Ephesians 3:7 NIV).

One comment we would often hear our Pastor Noble from time to time say, an elderly wise and godly man, "anyone who comes to Newark is on a detour sent by God." He goes on to say, "because there is no direct route here. You have to take a detour to get to this small town tucked away off of the major highways. You have to know this city exists and that it is located here."

After joining the church, Pastor Noble assigned First Lady Nora to be my spiritual and professional mentor. And I also believe Carolyn, the very knowledgeable personnel director, was sent by God to Ohio from Texas to provide me professional advice about how to handle personnel issues within the organization I inherited. Just at the right time, the center and base commanders devised a center-wide re-organization plan with all senior leaders, including myself, to implement.

The base did not have a chapel. After much prayer the Lord gave me wisdom on what to do. I requested the command HQs Chaplain's Office help us establish religious programs on the base. The Lord answered my prayer and I became the coordinator on site for religious activities, such as breakfast or noon-day lunch Bible Study.

My brother Ken and I both had our own separate challenges throughout this assignment but by God's grace my faith sustained me for the four years.

Preparing for the Next Assignment to Meet the God Sent Mate

Three distinct events happened prior to me leaving Ohio in preparing me for my next assignment. Nearing the end of my "detour" assignment, the first surprise call was from the Pentagon general's office and the voice of his military assistant, Lieutenant Colonel Everett to let me know about a job opening. He asked, "are you still interested in coming to work here?" The other was another surprise "out of the blue" call from a military counterpart, Major Leroy, on assignment in Washington, D.C. The focus of his call, while boasting about his church Ebenezer and his Pastors Grainger and JoAnn Browning's teachings, was to encourage me to visit his church, when I got to the D.C area. And the third event happened with my dear God-sent sorority sister and friend Beverly Warfield. She was founder of our book club "Chapter One." She and all of us book club members decided to go hear the author of a book we had finished reading "Just A Sister Away." The author Dr. Renita Weems was the guest preacher at a local Columbus Women's Day service. The book was brought to our attention by Beverly's husband Paul. Prior to the book being on our book club list, I had not heard of Dr. Weems. By the time I relocated to D.C. and visited Ebenezer, Pastor JoAnn mentioned that the Reverend Dr. Renita Weems had been the keynote preacher to kick-off the first night of her annual women's spiritual retreat conferences since its inception. God made it very clear Ebenezer was to be my church. God was directing me to become a member. Amazingly after I arrived and connected with my line sister Gwen who lived in the area, it was a confirmation. She also shared the names of the Pastors giving an endorsement of their ministry and sorority chapters in the area. I had visited several Baptist churches before finally joining Ebenezer.

Listening to My Inner Spirit & Outcome of Parents' Wisdom

It is evident how God works mysteriously in our lives from birth until the end. God knew in my mother's womb and he also knew the plans He had for my life. Just as He knows about the life of every human being on this earth. *"And we know that in all things God works for the good of those who love Him and who have been called according to His purpose" (Romans 8:28 NIV)*. Because once in college during the career decision phase of my life, right away, I chose Business Education with the primary option of practicing my business skills versus teaching them. Although it was still an education degree program, there was no teaching certification requirement. Shy, insecure, and afraid to talk in the public, I discovered I felt the most comfortable talking one on one with people and not in group or classroom settings. Once in college, if I had not listened to the spirit of God within me to "check out the ROTC program," there is no telling what direction my life would have gone.

My childhood dream, when we were "one big happy family," of joining the military also came true. Out of obedience to my father, I did not pursue a fashion designing career, but got a college education from a four-year university. His firmness left no doubt for me to obey what the Bible instructs, *"Children, obey your parents in the Lord, for this is right" (Ephesians 6:1 NIV)*. Yes, *"Children, obey your parents in all things: for this is well pleasing unto the Lord" (Colossians 3:20 KJV)*.

Dad's dream for his daughter to go to college was successfully achieved. Mom's desire for me to attend a college near home was also successfully accomplished in four years. Blessed be the name of the Lord for the provision came without the stress of where the money would come from and whether my parents would be able to pay. How convenient it turned out that I was able to go to college at home and not be limited to getting a teaching degree only.

I successfully earned an undergraduate degree solely with tuition assistance from the BEO grant (BEOG), which paid for my entire college. Amazing, how God's perfect timing works. Because unbeknownst to us the BEOG became law one year before we graduated from high school. Yes, God watches over His children to ensure His plans for our lives are fulfilled. The added bonus was the monthly AFROTC paycheck paid for my transportation and my part-time sales job paid for books and fun ways of celebrating Mom on special occasions with my sisters and brothers. Songs we used to sing in church came to my mind, and I started singing it every time positive things happened during those critical years of my life: "Oh yes, God will open doors you cannot see …" and "What God has for me, it is for me. I know without a doubt He will bring me out …"

"[T]he steps of a good man (person) are ordered by the Lord: and He delights in his (person) way" (Psalm 37:23, 24 KJV). *"And my God will meet all your needs according to his glorious riches in Christ Jesus" (Philippians 4:19 NIV)*.

A Love Letter from Your Heavenly Father

My Dearest Daughter, the Dreamer

The sky is the limit to what you can do. When you delight yourself in Me, I find joy in you. I will give you the desires of your heart and make all your plans succeed (Psalm 37:4, Psalm 20:4 NIV). I will instruct you, teach you, and counsel you in the way you should go with my loving eye on you (Psalm 32:8 NIV). I have given you the ability to bless others with your talents and spiritual gifts because I give you gifts to serve others to be faithful stewards of My grace in its various forms (1 Peter 4:10 NIV). I love you and I made you, I will not abandon you (Psalm 138:8).

You are valued by Me. It is not because of anything you have done. I knew you before you were born. When I formed you in your mother's womb, I set you apart and appointed you (Jeremiah 1:4-5 NLT). I fearfully and wonderfully made you for my divine purpose giving you talents and spiritual gifts.

Because of My great love for you, I am rich in mercy. I made you alive with Christ even when you were dead in transgressions—it is by my grace you have been saved and I raised you up with Christ Jesus who seated you with Him in the Heavenly realms. For it is by my grace you have been saved, through faith and it is not something you did, but My gift and not by your works, so that no one can boast (Ephesians 2:4-8 NIV). That is why I command you to be strong and very courageous. Be careful to obey all the instructions in the Bible. Do not deviate from them, nor turn either to the right or to the left. Then you will be successful in everything you do. Study the Book of instruction continually. Meditate on my Words day and night and be sure to obey everything written in it. Only then will you prosper and succeed in all you do (Joshua 1:7,8 NLT).

I have blessed you with privilege and authority, yet I also give this warning: don't think you are better than you really are. Be honest in your evaluation of yourself, measuring yourself by the faith I have given you (Romans 12:3 NLT).

You have a unique role in the body of Christ, which has many parts and each one is given specific spiritual gifts to serve Me and allow Me to work in all who believe in Me. Each one belongs to the other, and for you to build my kingdom on earth and bring glory to Me. Gifts are given to help others, such as the ability to give wise advice, or a message of special knowledge, or great faith, or the gift of healing, or the power to perform miracles, or the ability to prophesy or discern whether a message is from the Spirit of God or another spirit; or the ability to speak in unknown languages or the ability to interpret what is being said. My one and only Spirit distributes all these gifts to each person (1 Corinthians 12:7-11 NLT). Use your gifts of motivation to speak prophesy with as much faith as I have given you or the gift to serve others well, teaching, encouraging, giving generously, leading others, showing kindness. Whatever the gift—do it well (Romans 12:4-8 NLT). Perfect your gift, and your gift will open the way for you and usher you into the presence of the great (Proverbs 18:16 NIV). Use your gifts and talents to honor Me and bless others, and when you do that, you are loving Me with all your heart, all your soul, and all your mind in obedience to the first great commandment. The second is equally as important: love others as yourself (Matthew 22:37–40 NLT). I will strengthen you with all glorious power to have the endurance and patience you need to share in the inheritance, I have given you. I have rescued you from Satan's kingdom of darkness. So be confident of this very thing that I began this good work within you, and will continue the work until it is finally finished on the day when Christ Jesus returns (Philippians 1:6 NLT).

Your El Shaddai, God Almighty

Self-Discovery / Self-Reflection

Application

(1) *Find photos of yourself participating in your favorite activity that highlights your gifts, talents, and strengths or limitations and add to vision board.*
(2) *Reflect and chat about the questions below with your mother or close adult female friend (mentor).*
(3) *Look up and write down on your vision board the Bible verses from this chapter that inspired you and use them to also answer the questions.*

Thinking about Me: What's Right With Me? Born with Dreams, Gifts, and Talents

1. What are your God-given gifts, talents, abilities, strengths, and limitations? How do you know?

_____
_____

2. What are your dreams and aspirations? Why? Are you a negative or positive, doubtful or hopeful about accomplishing all your dreams? Why?

_____
_____

3. Have you or anyone in your family graduated from high school and/ or college? is this your dream? Why or why not?

_____
_____

4. Do you know what it means to have a broken heart in the midst of achieving your dreams?

_____
_____

5. Have you been challenged in achieving your dreams? Were these the times you prayed to God for help? How did God help you be successful?

_____
_____

For you are a people holy to the Lord your God. The Lord your God has chosen you out of all the peoples on the face of the earth to be his people, his treasured possession.
—Deuteronomy 7:6

You are special! God made you with a unique plan and purpose.
—Anonymous

I am a princess not because I have a prince but because my Father is a King and He is God!
—Author Unknown

CHAPTER 7

You Are Special...
Born into Royalty!

Valued by God

Unlike any other creatures, you are God's special daughter. He has given you royalty privileges. You are costly, valuable and a rare jewel to Him and your value is as vast as the heavens and the same vastness is God's love towards you.[51] When we value ourselves, the same way God does, then we are able to relate to and value others in a more positive way, thereby boosting our own self-esteem.[52]

Just about every girl likes diamonds. But the more rare and valuable gemstones than diamonds are tanzanite, Burma ruby, jadeite, alexandrite, and others including the natural pearl. The story of the birth of natural pearls is fascinating and miraculous. Why, because natural pearls are created in live oysters below the sea surface in an usual way. A pearls' life begins as a foreign object lodged in an oyster. The object is either a parasite or piece of a shell or irritant that accidentally lodges itself in an oyster's soft inner body and once in cannot get out. A mollusk produces layers of nacre (pronounced NAY-kur) around the foreign object inside its shell and therefore producing a beautiful pearl.[53] Other gemstones worth thousands of dollars such as diamonds, tanzanite, black opal, red beryl, musgravite, emerald, ruby, pink diamond must be cut and polished to bring out their beauty. But not so with pearls found in oysters because they are already complete with a shimmering iridescence, lustre and soft inner glow. Natural pearls are rare, valuable and costly.[54] Jesus tells His disciples a parable story about *"The kingdom of heaven is like a merchant looking for fine pearls. When he found one of great value, he went away and sold everything he had and bought it* (Matthew 13:45 NIV). The merchant pays the ultimate price in order to have the pearl, which is the sacrifice God made with His Son to pay the price to redeem humanity back to Him.

What does "special" mean?

You are just that special as a rare natural pearl. The definition of *special* in the Webster dictionary is better, greater, or otherwise different from what is usual; exceptionally good or precious. When someone says a person is special, they are expressing a feature about the person having quality, character, identity, distinctness and uniqueness as an individual.

The first place we may notice the word "special" is usually during holiday greeting cards to someone special, during television commercials or on marketing signs advertising the sale of select products and creative gift ideas.

What about when you hear the words, "You are special," do you know what the person means when they say it to you? How do they know? Do you believe them? What is it about you that they say those three words to you? Do you take them at their word or do you need to know their reasons for saying it?

When and how do you feel special? Is it when you feel loved in your relationships with family, friends, teachers, pastors, priest, or others? Are they complimenting your inner and outer beauty? Or are there certain times of the year you feel special? Most girls feel special when they get jewelry or their first string of pearls. When you dress up for birthday parties, prom, weddings, cotillion "debutante" balls and holiday festivities, such as Christmas, Valentine's Day, and Easter. Do you feel really good as I do with a favorite outfit on and accessorized with beautiful jewelry, shoes, and scarves? You can catch me making turns and dancing all in front of a long length mirror.

Are you naturally quick to tell others, "You are special?" Being self-aware of your own uniqueness, value, beliefs, strengths, and weaknesses (or limitations) will help you decipher the intent of others when they say things you have not heard or experienced first at home by your parents and family.

Although, we may not have heard those words growing up, I do remember the first time I actually heard those precious words. I was taken by surprise because it did not come from a family member or even a boyfriend, but a co-worker and devout Christian young adult woman. During a conversation at the lowest point in my life, she said, "You are special." She got my attention. Why at that particular time and on that particular day, did she say aloud in the midst of our conversation, "You are special?" It did seem odd. However, we had already been getting to know each another and she knew I was a Christian also. My boyfriend and I had broken up. At the time, she was God's messenger who shared with me words of encouragement from the Bible. As we talked about God and the Bible, I felt the spiritual void in my life. The Spirit of God was convicting me. God used a Christian female peer to inspire me with words of God from the Bible. I needed to start reading, studying, praying, and applying God's words in the Bible to my everyday life and going back to church regularly. She eventually brought to my attention and made the statement, "you need to see yourself the way God sees you."

As I think about it, my sisters, brothers, and me had not heard, "I love you," or "you are special," spoken at home, but our parents' actions did it, such as letters or cards signed "love, Dad" and Mom making us feel loved by doing special things for us.

Born in an Earthly Royal Family

When I think of special, I also think of royalty and immediately the British royal family of England comes to mind. A royal person is the member of a family with status. Persons of royalty status are the most successful, famous, or highly regarded members of a particular group and have titles such as King, Queen, Prince, Princess, Duke, Duchess, Earl, and Countess, to name a few. Queen Elizabeth is the current British head of state and monarch. Her son Prince Charles is the next in line to succeed to the throne and become king. Queen Elizabeth was born into royalty and the first of two daughters to King George, VI. When her father died she became the Queen and longest reigning monarch. Royal families live their lives in the public eye with no choice from the day they are born until their death. Their destiny is to become the leader in their native land and the other territories they own. Around the world, there are twenty-six royal families, who achieved their royalty status by acquiring and owning a number of territories. Specifically, the British royal family is the owner of sixteen commonwealth realms comprised of seven sovereign states of the United Kingdom, Canada, Australia, New Zealand, South Africa, Pakistan, and Ceylon.[55] A royal family's whole purpose is to procreate by having at least one child heir to the throne who guarantees the survival of the monarchy, which began in AD 926.

I recall the British royal families' pomp and circumstance on three separate occasions. Over millions watched on television the United Kingdom celebrating the British royal weddings in London, England. Glued to our television sets on July 29, 1981 and in awe we watched the beautiful bride, Diana Spencer, an English schoolteacher, and her waiting groom, the royal Prince Charles get married at Saint Paul's Cathedral. They had two sons. Three decades later, on April 29, 2011, millions gathered again to watch the bride Catherine "Kate" Middleton, former accessory buyer and photographer grace the aisle of Westminster Abbey to wed the royal firstborn Prince William. Kate, was born to ordinary parents. Her father was a coal miner who, later in life, with his wife, became a very successful business owner. Both Princess Diana and Duchess Kate married into royalty. As soon as Kate's three children, Prince George, Princess Charlotte, and Prince Louis were born, they entered into the world living in the public eye. Their lives are very far from being ordinary. The firstborn baby boy, Prince George becomes the heir to the throne and the next king after his father, Prince William. Prince George and his siblings will receive a substantial inheritance just by being born into a royal family, whether they like it or not. Their inheritance is the possessions and property belonging to the family, which will be passed down to the children, from their parents.

Yes, when a child is born into the British Royal family, it means he or she is a member of a royal family line with the status or power of a king or queen coming from a generation and a line of royal family ancestors dating back over thousands of years. Royalty is not as much about the pomp and circumstance as much as it is about the person and their relationship to the king or queen and their lineage or nobility and their elite class inheritance. A royal family usually includes the spouse of the reigning leader, such as a king or queen who rules a kingdom. Also, the royal family includes the surviving spouses of a deceased king or queen, all their children, grandchildren, brothers, sisters, and paternal cousins of the reigning king or queen, as well as their spouses. According to Wikipedia, "the Royal Family," membership usually extends to great-grandchildren and more distant descendants of the king or queen.[56] The best of everything is prepared for the royal child when he or she is born into the world.

Most recent about seven years later, eyes turned back to the British royal family on May 19, 2018 for another royal wedding with millions glued to their television sets to be eyewitnesses to the marriage of Princess Diana and Prince Charles' last-born son, Prince Harry. Prince Harry dressed in his military apparel waited at the altar of Saint George's Chapel of Windsor Castle for his lovely bride, Meghan Markle, an American actress who gracefully strolled the aisle to join and wed her waiting groom at the altar. As I watched and listened to the officiating bishop preach about love, he convincingly remarked "two people fell in love, and we showed up."

Interesting, right? You may say that is all good to know, yet what does royalty have to do with me? "I am not royalty. I do not feel like royalty. My parents are not wealthy, not even close to it. We are poor or middle class, or we live in an apartment, house, or shelter. No way can I be royalty." You may go to a public school, charter school, or private school. Or you might say, "I have no father. I do not know my father. My father left my mother. I do not know my mother or have a mother. She works two or more jobs almost around the clock to make sure we have food to eat, clothes to wear to school, and a house to live in." Or you may even be thinking, I don't even know my parents. No, you are not talking about me! There is no way I even live like royalty.

Royalty Status of the Parentless

I also think of a young orphan girl in the Bible who rose to royal status. Her name is Esther. Only two books in the entire Bible are named after a woman. Esther did not have a father or mother. She was adopted and raised by her cousin, Mordecai. When Mordecai heard about King Xerxes edict in search for beautiful young virgins to come to the citadel of Susa to participate in a twelve-month long beauty contest. Esther won the king's favor and approval more than any of the other virgins. King Xerxes, the ruler over 127 provinces stretching from India to Ethiopia made Esther his wife, crowned her queen of Persia, and gave her a great banquet. Queen Esther was a beautiful woman inside and out with godly character. She was respectful, wise, courageous, hospitable, open to advice, willing to act, a careful planner, a risk taker and a woman of faith.

She received troubling news from her cousin Mordecai about one of the leading men in her husband King Xerxes kingdom, named Haman who had devised a plan to kill all the Jewish people. She told Mordecai of the king's law that anyone who approaches the king without being summoned would be put to death. Mordecai responds, *"do not think that because you are in the king's house you alone of all the Jews will escape. For if you remain silent at this time, relief and deliverance for the Jews will arise from another place, but you and your father's family will perish. And who knows but that you have come to your royal position for such a time as this?"* (Esther 4:13,14 NIV) Esther then requested all the Jews in Susa fast and pray for her with no food or drink for three days. She and her attendants would do the same. When the fasting and praying was done, she committed to going to the king even though it was against law by saying, "and if I perish, I perish." After praying and fasting, God gave Esther the wisdom to approach the king. The king granted her wish by summoning her to come and touch the scepter and promised to give her up to half of his kingdom. He gave her what she asked for and she graciously planned two banquet parties for the King and Haman. At the second banquet, she disclosed Haman's secret plan to annihilate the Jewish people. When King Xerxes realized the scheme of Haman, he ordered the same plot be used to destroy him. Queen Esther successfully saved her people from being killed, she remained Queen and her cousin became 2nd in charge of the King Xerxes kingdom.

This is the Cinderella story of the Bible, where Esther was a woman of good character who became royalty. Not on her beauty alone but the purpose God created her to accomplish. In honor and respect for the cousin Mordecai who raised her, she listened to him and obeyed him in participating in the beauty contest, not knowing her royal position ultimately was to save her people from annihilation. God values His people.

Royalty & Our Lineage in the Identity of Jesus Christ

As a child of the Almighty God, the Creator of the whole wide world and everything in it, human beings are given dominion and rule over all His earthly creation. Therefore, men and women together are kings and queens in God's royal family. Children of God are born to receive an inheritance, which makes you royalty. Children of royalty status are to be trained how to live of royal position. *"Train up children in the way they should go, and when they are old, they will not turn from it (Proverbs 22:6).* Children born with a royalty inheritance know who they belong to and who they are. We, humans are created in the image and likeness of our Creator God, who breathed His breath of life in us. *"We are his offspring"* (Acts 17:28 NIV). Then, if we are offspring and children of the Almighty God, we are also joint heirs or co-heirs with Christ Jesus, the first-born Son of God.

Our royalty benefits are given to those God created at birth. You were born into the heavenly royal family. This royalty is not about being born into wealth or possessions. Your royalty is the promised inheritance that waits for you to accept through your identity given in a relationship with Jesus Christ. Just as the royal family teaches their children from birth who they are and the history of their family lineage so are we the children of God to be taught to know our Heavenly Father and His Son's royal bloodline. Our royal bloodline comes through the lineage of Jesus Christ. He connects us to the Heavenly Father, who is sitting on His throne watching and waiting for us to accept His gift of salvation in Jesus Christ. You have access to your royal position. It is a rich heritage, and it's in your bloodline!

Royalty means you are a person or group, who has regal character and family bearing. Our royalty status comes through the lineage of Abraham and Sarah (mother of Isaac), Salmon and Rehab (mother of Boaz), Boaz and Ruth (mother of Obed), Jesse and an unknown woman (mother of David), King David and Bathsheba (mother of King Solomon), and several generations later Mary (mother of Jesus with the Holy Spirit). *"The LORD swore to David a sure oath from which he will not turn back: "One of the sons of your body I will set on your throne (Psalm 132:11 ESV).* From the lineage of King David is the genealogy of God's Son, the Messiah and King Jesus was born about 480 years later (14 generations).

After the Fall of Humankind

However, sin entered the world after the "Fall of Humankind." First, God's original plan for humans was for us to live forever in a loving and caring relationship with Him and each other. We were to multiply and have complete dominion over all God's creation on earth together, male and female.

Second, after the first humans disobeyed God's command and ate from the *"tree of knowledge of good and evil, for when you eat from it you will certainly die" (Genesis 2:17 NIV). They were separated from God. "At that moment their eyes were opened, and they suddenly felt shame at their nakedness"* (Genesis 3:7 NLT). Then Adam and Eve knew the difference between right and wrong. They ran and hid from their Creator God, which is the resulting sin of fear, shame, and guilt entering the world.

Third, humans will live and humans will die. The act of disobedience in the Garden of Eden broke human's relationship bond with God and death entered the world. As a result, Adam and Eve passed on their sinful condition to all humans, starting with their own offspring. The New Testament Greek word for sin is amartia.[57] Amartia means a failing to hit the mark; failing to meet an objective, maintain a standard, or fulfill an obligation.[58] Sin is defined in relation to God, which is the lack of conformity to, or the violation of the moral will of God.[59] Sin is a serious matter; it has far-reaching effects upon our relationship with God, with ourselves, and with other human beings.[60] However, being depraved (morally corrupt) or totally sinful does not means that one is worthless.[61] The underlying dynamic for our self-esteem or worth is the unconditional love of God when He expressed it in His redemptive act on the cross of Calvary.

What should human beings living in a sinful world of pain and suffering do to be reconciled to God and regain their relationship with Him? We were once imperfect human beings, however, when we accept the fact that we all have sinned and come short of the glory of God (Romans 3:23 KJV) and that we do have a sinful nature, we need to no longer hide from God.[62] We should receive the free gift of salvation and be reconciled to God through, Jesus Christ. God prepared a plan for humans to be able to return to Him. The only way to live forever again with God as He originally intended is to choose to obey God. This means to choose first to believe He loved His children so much that He made a special sacrifice for us. God said in John chapter 3 verses 16 and 17 (MSG) *"This is how much God loved the world: He gave his Son, his one and only Son. And this is why: so that no one need be destroyed; by believing in him, anyone can have a whole and lasting life. God didn't go to all the trouble of sending his Son merely to point an accusing finger, telling the world how bad it was. He came to help, to put the world right again."*

Christ comes from God to judge and destroy sin. "God made him who had no sin to be sin for us, so that in him we might become the righteousness of God" (2 Corinthians 5:21, NIV). The sinless Jesus became sin and the substitute atonement for humans through His crucifixion and resurrection. Erickson writes, it is important to know and understand, sin is not caused by God (James 1:13 -15).[63] No, the responsibility of sin, amartia, is placed squarely on the humans themselves based on the first human beings' act of disobedience. One must receive the new birth and regeneration, which is what being born again means. *Jesus answered, I am the way and the truth and the life. No one comes to the Father except through me" (John 14:6 NIV).* Jesus shared with Nicodemus However, *"Jesus replied, very truly I tell you, no one can see the kingdom of God unless they are born again" (John 3:3 NIV).*

The only way to have direct access and a personal relationship with God, our Heavenly Father is to believe God's Word about His Son. Jesus Christ is God's Son conceived by the Holy Spirit and born of the virgin Mary who came to earth to show us how to love God the Father and how to live in our true identity. Your new life in Christ is not like your old life. Your birth came from mortal man your new birth comes from God's living Word, name Jesus. Just think a life conceived by God Himself (1 Peter 1:23 MSG). Therefore, just as sin entered the world through humans, righteousness entered the world through Jesus Christ, the Son of God. Jesus Christ is the true image of God, par excellence.

The Apostle Paul also writes in 2 Corinthians 4:4, "In their case the god of this world has blinded the minds of the unbelievers, to keep them from seeing the light of the gospel of the glory of Christ, who is the image of God." Both the New Testament Greek word for image have the same meaning as an image, figure, likeness.[64] Christ was totally without sin and in Him was the perfect image of God. "He is the image of the invisible God, the firstborn of all creation" (Col. 1:15). Therefore, through Christ Jesus, God atoned for the sins of His created beings. Christ represents humanity and the one who overcame sin for all humanity. He is the image-bearer of God, the Father.

The Apostle Peter also comforts all who would believe in a God of second chances in Second Peter 3:9 "The Lord is not slow to fulfill his promise as some count slowness, but is patient toward you, not wishing that any should perish, but that all should reach repentance." Repentance (metanoia) means a change of mind: as it appears in one who repents of a purpose he has formed or of something he has done; especially the change of mind of those who have begun to abhor their errors and misdeeds, and have determined to enter upon a better course of life, so that it embraces both a recognition of sin and sorrow.[65]

Jesus sacrificed His life out the love for His Father and determined to do exactly what His Father commands Him to do (John 14:31 NIV). Jesus' ultimate sacrifice on our behalf was to take all our sins and transgressions to the cross of Calvary by suffering, be crucified, die, and be buried, for us to have life everlasting with the Creator and King. Jesus defeated Satan by taking back life over death. On the third day, Jesus arose from the dead, He resurrected the King of kings. He took authority and dominion over the earth once again for God and gave the authority on earth to His disciples who were called to follow Him (Matthew 28:18-20). Jesus is saying that His own earthly biological family is not as important as being a part of His spiritual family and blessings. *"Praise be to the God and Father of our Lord Jesus*

Christ, who has blessed us in the heavenly realms with every spiritual blessing in Christ" (Ephesians 1:3 NIV). God's commands us to love Him first with everything we have and secondly love others as we love yourselves. *"That's what Christ did definitively: suffered because of others' sins, the Righteous One for the unrighteous ones. He went through it all-was put to death and then made alive-to bring us to God"* (1 Peter 3:18 MSG).

Also, the Apostle Paul writes in First Corinthians 15:3 *"For what I received I passed on to you as of first importance that Christ died for our sins according to the Scriptures, that he was buried, that he was raised on the third day according to the Scriptures, and that he appeared to. Cephas, and then to the Twelve. After that, he appeared to more than five hundred of the brothers and sister at the same time …"*

Fourthly, After Jesus' miraculous birth, life, ministry, suffering, death, burial, resurrection and ascension, Jesus was given the authority in heaven and on earth to take back what belonged to God. Jesus came to the earth to reign as our earthly King of the children of God! Father God encourages us with these words *"if you openly declare that Jesus is Lord and believe in your heart that God raised him from the dead, you will be saved. For by believing in your heart that you are made right with God, and it is by openly declaring your faith that you are saved"* (Romans 10:9,10 NLT). But in order to openly declare your faith that you are saved, *"I tell you the truth unless you are born again* (John 3:3 NLT), which means a person enters the Kingdom of God by *being born of water and the Spirit … the Holy Spirit gives birth to the spiritual life* (John 3:5 NLT).

Finally, our royalty status is our inheritance and identity in the bloodline of Jesus Christ given us once we are born again. Then *"you are no longer a slave (to sin), but God's own child; and since you are His child, God has made you an heir with complete access to the inheritance (Galatians 4:6–7 NLT)*. The Spirit calls out, *"Abba, Father! You received the Spirit of sonship/daughtership." "And by Him we cry, 'Abba (Daddy), Father"* (Romans 8:15). We are God's very own children, and our royalty status is bestowed upon us because of who He is. Children of royalty are chosen to represent Christ to others. Our value is a character trait given us by God and does not come from what we can achieve. We have to choose to live a life of obedience to God through the only way, the truth, and life. *"Because we are united with Christ, we have received an inheritance from God, for he chose us in advance, and he makes everything work out according to his plan"* (Ephesians 1:111 NLT). Our worth is in what God does by His character and nature in us. We cannot do it all by ourselves. Children of royal lineage will reign with Christ, the Messiah forever. Why? *Behold, children are a heritage from the LORD, the fruit of the womb a reward* (Psalm 127:3 ESV).

Relationship with Christ, the Head of our Royalty Bloodline

By being in a relationship with the head of the family, God and His Son, and in fellowship with other believers of the royal family, we are heirs and co-heirs with Christ. As a child of God, His daughters are co-heirs of His kingdom through His Son Jesus Christ, the King of the whole wide world. His Son breathed His breath of life back into humans' hearts. Everyone is born to inherit the royal heritage as co-heirs with Jesus. Royalty and co-heirs live in the public eye, prepared to assume positions as children of the King of kings and being a King's kid. Therefore, we must believe His words *"If you belong to Christ, then you come from the generation of obedient offspring of God starting with Abraham's seed and heirs according to the promise (Galatians 3:29).*

The Heavenly Father, the Creator of every human being from the beginning of time, gives us identity, royal status, access, an inheritance, ownership, and earthly responsibility to care for all that belongs to Him. We belong to Him. We are to grow in the knowledge of who He is by living out His commands in His kingdom on earth. When Jesus resurrected from death to life again, He appeared to His disciples

"Then he breathed on them and said, "Receive the Holy Spirit" (John 20:22). "The Spirit himself bears witness with our spirit that we are children of God, and if children, then heirs—heirs of God and fellow heirs with Christ..." (Romans 8:16,17a ESV).

"But you are a chosen people, a royal priesthood, a holy nation, God's special possession, that you may declare the praises of Him who called you out of darkness into his wonderful light. Once you were not a people, but now you are the people of God; once you had not received mercy, but now you have received mercy" (1 Peter 2:9–10 NIV).

Kingdom Royalty in Christ Jesus

You are God's princess. Just as the children of earthly royalty are taught at a young age about who they are and receive instruction preparing them to reign as heir to the throne, so should the children of God be trained. You should know who you are from the time of birth until you receive your eternal inheritance of royalty.

Once we know the *truth*, we are free. No, our lives are not perfect. Yet when God speaks from His Holy Word that endures for generations, He declares, *"For you are a holy people, who belong to the Lord your God. Of all the people on earth, the Lord your God has chosen you to be his own special treasure" (Deuteronomy 7:6 NLT).* And *"Since you are precious and honored in my sight, and because I love you, I will give men in exchange for you, and people in exchange for your life" (Isaiah 43:4 NIV).*

The truth is God designed you for His purpose that guarantees your inheritance and you entering His kingdom forever. When God gives those whom He loves access to His kingdom, it is given through the lineage of the one who reigns as King, Jesus Christ. God has no favorites only those who choose to please Him and He rewards those who diligently seek Him (Hebrews 11:6). God calls each one of us out of brokenness and our perceptions of the world.

What makes you special and royalty to God is not that you have a mother or father or sister or brother and not where you live—in a home or shelter—or that you wear brand-name or second-hand clothes; it is about your desire to know and honor Him and to also get to know yourself through the love of His Son, Jesus Christ. Jesus addressed this truth while speaking to the crowds. *His mother and his brothers appeared outside, wishing to speak with Him. Someone told him, "Your mother and your brothers are standing outside, asking to speak with you." But he said in reply, "Who is my mother? Who are my brothers?" And stretching out his hand toward his disciples, he said, "Here are my mother and my brothers. For whoever does the will of my Heavenly Father is my brother, and sister, and mother" (Matthew 12:46–50 NIV).*

Jesus is saying that He is not concerned about the privileges that come with the earthly bloodlines. But the only way to achieve your royal status and inheritance of a son or daughter is through a relationship with Jesus and God, the Father, who are one. And we are to live as He did on earth, as heirs of God's kingdom.

Bottom line in God's kingdom, royalty is not about being in the upper class in wealth bound to the government of the country they live and rule. But, royalty in God's kingdom comes directly from you knowing who you are, what your value and worth is based your identity and relationship with His Son and coming King Jesus Christ. We are His princesses and princes. God loves us. *"and if God is for us who can be against us...There is nothing that can separate you from God's love* (Romans 8:31,35 NIV). We are all very special to God and have been born into royalty.

There Is No Greater Love

Can you imagine the love the Heavenly Father has for us?
One to give His beloved Son, Jesus
The Son whose blood was shed for us; Oh His love and grace

What does that mean to you?
When someone loves you that much, don't you
want to give that love in return?

We are not asked to die a physical death
Our Father says, just accept and believe in your
heart that my Son died and arose again.

At the cross, the bloodshed, the pain and agony,
the shame, and the weeping mother.

The Son, Jesus had a purpose to fulfill, being obedient to His Father.
Aren't you obedient to your natural father? Why? Because you love him.

Why not be obedient to your Heavenly Father
and believe He loves you too?

The Son, Jesus, saying, "It is finished." He died with
our sins and sicknesses on that cross.

He arose again, a new life. We don't have to be slaves to any sin or illness.

Believe in the Savior, Jesus Christ. Receive your Heavenly Father's love.
Bury your old self and accept Jesus and be renewed, be transformed.

Jesus' mother wept as she saw her own son on that cross, the
ridicule by the unbelievers ... God's chosen people.

Imagine you at the cross and your mother weeping for
you because she loved you and could not help.

And her son's last words being, Father forgive
them for they know not what they do.

Accept Jesus in your life, accept the Heavenly Father's love. It's free. All you have to do is believe.

The Holy Spirit will do the rest in Jesus' name.
At the cross, it symbolizes our Heavenly Father's *love*.

There is no greater love!

A Love Letter from Your Heavenly Father

My Daughter of Royalty,

My sweet Princess. You are very special to Me! From the beginning, I created you to be loved and to give love. I chose those who are poor in the eyes of the world to be rich in faith and to inherit the kingdom I promise to those who love Me (James 2:5 NIV). Then the royal rule and the authority and the glory of all the kingdoms under heaven will be handed over to My people chosen by Me. Their royal rule will last forever. All other rulers will serve and obey them (Daniel 7:27 MSG). I chose you to be saved through the sanctifying work of the Spirit and through belief in the truth (2 Thessalonians 2:13 NIV). I chose you, called you, predestined and elected you to accept My gift of salvation offered to you. You can receive it and be saved from the consequences of sin and guilt that separated you from Me. Yes, it was a long, long time ago that I decided to adopt you into My family through Jesus Christ. What pleasure I took in planning it (Ephesians 1:5 MSG)! I loved you so much that I gave my firstborn Son, Jesus Christ to be the Messiah, for you to come home to live with Me in my kingdom with your heavenly Father forever. Your worth is in My Son and that makes you co-heir and very special. Everyone who believes that Jesus was born of Me, God the Father, and everyone who loves Me has been born of Him.

By making the personal decision to accept My gift of Jesus Christ and seek His forgiveness. I chose you in Him before the creation of the world to be holy and blameless in My sight. In love, I predestined you to be adopted as My daughter through Jesus Christ, in accordance with His pleasure and will (Ephesians 1:5 NIV).

When you accept Him, I give you a new identity in Christ Jesus to do the good things I planned for you long ago (Ephesians 2:10 NLT). But to all who believe Me and accept Him, I give the right to become My children (John 1:12 NLT). At birth, you were guaranteed this royal inheritance in My kingdom. You can be sure of this: I have set you apart for Myself. I will answer when you call on Me (Psalm 4:3 NLT). You are predestined for greatness. For you are holy and set apart to Me, the Lord your God. You are a chosen vessel, who belong to the Lord God. Of all the people on earth, I have chosen you to be My own special treasure (Deuteronomy 7:6 NLT). I crowned you, Princess with My everlasting love, compassion and unspeakable joy at birth.

Will you hear and receive this good news of the gospel of Jesus Christ, My earthly firstborn Son? This means that anyone who belongs to My Son loves Me and has become a new person and receives the royalty status. I have called you to live in freedom and royalty inheritance, Princess. But don't use your freedom to satisfy your sinful nature. Instead, use your freedom to serve one another in love (Galatians 5:13 NLT). The sinful nature to name a few results in sexual immorality, impurity, lustful pleasures, idolatry, witchcraft, hostility, quarrelling, jealously, outbursts of anger, selfish ambition, dissension (disagreement that leads to discord), division, envy, drunkenness, wild parties and other similar sins. Anyone living this kind of life will not inherit the kingdom of God (Galatians 5:19-21 NLT)

Your old life is gone; a new life has begun (2 Corinthians 5:17 NLT)! You are the ambassador of My Son (2 Corinthians 5:2 NLT). Reach out, and welcome one another to My glory. Jesus did it; now you do it! (Romans 15:7 MSG). You are Christ's body—that's who you are! You must never forget this. Only as you accept your part of the body does your "part" mean anything (1 Corinthians 12:27 MSG). Every believer in Christ belongs to one body and one Spirit, who have been given My abilities to contribute to the strength and health of the body united by one Spirit (Ephesians 4: 4).

I love you, Princess, because I am God, your personal Heavenly Father ... Your Savior. I have called your name. You are mine. I paid a huge price for you. That is how much you mean to me! That's how much I love you! I'd sell off the whole world to get you back, trade the creation just for you and to have you live with Me forevermore (Isaiah 43:1,3,4 MSG). To know your identity first and foremost is in knowing who you are, which means you are My child and you are royalty. You have My Spirit who confirms who you really are. Know that you are mine and know who you are, the Father's child, who is giving you an unbelievable inheritance! As you go through the hard times with your co-heir Jesus walking alongside you, then you also will certainly go through the good times with Him (Romans 8:16–17 NLT). You are not another statistic. Your life matters as a girl because you were designed to know who you are. Being a daughter of value and worth makes you royalty. I love, value, and treasure you. Therefore, nothing can separate you from Me, neither death nor life, neither angels nor demons, neither the present nor the future, nor any powers, neither height nor depth, nor anything else in all creation. Nothing will be able to separate you from My love that comes from your status as a child of the Messiah in Christ Jesus, your Lord and King (Romans 8:30 NLT). You are my Special Daughter. That makes you Royalty, Princess!

Lovingly, Your Father, Savior, and Reigning King

Self-Discovery / Self-Reflection

Application

(1) *Find your salvation or baptism certificate, a photo of someone or something special to you or an event where you felt like royalty. Add it to your vision board.*
(2) *Reflect and chat about the questions below with your mother or close adult female friend (mentor).*
(3) *Look up and write down on your vision board the Bible verses from this chapter that inspired you and use them to also answer the questions.*

Thinking about Me: *Your Are Special!* Born Into Royalty

1. How do you know and feel about being special? How does being a Christian make you special?

_____

2. What is royalty? Who do you know is born into privilege and wealth?

_____

3. What is the difference between earthly royalty and the royalty you inherit in Jesus Christ? When do you feel special? How are you born into royalty?

_____

4. Are you a Christian? How do you know? If yes, when were you saved? Were you baptized?

_____

5. If you are not saved, would you like to become a Christian, become a disciple of Jesus Christ, and grow in a relationship with Him?

_____

Pray now: Admit you are sinner, believe God loves and forgives you, then ask Savior Jesus to come into your heart to help you live obeying God in the power of His Holy Spirit. AMEN! Write date & time prayed.

Part Four

**You Are His Bride, Our Marriage Relationship …
Becoming His Bride on Earth as it is in Heaven**

Look in the scroll of the Lord and read: None of these will be missing, not one will lack her mate. For it is his mouth that has given the order, and his Spirit will gather them together.
—Isaiah 34:16 (NIV)

Blessed is she who has believed that the Lord would fulfill His promises to her!
—Luke 1:45 NIV)

Marriage ... Finally! Becoming A Bride on Earth

You Are His Bride

Marriage is typically every girl's dream. The long-awaited love of her life, Prince Charming finally arrives. Arrayed in a gorgeous wedding gown, strolling down the aisle on her beautiful fairy-tale princess wedding day, she joins the love of her life at the altar, her bridegroom. And with great anticipation, they will live blissfully in love and happily ever after.

Marriage, as defined by the Oxford dictionary, is the legally and formally recognized union of two people as partners in a personal relationship, specifically a union between a man and a woman. God designed the marriage covenant to be between male and female.

> "Haven't you read," he (Jesus) replied, "that at the beginning the Creator 'made them male and female,' and said, 'For this reason a man will leave his father and mother and be united to his wife, and the two will become one flesh'?[6] So they are no longer two, but one. Therefore, what God has joined together, let man not separate" (Matthew 19:4-6 NIV).

Two people male and female fall in love, get married, make plans to have children, become a family, and live together happily ever after. Although, the reasons for getting married may vary, marriage is a very big decision. By deciding to marry, a man and woman are making a lifelong commitment to each other. Love is the key ingredient of their commitment. Because deep within their hearts is the innate desire of the bride to love and be loved and of the bridegroom to love and to be respected. Marriage is friendship, trust, honesty, humility, frequent communications and intimacy between two people in love.

Dream Assignment Come True

Back in Colorado while creating the vision board" I gave the dream assignment and dream husband over to God. I trusted and surrendered my career, love life, and mate selection over to Him. Six years later, too good to be true, I finally arrived to my dream assignment in the nation's capital, Washington, D.C. What an honor! God answered my prayers. I was elated about being selected for such a prestigious job in "the world's largest office building," the Department of Defense (DOD). A building where more than twenty thousand civilian and military employees worked.

I became one of the many "action officers," who took my job seriously in preparing information and submitting recommendations to senior military leaders and decision makers.

Finding a place to live among the many choices of new and old townhomes in Virginia, Maryland, or W.D.C was a bit overwhelming. I was grateful for cousin Amanda and her husband Colonel Joe's hospitality. They allowed me to stay with them in Maryland until I found and settled into a very nice two bedroom in northern Virginia. With my job and housing in place, the next decision made was what church would I attend to worship in Maryland or Virginia or D.C? After visiting various churches of the Baptist and Methodist denominations, I prayerfully decided on Ebenezer remembering God's intervention with the call from Major Leroy. Having become accustomed to attending the mid-day Bible Studies on military bases, I discovered something significant while walking from the Pentagon parking lot into one of the building entrances. Out of the corner of my eye an image of a cross caught my attention on a bulletin board as I whisked by. Stopping right in my tracks, I backed up to verify I had seen a cross and began reading the words on the paper. Surprised, yet excited to learn in this huge office building weekly Bible Study groups were conducted by the Christian Embassy. I had a choice of either the weekly early morning or noontime studies. With all the squares filled and priorities met, so to speak, the job of my dreams, a home, a church and Bible Study on the job, I started living the dream.

Remembering the "Pass Over"

Until, about six months into the dream, when I received the news of my promotion non-selection to the next rank. My immediate boss a Colonel and I were called into the general's office. The one star brigadier general solemnly shared with me that my name was not on the promotion list. Then allowing me a few minutes to absorb the shocking news, as we discussed options on how to proceed. He also gave me permission to take the next day off when the promotion list would be officially released to the public. I could only imagine the joy of everyone gathering to look at the prominently displayed lists of selectees in the office corridor. They would all be celebrating their victory without me being one of them.

From the onset of the "pass over" news, I began feeling intense feelings of failure and rejection. I was not able to eat or sleep. It was the lowest and most difficult time in my entire career. I began speculating about all the possible reasons why I had been "passed over." I believed I was on the right career progression track. Because prior to me being selected to join the Pentagon staff, my records had been scrutinized by leadership. The standard criteria for selection to work in the Pentagon was a person's "promotability." I had questions. Why wasn't my name on the list? What happened? Quite naturally other thoughts flashed across my mind, such as could this be discrimination?

In making calls to the selection board administrator, I discovered they too were perplexed. They reviewed my records, the scoring sheets, and the record of others in my peer group and found nothing that stood out to substantiate the "pass over."

I prayed. I cried. I prayed and I cried because at that juncture in my life, it was all I knew to do. I was totally defenseless and helpless. I searched the Scriptures and sought God for answers. One scripture, in particular, came to mind, as I remembered a Colonel in Ohio at my base welcoming party. While I was greeting everyone passing through the receiving line, he was humbly serving others cake and refreshments. I was two ranks less than him. I should I have been serving him cake and refreshments. I was anxious to find out who he was and get to know more about him. I had made an appointment to meet with him. He shared he was a Christian. He also, brought to my attention a verse in the Bible that I did not know was there. *For promotion comes neither from the east, nor from the west, nor from the south. But God is the judge: he puts down one, and sets up another (Psalm 75:6, 7 NKJV).*

With this verse and others, I began to discern God speaking into my spirit about the "pass over." A number of times I hesitated to say those two words or I would cringe at the sound until I discovered another revelation in Exodus chapter 12 verse 13. *God said, "I will pass over you"* (Exodus 12:13 NIV). The "pass over" declared by God was significant. God performed a miracle in the midst of His chosen Hebrew people. The people who chose to obey, love, and worship God. However, when the Egyptian Pharaoh (ruler) oppressed God's people by doing harm to them, God devised a plan of protection. In Pharaoh's ninth refusal to release God's people from the cruelty of oppression, slavery, and bondage, God gave His people special instructions to follow. The parents of the Hebrew firstborns were to place an identifying mark above their house doorposts that sets them apart from Egyptian firstborns. And no harm would come to the firstborns in the Hebrew households. The Pharaoh refused to obey God's command to stop treating and doing harm to His people. All who obeys God's commands, worships and loves Him, and who loves others are called His children and His people. The Hebrew children obeyed God's instructions and God blessed their firstborn by not allowing any harm to come to them.

Therefore, the revelation I received in the "pass over" was about God setting me apart, my parents' firstborn to receive a blessing from Him and to use it to bless others.

During my "pass over" uncertainty and in much despair, I mustered up the courage to make an appointment with my pastor. I needed godly direction about keeping the faith and relying on God's Word. Since my pastors were a pastoral team, the Holy Spirit prompted me to make the appointment with the female co-Pastor. I met with Pastor JoAnn. The church membership was very large and she did not know me. After our introductions, she prayed. I shared with her about my faith journey in Christ and the dilemma I was facing. Her words of encouragement, *"well, you just continue seeking God in prayer and do not leave His presence until He answers."*

A colleague also shared, *although this is a tough time for you, it is also a time when you will discover who your true friends really are.* His words of wisdom held true. Through months of quiet withdrawal to myself praying, researching regulations and Scriptures, writing letters to current and former bosses, seeking counsel about what to do, calling and sitting with mentors for sound advice, I finally put the promotion "appeals" package together. I had one of two options, either to request the convening of a special selection board or an appeals board. I chose the special selection board (SSB).

Whether living and working in and out of the continental United States, former bosses, general officers, and colleagues seeing my potential took the risk and stepped up to the task in response to my request. By continuing to invest in me and my future in the active duty military, they wrote convincing letters of support about my job performance. Their underlying message became my mantra "Let my performance speak for me." It also became very clear how I was to proceed on this journey until victory is won. One word, I ran across, written in large black font on a white thick stock of paper prodded me to, "PERSEVERE!"

One Sunday during my "pass over" season, God's timing was perfect. After our pastor rolled out the title and theme of the sermon, he asked everyone to stand, while he called out the various and specific types of setbacks we were facing. When he named promotion setbacks, I instantly stood up. God was speaking to me and I believed the message was just for me. He said, repeat after me (words similar to these) *"my setback is only for my victorious comeback, the promotion is mine."*

During this disappointing season and much prayer, sins were revealed to me by God. It was separating me from Him. In my excitement about God answering my dream job prayer, I had forgotten about my vision board and also the promise of God to send the mate He has for me. Since Denver, counterfeit men were subtly coming in and out of my life. At first it was easy to pray and ask God if he was the one. Sometimes it was clear and easy to decide to not enter into a relationship with a certain guy. But when I unintentionally ignored the still, quiet voice of the Holy Spirit warning me, I began making wrong choices. Sin comes with consequences. Once the spirit revealed what they were I surrendered to God with remorseful regret because He had gotten my attention. Therefore, sins consequences caused a delay in me receiving His promises. After this spiritual awakening, I found strength to have faith in God in a verse in Genesis chapter 50 verse 20 (NIV), *"you (the enemy) intended to harm me, but God intended it for good to accomplish what is now being done, the saving of many lives."*

I was not to put any blame on anyone else, but acknowledge my sins before God alone. *"But if we confess our sins to Him, He is faithful and just to forgive us our sins and to cleanse us from all wickedness. If we claim we have not sinned, we are calling God a liar and showing that His word has no place in our hearts"* (1 John 1:9,10 NLT). Through this life challenge, I thirsted for a deeper and more intimate relationship with Jesus. I was learning to hear, recognize, and respond to His direction and counsel. God really never leaves or forsakes His children. I was getting to know Him in a new and different way through the promises of His words in the Bible. *"How blessed the man you train, GOD, the woman you instruct in your Word, providing a circle of quiet within the clamor of evil, while a jail is being built for the wicked. GOD will never walk away from his people, never desert his precious people (Psalm 94:12-14 MSG).*

I should have held myself accountable by going to my vision board and "the list" to remind myself about what type man I was praying, watching, and waiting for God to send to me.

However, as a part of daily devotions and quiet time with God, I listened to the daily WAVA radio station broadcasts, one of my favorites, Chuck Swindoll's Insight for Living. However, one particular morning he was followed by a special radio program with the voice of Bishop T.D. Jakes. He was teaching about father – daughter relationships (Daddy's Girl). As I listened, I was prompted, while it was still fresh on my mind, to call Dad. The call resulted in the unrehearsed first-time verbal expressions to him of my pain in a tone of anger, hurt, and disappointment in myself. I said, *"Dad, it's because of you I do not know how to be in a relationship with a guy."* Prior to that day, I was use to keeping my broken heart and feelings of hurt to myself. No one knew how I dealt with hurt feelings and rejection, but my heavenly Father. God had become my confidant, who I went privately to in prayer. It was easy for me to go to Him to share and vent my feelings usually in tears and prayers. I was at my wits end. Apparently, very full and unable to any longer contain the hurt and brokenness. I did not know what to do with those feelings any longer. However, Bishop Jakes' teaching on the radio broadcast gave me the courage to say aloud my feelings to Dad. It was right on time for me. I had not heard the father-daughter topic presented in a way I completely understood. I wished Dad had heard the broadcast as well to put in perspective what I was saying. No disrespect to Dad was intended, but I blurted out my feelings and emotions. Thank God, Dad did not scold me. He listened as I vented all that was in my heart. And a peace came over me, I was no longer privately suffering.

Not sure how many months after pastor's sermon, but amazing is our God who answered my prayers again. For a total of 18 months, after preparing and submitting the appeals package containing documents and letters with the theme "let my performance speak for me," I finally received the news the wrong was made right.

By faith, the "pass over" for promotion to the next rank was corrected as requested, the special selection board (SSB) and President of the United States of America granted me with a very rare "direct promote" and retroactive pay all the way back to the date I should have originally been promoted with my peers. My records were corrected. Yes, my job performance spoke for me and God blessed beyond anything I could have ever imagined. I was promoted as if I had never been "passed over." *"My setback is only for my victorious comeback, the promotion is mine."*

God did not leave me, but had set me apart the "firstborn" of my parents and a born-again believer of Jesus Christ for a specific purpose. As the firstborn children of Israel obeyed God, the "pass over" was my test to see if I would trust God, love God, and obey Him in every area of my life. Enduringly tough, I still held on to the fact that Jesus had already fought my battles. Just as God chose and set the Israelites (Hebrew people) a part to do a specific work for Him, so has God done the same for believers of Jesus Christ, including me. In the "pass over" process, God refined me. His jar of clay is being disciplined and molded in His image. *"Because the Lord disciplines those He loves"* (Hebrews 12:6a NIV). *"Blessed is the one whom God corrects; so do not despise the discipline of the Almighty" (Job 5:17 NIV).*

The "Crisis Project"

The phone rings. I pick up to answer. There is a pending crisis. Anxiously scurrying around to find answers, this is one of Melissa's project, but she is away on business travels and I am her backup "action officer." She is out of office on business travels and I am in charge of her projects. This one is not one of her "hot issues." What is going on? This one project, in particular, is inactive and at the bottom of her priority list. Nothing is happening with it. How did this one manage to rise from the bottom of the list to the top and become the "crisis project." I was dumbfounded and caught totally off guard. Not only was I summoned to brief the front office as the back-up action officer, but also my immediate supervisor, Colonel Delorean and her boss, Colonel Southman.

As soon as we arrived to her office, we checked in with the military assistant for our appointment. I thought to myself, *I have not seen him before.* After going into Mrs. Weatherly's (civilian equivalent to a general officer) office, clueless about "the project" with no significant past history, we were dismissed to go, do the research, and take appropriate action to resolve it. Why was this one of all the projects to rise to the limelight, we did not know?

Was there something else going on? Was this God's providence for the man sitting behind the desk, the military assistant, and me to meet face to face? He now knew my name in the building of thousands of people, all because the Lord used "the crisis project" to bring me to him. *"Then the LORD God (who) made a woman from the rib he had taken out of the man, and <u>he brought her to the man</u>" (Genesis 2:22 NIV).*

Thereafter, we interacted on several occasions. One time, when I was serving as the acting executive officer for my one-star brigadier general. And weeks later, while I was on weeklong TDY (travel duty) to Florida. I was also in the throes of planning my "pin-on' promotion ceremony and party. Oh no, this one will not be a traditional ceremony. Why not? For God is to be praised for the miracle He performed on my behalf. The news was publicly and prominently displayed for all to see on the promotion board in the office corridor. Not a list of names, but this time only one name…mine! Praise God! It's time to celebrate the "wrong made right." My mentor, friend, and artist, Reverend Benton, affectionately nicknamed the "Bible Man," called me to get the last remaining details to add to the invitations he was designing for my celebration.

I called the front office, and Kenneth (aka Whit) answered the phone. I explained to him I am planning my promotion party and asked if he could help me reserve the big conference room. I wanted to make sure I would have the space to accommodate all my guests. Whit commented, he wondered why only one name was on the promotion list. When he heard the brief story, he congratulated me and wished me the best and shared his heartfelt pride for my victory. He agreed to see what he could do to reserve the conference room and get back with me.

By Friday of the same week and still in Florida on TDY, he made it happen. The big conference usually reserved for senior officers and leaders was reserved for my promotion ceremony. He gave me the room number for the invitations. And as we closed the business part of the conversation, he said, "Before you hang up, I would like to ask, if there is no husband, no boyfriend, or significant other, would you go out on a date with me tomorrow?" I replied with glee, "Oh yes!" He asked for my phone number and said he would call me on Saturday to get my address and pick me up. As soon as I put the phone down, I thought, what is wrong with me? I do not know this guy or what his expectations are of me. Oh no, I will not get my heart broken again. It takes too long to recover.

On Saturday, the phone rang. He called just as he said he would. He called to get my address to pick me up for our dinner date. However, I thought to myself before I give him my address, I have to find out more about him. I began asking a series of questions. Our conversation continued for about two hours or so on the phone. We both enjoyed getting to know a little more about each other. One absolutely remarkable fact, he was a career military guy who had never married nor had any children. He was also an only child of his divorced parents. I thought, then he must be a "mama's boy?"

Our First Date

Whit was prompt. At about four or five o'clock on July 24th, the doorbell rang. He arrived from northern VA to pick me up in southern Maryland for our dinner date in Washington D.C. Now it makes sense why one month earlier, God put the urgency in me to have the house blessed by the Benton's. Whit was the first man to cross the threshold of my new home. A gentleman extraordinaire and very polite. Chivalry is still alive. He made me feel special in a new and wonderful way. He opened and closed doors for me, pulling out the chair from the table for me to sit at Phillip's Seafood Restaurant on the marina in D.C.

We had a delightful time together. He did all the talking as I listened. A lot of firsts happened for me during the course of the night. Usually, I am the talker. With him, I enjoyed being quiet and listening. But when I almost slipped to ask if we could say grace for the meal, I listened to the spirit of God within me say keep silent, just listen, and do not to say a word. At that moment, he asked if he could pray over our meal. Praise the Lord! This was the very first time ever seeing or hearing a guy on a date take the initiative to pray and to do it publicly. This was significant. This guy is different.

During dinner, Whit and I finally got to the topic about our Christian journey to becoming believers of Jesus Christ. We also discovered a common interest around finances. We chatted about a few of the verses in the Bible related to finances. His pastor in North Dakota once challenged him to design a biblical finance curriculum for the new young military personnel members of their church. Wow I said, "have you heard about the Crown Financial Ministries Bible Study? I just completed the Bible Study six months ago." After our dinner, he drove me back home and I asked him to come in. I gave him the Crown Bible study books to review. Before leaving for the night, I invited him to go to church with me the next day. He accepted.

Our Second Date

On the next morning, Sunday July 25th, he was back again to pick me up at my home almost twenty miles away across the bridge in Virginia to take me to church. I was a princess, who was having doors opened and closed for her. How refreshing and obvious, he was different. From the parking lot to the worship services about to start inside "Friendly Ebenezer" the energy and move of the spirit was present. This was the Multi-Cultural Heritage Sunday with everyone dressed in colorful African apparel. The spirit was high and celebratory from the preached word to the anointed choirs and vocalists singing uplifting songs with the band.

From that weekend on, Whit and I were inseparable. Early in our relationship, I witnessed Whit's caring, compassionate, thoughtful, and selfless traits. I received an emergency phone call from Ohio about my brother Ken having been hospitalized. As I was talking to the doctor on the other end, Whit signaled for me to pause, he calmly asked if I wanted to go to be with my brother? I said, yes. When I hung up the phone, he said, he had made reservations for me to fly to Ohio and reserved a rental car for me. I immediately called some friends in the area. They agreed I could stay at their home. He asked if I would want him to come with me. I said yes. Amazing, a man in my life with a great big heart.

I was overjoyed because for the first time in my dating history, he showed me how much he cared about me first. He observed and listened well. He intuitively acted, even before I would think about or ask for anything. Our friendship naturally evolved into a special relationship.

Mate Revealed

On a Sunday after church, Whit came by the house and volunteered to hang new window blinds for me. Since I had only been in the house about three months, any help with manual labor was much welcomed. It was a beautiful day! While I was downstairs preparing a snack—actually warming up a leftover seafood dish prepared by my mentor's daughter, Crystal — Whit came down to let me know it was raining outside. As soon as I heard those words, I rushed outside, leaving him behind in the kitchen, while also saying, "Oh God please let me see a rainbow!" I opened the garage door and stood looking to my right to see the sun brightly shining and the rain drops falling. Then I turned to the left and in the midst of the overcast sky was a rainbow. By that time, Whit was standing quietly next to me looking at the rainbow, too. I rushed back into the house with joy in my heart having seen the rainbow. I had not seen a rainbow at all since moving to Washington D.C. I did not say a word to Whit about what seeing the rainbow meant to me. God heard my quick prayer to let me see the rainbow and He answered. By answering my prayer, God was reminding me of His promise made to me back in Denver.

With the joy in my heart and pep in my step, I went back to what I was doing in the kitchen. Whit went upstairs to finish installing the window treatments. As the day drew to an end and he was preparing to leave, he took me by the hand and asked if I would humor him. We knelt on our knees, and he prayed. When the first words from his mouth began with thanking God for letting me see the rainbow, tears welled up in my eyes and I wept. I was amazed because we had not talked about the rainbow and its' meaning to me. Everything else he prayed about, I do not recall his exact words. But he definitely prayed an unselfish prayer, full of thanksgiving. No man had ever taken this type of godly leadership with me before. Tears of joy streamed down my face. I choked up with much gratitude to my God & Savior for sending this man into my life.

God had put a man in my life, who was putting into practice what the Bible tells us about how husbands should treat wives. I know I was not his wife at that time, but this is how God sent Whit into my life. Whit may not have known that was what he was doing, but he just made me feel so very special, again unlike I had in past relationships. *"Husbands, in the same way be considerate as you live with your wives, and treat them with respect as the weaker partner and as heirs with you of the gracious gift of life, so that nothing will hinder your prayers"* (1 Peter 3:7 NIV). It seemed to me, he was treating me as his wife even though we were not married.

A few weeks later, during my morning quiet time and devotions with God, He placed before me a flashback of the scene when Whit and I were standing together in the garage gazing at the rainbow. Then God whispered the words in my heart, "he is your husband."

Journey to the Premarital, Proposal, and Marriage Covenant

Six months into our relationship, Whit took me to his hometown, Philadelphia, to meet his mother and father during the Christmas holidays. With his parents being divorced, it did not interfere with his father, family, and friends gathering on Christmas Day at his mom's home to eat, fellowship, and exchange gifts. His mother and I connected quickly with our common interests of sorority involvement, love of travel, love of teaching and children, southern roots, and female independence. She made me feel accepted and like a daughter in no time.

In my family, receiving gifts on Christmas was a big deal. My sisters and brothers looked forward to the Christmas holidays. However, since Whit was the only child, I quickly learned how practical he was in gift giving. Visiting his parents for Christmas and all the other tell-tale signs of our unique and special relationship, I have to admit I was surprised by his Christmas gift given me. In slowly removing the bow and tearing the paper off the large box, I looked closely to read the words "bread-maker." My heart began to settle down and surrender to the fact that even though he brought me home to meet his parents, it was not an automatic sign. No, I was not getting a piece of jewelry or even be proposed to with a ring.

The next Christmas was wonderful with both of our mothers spending time with us for the holidays in the Washington D.C. area. We introduced them to each other and enjoyed exciting and fun outings over dinner and a musical play.

During our courtship, friends, family members, church mentors, and ministers, all observed and commented how much of a match we were for each other. Brother and Sister Hunigan, a retired military and mentor couple made a bold statement once, you are the most "deliberate couple" we have ever known. To get us thinking more deeply about our relationship, they resorted to sharing with us about their beautiful love story of how they met, fell in love, and had been married for almost 40 years. Reverend Benton and his wife, Beverly, noticed every time Whit and I were together, the "we" statements made as if we were already married. They started calling us by the name "we," every time they saw us.

Why was it taking him so long to propose? God had already given me the confirmation Whit was the one. My mind was made up, however, I had to wait on him. I was not going to get ahead of God and get my feelings hurt. The word of God says, *"He who finds a wife finds what is good and receives favor from the Lord" (Proverbs 18:22 NIV)*. He needed to be sure and hear from God as well, which may explain the reason for a number of wonderful things he did to make me feel special to him, yet, he needed to be sure. He was the deliberate one in his approach to dealing with what he perceived a very independent woman. Like the surprise trip, he planned for my first time visit to New York. I had never ridden a train before. Although, we caught the train from Union Station, Washington D.C., I did not know our destination would be New York City, "the Big Apple" until we detrained. It was a thrilling visit of exploring sights I had never seen before to include the Rockefeller Center and attending the annual Radio Music City Hall Christmas Musical featuring the Rockettes.

Back in northern VA area, Whit began inquiring and finding jewelers who actually could create a ring based on a design I had in mind. He found and then decided on the jeweler. The timing was great. Because at an Ebenezer worship service, an announcement was made inviting engaged and married couples to the upcoming February retreat. Without hesitation immediately after church, I made my way to the pre-registration table to ask the question, "If we do not have a ring or a wedding date, could we attend the engaged couples' session at the retreat? We are trying to decide about getting married?" The young woman at the table said, "Yes you can, but like engaged couples you will have to sleep in separate rooms."

Looking at Whit in excitement, I asked what he thought about it. He agreed. Sleeping in separate rooms would definitely not be the problem, since our relationship was platonic. We had both agreed at the outset to trust and obey what God said in the Bible about girl-boy relationships before marriage, unlike in our past.

We signed up to go to the retreat. Oh my, it was the best decision we ever made together. We were tremendously blessed by the workshops and the experiences shared by renowned couples of the Christian faith. Our eyes were opened to a better understanding of what to expect in marriage. The pastor couples workshop facilitators openly and candidly shared the practicality of marriage and their own personal experiences. The Flakes' from New York, the Robinson's from Tennessee, the Weems-Espinosa's from Georgia and the Browning's from Maryland were the retreat workshop facilitators. With Whit's and my parents having been divorced when we were teenagers and not having an example of what a marriage for a lifetime would be like, we walked away with a wealth of knowledge and hope.

Not soon after, my military contemporary Jackie and her husband had just completed premarital group sessions at her church. "From the Heart of Ministries," led by the pastoral husband and wife team, the Cherry's taught us in fourteen pre-marital group sessions. However, prior to non-members of the church enrolling in their group sessions, we were required to get an approval letter from our home church pastor consenting to us being taught by them. Our pastor gave consent in a written letter to the church pastor. Once the fourteen sessions were completed, we joyfully provided our pastor a written summary about what we learned.

In the first session, couples were encouraged to not set a wedding date until after the course was completed. We were taught what dating and its' relationship to marriage really meant, how to distinguish whether the other person was our soul mate or not, and once married how to honor our marriage vows.

By the time Whit and I completed the fourteen sessions, we were much more informed and had a better understanding about God's plan for the covenant of marriage. However, now we were on a roll and we wanted more. I needed to be sure, and it seemed Whit did too. The next request, we made was to receive individual couples counseling. We contacted our church. We were assigned Reverend Al Deas, an associate minister on the ministerial staff. He met with us weekly. We discused the practical situations of marriage. He allowed us to ask the real questions, especially about specific topics mentioned at the retreat or group sessions.

As a result of having participated in the three marriage preparation resources, we felt equipped. It helped us tremendously. We finally made the decision to get married. From the teaching moments of the engaged couples retreat, the fourteen premarital sessions, and the ministerial pre-marital counseling, then the skeletons (secrets) slowly came out of the closet.

Through these resources, we came clean by telling the truth, being honest, and real with each other about our past relationships.

Because deep down in my heart, I still had some residual hurt and wounds. I would agree by the time we went on the church engaged couples retreat, the group pre-marital classes, and the personal couples counseling, little by little we disclosed the secrets while thinking, what will he think of me after he learned of my transgressions. Yet, with what I was experiencing with God and feeling about Whit, it seemed natural to tell the truth. But, the real "acid test" was will he still love and want to marry me? For some strange reason, I felt most comfortable opening up and talking with him. He was easy to talk with and a good listener. From what I could tell, he was not judging me and I certainly was not judging him. Believing that if he was sent by God, he would know how to handle the truth about me and I about him. As he openly shared his secrets, I fell more in love with him. By being honest, not only did we know God forgave us both, we forgave each other. I understood how important it is to let go of fear of what another person will think of you and tell the truth. At this point in my life, I was ready and strong enough to believe the quote *"If you love something, let it go. If it comes back to you, its' yours forever. If it doesn't, then it was never meant to be."* I was finally freed from the bondage of strongholds of rejection and being unloved. I discovered the benefits of really trusting and obeying what God tells us to do in His Holy Word. *"Do not lie to each other, since you have taken off your old self with its practices and have put on the new self, which is being renewed in knowledge in the image of its Creator" (Colossians 3:9 NIV).*

Victory in Facing the Past

Would he still be interested? My relationship with Jesus became a priority. Since I had read the entire Bible, attended Bible Studies, and heard the preached word on Sunday's I was determined my past lifestyle was behind me and not to live that way again. Jesus had forgiven me for succumbing to the temptation of giving my heart away to others even as I believed I was giving Him first place in other areas of my life. However, I did not understand how and failed to keep God first place in my love life. It took time and required focus on what His Word says about sin. I had sinned against God. I confessed to Jesus, repented of my sins and as He promised, He forgave me and cleaned me up of the residual of shame and guilt. Jesus set

...e free and allowed me to be at peace. He had restored my relationship with Him once again. Now I had to put into practice what I learned. Once you confess and repent, you are forgiven. Therefore, can you honestly share with your future mate what needs to be shared? Trust is important in committed relationships. If God sent Him in my life, then I have to trust God and be honest and not afraid.

I was getting my life right with God, my heavenly Father. I had learned from reading and studying the Bible that we must forgive 70 times seven. Forgiveness was one of God's greatest commands. Every time I prayed the prayer the Lord Jesus taught His disciples to pray, a specific verse stood out for me to do what it says to do in Matthew chapter 6 verses 12 and 14 (NLT) *"our Father in heaven .... and forgive us our sins, as we have forgiven those who sinned against us."* In being convicted by the Holy Spirit of God, I took responsibility for my actions and did not put total blame on another person who hurt or offended me in my past. I had to look at myself as well. I learned how to go to the person one-on-one and ask for their forgiveness.

God instructs in His Word about our relationship with Him, with ourselves, and with others. There is power in forgiveness and being honest with others. I began to understand what was meant by Colossians chapter 3 and verse 13 *"we should make allowance for each other's faults, and forgive anyone who offends you. Remember, the Lord forgave you, so you much forgive others."*

Along the journey of maturing in my faith, I learned more about who I am in the eyes of God and His Son and Savior Jesus Christ. I also learned and experienced the power of forgiveness. Yes, it is hard to do. Forgiveness and love must be given to others for the sake of peace and freedom within ourselves.

Only God could have orchestrated opportunities for me to live out His command to *"make allowance for each other's faults, and forgive anyone who offends you. Remember the Lord forgave you, so you must forgive others"* (Colossians 3:13 NLT). And I was able to freely forgive, by the time Whit came into my life. Jesus had forgiven me for the baggage of my past.

Several relationships come to mind from my childhood on into adulthood, where I intentionally asked others to forgive me or I forgave them whether they asked for it or not. From the first boyfriend who married years before I did, we eventually talked about the past, forgave each other, and moved on with our lives. Forgiveness is also important when someone who broke my heart in the past calls me for help during a crisis in his life. How did he find me? He had to have done some extensive research to find me. He called to ask for my help. What should I do? After listening to him explain his dire circumstances, my heart went out to him. God knew and must have dropped my name in his spirit to call me. I had forgiven him. I hung up the phone with him and immediately called my mentor, Sister Noble. She listened and then as usual she prayed. He is an hour and a half away and the weather conditions were adverse with a pending snow storm. I did not hesitate to go to his aide, despite others cautious concerns in trying to discourage the drive in the snow storm. It did not matter, after Sister Noble's prayer of protection I believed I was to trust God for my safe arrival. Because God knows everything. This was God's child also and He must have put me on his mind for him to call me. He was at his wits' end. By faith, once on the highway, the snow storm was not as bad as predicted.

This was evidence of how God wants us to understand that people will hurt us, but do they really know that is what they are doing at the time? We are to take the same attitude that Jesus did when from the cross, He prayed *"Father, forgive them for they do not know what they are doing"* (Luke 23:34 NLT). I forgive as Jesus does. I do not believe the former boyfriend would have taken the chance to call me for my help if in the past he had really intended to hurt me. My faith helped me to understand why Jesus commands us to put into practice the second commandment to love one another as we love ourselves (Luke 10:27 NIV). Because" *If you forgive those who sin against you, your heavenly Father will forgive you. But if you refuse to forgive others, your Father will not forgive your sins"* (Matthew 6:14 NLT).

I had a clear conscience after having dealt with the pain of my past. God forgave me once I admitted my sins to Him, whether they were knowingly or unknowingly committed against God's biblical instructions for living a moral life. I was free from the burden of sin. I was forgiven and therefore, prepared to receive the mate God had sent me and not withhold any secrets. Getting them out in the open was liberating. I did not know if Whit would still want to marry me, but I was obedient to God first and made up my mind I would trust Him this time with His mate selection. Once I opened up and shared… a peace came over me. I did not need to hide or keep secrets anymore. *"Do not steal. Do not lie. Do not deceive one another"* (Leviticus 19:11 NIV).

I also learned that as much as he was a gentleman to me and treated me like a special woman of God, amazingly, he likewise shared his baggage from the past as well. He trusted me enough to tell me about his. Relieved that the secrets were out. I knew that God was loving me unconditionally and forgiving me through this earthly person. As much as I knew I was not the only person who ever sinned. It was hard to believe that when my sins seemed so great, God still sent a husband to cherish me despite my faults. *"Confess your sins to each other and pray for each other so that you can live together whole and healed. The prayer of a person living right with God is something powerful to be reckoned with"* (James 5:16 MSG).

The Wedding Gown Revealed

The man of my dreams is in my life, but why has he not proposed? The heat was turning up. My Pentagon assignment of four years was about to come to an end. I needed to be preparing for the move to my next assignment. Would it be with or without him? A lot depended on my marital status and the needs of the Air Force whether they would look for jobs to accommodate us as a couple or separate us.

I needed to make some decisions. But yet I was stuck. Has he changed his mind since having spoken with various jewelers about designing my rainbow ring? I was waiting for his proposal before shopping for my wedding gown. However, on the first Saturday in December, I received a surprise call from the wife of our mentor, Mrs. Beverly. She said she was coming to my house right then to pick me up. We were going wedding gown shopping. I said to her with disappointment in my voice, "But Whit has not proposed to me yet."

Ignoring my comments, she said, "Be ready. I will be there in a few minutes." Hurriedly, I grabbed the tote bag with all the bridal books and materials I had collected over the years for this very day. The doorbell rang, and I rushed out and jumped into her car. Moments into our drive, it began to snow. At that point, I knew she was determined that nothing was going to keep us from accomplishing our mission for the day.

Reflecting back in that moment, I saw how Father God worked everything out in His timing. I had purchased my brand-new home in May the year before, then with urgency the Holy Spirit led me in June to have the house blessed. It was Mrs. Beverly and her husband, Rev Benton who conducted the "House Blessing" one month before meeting Whit. The "crisis project" surfaced for Whit and me to meet each other, the planning of my out-of-cycle "passed over" promotion party and Whit asking me out on our first date, July 24th. When Jesus speaks to those called by His name, Christian or believer of Jesus Christ, the Bible reinforces our actions. *"My sheep listen to my voice; I know them, and they follow me"* (John 10:27 NIV).

Beverly and I visited several shops, suddenly she stopped to pull over to call her friend, the wedding planner, Ramona. She gave us more names and addresses of other stores. Nothing strikingly unique had yet caught my attention. Next stop, we drove into a strip mall plaza. The bridal shop was going out of business. Signs were prominently displayed. We got out of the car and went in to be greeted by a friendly and polite sales-lady. Browsing was really easy in the shop because the racks were almost empty. However, one gown caught my eye. It was my size. Beverly and the sales-lady encouraged me to try it on. I did. Oh, it's beautiful, absolutely beautiful on you, they said. And as I stood on the platform, turning, and posing, and smiling while looking into the three-way mirror, I asked, "How much is it?"

The saleslady responded with, "The shop is going-out-business and it was on sale for four hundred dollars. Yet, I was not convinced this gown was the one. This was the first-ever wedding gown I had tried on. Nor did I really appreciate how much of a bargain it really was. I said, Beverly, let's go to another shop on your list before I make a final decision.

We left the shop. And in the car, after she drove a few miles down the street, one of the *Bride* magazines fell open in my lap to the page with the picture of the exact same mermaid gown I had just tried on. I took a double look at the page and picture. In almost disbelief that this was the same exact gown as we had just left. Beverly stopped the car to look at the picture of the gown for herself and said, "We are going back. That is your gown."

When we arrived back at the shop, the owner was waiting for us. She said, "I knew you would come back." The lacy, long-sleeved mermaid-style wedding gown with a heart shaped back and two trains was originally $1,200.00. The owner also threw in the white satin shoes and a handbag. Beverly and I left that shop excited and jubilant about her mission accomplished. She helped me find the right dress. Since she had me out shopping and one victory accomplished, I said, "Let's shop for the bridal party dresses." As soon as we walked into another store looking for the bridal dresses, I immediately began having cramps. I said to Beverly, "I do not feel well." She was relieved and said, "Let's go." We left the store, and she took me home. Her mission was accomplished.

Back home with my beautiful wedding gown, still one problem Whit had not proposed nor did we have a wedding date. My Dad and others started calling me to find out if they should be making plans to take off work and travel to Washington, DC for a wedding. I could not tell him yes or no. I said, "He has not proposed yet."

It seems everyone who had interacted with the both of us knew we were meant for each other. We just naturally acted like it.

New Year's Eve and the Call

On New Year's Eve, December 31, I received a disturbing phone call from Mom asking questions about the intentions of Whit in my life. She was concerned about the emotional well-being of her firstborn daughter who was in a relationship with a young man she and the family definitely approved of. I guess she was hopeful, but about to give up on him. She may have just been tired of my heart being broken.

I was vulnerable. Why was she bringing this question up now? We are fine. Her words caused me to doubt. My first inclination was to pick up the phone, call him, and let him know I was upset. I was ready to break up with him first before he broke up with me. However, my mind was changed instantly while I was sobbing to God as I usually do. I went to my "prayer closet," which was a large bedroom converted and decorated solely for the purpose of spending quiet time with the Lord. I fell on my knees then I laid out prostrate before God in tears, seeking His help in deciding what to do. Should I break up with Whit?

Time was drawing near for Whit to arrive to pick me up for the Watch Night service at our church, "Ebenezer, the Beautiful." When he arrived, we embraced, and I had to do all I could to refrain from getting into a conversation about our relationship and where it was going. We headed to the Watch Night Service.

Watch Night Service Proposal

On December 31st, Watch Night service at Ebenezer was celebratory as the clock moved closer and closer to the stroke of midnight bringing in the new year. Everyone rejoicing in prayer and thanksgiving about all the Lord God had done for us over the previous year. I jotted down thoughts in my journal that reminded me of the Lord's goodness especially since Whit came into my life. God had been good to us as individuals and as a couple. The preacher preached and the musicians played their instruments with the choirs singing songs of praise as the countdown began—ten, nine, eight, seven, six, five, four, three, two ... and at the stroke of midnight, we all shouted joyous praise unto the Lord, our God and Savior, Jesus Christ for another blessed year. In the midst of rejoicing, Whit grabbed my left hand and slid a solitaire engagement ring on my finger. While I was gazing at the ring, he asked me a few questions for affirmation. Then he asked, "Will you marry me?" "Oh my God, yes!" I said.

We embraced with a big, tender, loving hug. And I danced all around in the pew area as much as I could hugging and flashing my left hand to everyone around us. I am engaged. Congratulations, I heard in return.

Wedding Date Decision

We chose the date March 9th. With only two months to plan our wedding, God intervened with snow storms every weekend in January. Since we were snowed in, Whit and I were forced to decide on a budget, coordinate with our mothers about who they wanted to invite to the wedding, consolidate all our guest lists, and together make the final plans for our big day. We did it. Finally, all the invitations were put in the mail. We met with our wedding planner, Beverly's friend Ramona along with my sorority sister Jervie and started planning the big day for family and friends to celebrate with us God's answer to our prayers.

My fiancé loved photography as a past-time. He remembered my childhood dream of getting married on the capitol steps in Montgomery, Alabama. So as a special gesture, he arranged for us to take pre-wedding photos on the steps of the nations' Capitol building. Because for security reasons, we could not have a wedding ceremony there.

Look at God and His words coming to life in Psalm 37:4: *"Delight yourself in the Lord and he will give you the desires of your heart."* The wedding was not happening at the state capitol, my childhood dream. But *"now to him who is able to do immeasurably more than all we ask or imagine, according to his power that is at work within us"* (Ephesians 3:20 NIV), God took my dream beyond anything I could have ever imagined. From a childhood comment, God heard me and my prayers while creating the vision board for Him to choose the mate He had for me. God arranged for us to meet at the Pentagon in the nation's capital. Wow! What an amazing God!

Engagement Afterthoughts ...What About Me and My Career?

A few weeks away from the wedding day, the reality set in that I had my God-sent mate. While, I was driving my car and leaving McDonald's early one morning in late February and listening to Chuck Swindoll's *Insight for Living* radio broadcast, I began to cry at the thought and prayer, "now what about my career?" I was finally about to be married, receiving the man God had chosen to be my mate for a lifetime and had been victoriously promoted to the next rank. I prayed and heard in my spirit the words, "You are to be a colonel's wife." Immediately, I calmed down and drove right over to the military clothing sales store at Andrews Air Force Base (AFB) and purchased the male "colonel" insignia.

I had a tradition of placing photos, images from magazines, or other significant items on my vision board to use as my point of reference to rejoice when God answered my prayers. After hearing those seven words, I was clear this time what to do. After work I went home excited about what I heard. I obeyed and prepared my vision board as I usually did for future promotions and so on. I glued the male "colonel" insignia (there was a difference in the male and female; we were the same rank at the time) on the board and dated it February 20th. I was at peace about proceeding with the wedding and trusting this was God's divine will.

Countdown to two weeks away, all the final details had been coordinated with the "Ebenezer, the Beautiful" wedding director. The program was reviewed and printed, RSVPs were in, photographer and videographer in place, and the reception location and contract signed.

On the eve of my wedding, my mother and I spent precious time together at my home talking about my new life. With love and joy in our hearts, Mom and her firstborn bonded on a whole other level and I was about to be married.

Finally, Here Comes the Bride!

With light snow flurries, cold temperatures, yet a gleam of sunshine, the much-awaited marvelous day was finally here. Invited guests from across the nation arrived at "Ebenezer, the Beautiful" and were greeted by hostesses and escorted to their seats by ushers. Wedding coordinators Ramona and Jervie finished the final touches ensuring every aspect would be executed without a glitch. Best man, Gary chauffeured the bride and Mom from my house to the church to join my nine attendants, Theresa, Bonnie, Carolyn, Mary, JoAnna, Janice, and sisters Sanchelesresa, Teresa and Michele for photos. The musicians playing softly in the background signaled the start of the ceremony. Both Whit and my parents were escorted to their seats to the song "Jesu, Joy of Man's Desiring" by Joann Sebastian Bach. At the front of the church along with the officiating pastor, Whit and his nine groomsmen dressed in back tuxedos took their places at the altar with our Pastor, the officiant. The ceremony continued with the Ebenezer liturgical dancers ministering in dance to the song "Order My Steps," and the soloist, Gwen and choir singing "My Tribute."

Doors opened and the center aisle was graced by the nine attendants led by the bride's sisters and matrons of honor Michele and Teresa. Each wearing red shoes and red chiffon and sequined evening dress clutching their floral bouquets. The cute little flower girl, Simone (daughter of deceased BFF Felicia) nervously followed them sprinkling rose petals on the runner.

Then a quiet pause was interrupted with an announcement. In their little-men tuxedos, both her six- and five-year-old nephews, Robert and Jaylon, paraded down the aisle, excitedly ringing bells and the six-year old shouting to the top of his lungs, "The bride is coming! The bride is coming!"

The guests smiled as they stood to their feet for the grand entrance of the bride. Turning their faces to the center aisle and to the back of the church, the double glass doors swung open. There stood the bride dressed in a beautiful white mermaid-style wedding gown with a long veil and flowing train.

Walking slowly down the aisle nervous with Dad, to the chosen bridal march song "Real Love," my heart was melting as I made eye contact with my bridegroom. Dad was about to transfer ownership of his firstborn daughter to the man God-sent to be her husband. Our officiating Pastor asked, "who gives this woman to be wed to this man?" Dad was giving the bride away as traditional calls it. Dad responded, "Her mother and I do." *"Then the Lord God made a woman from the rib he had taken out of the man, and <u>he brought her to the man</u>. The man said, 'This is now bone of my bones and flesh of my flesh; she shall be called "woman," for she was taken out of man.' That is why a man leaves his father and mother and is united to his wife, and they become one flesh"* (Genesis 2:22–24).

With tears of joy, I grasped my groom's hand and nervously brushed it with my thumb throughout the enitre of the ceremony. Love songs were sung by the gospel Chancel Choir and symbolic Scriptures read by my grand-uncle, Reverend Dr. V.C. Provitt, my grandmother's brother, and my god-daughter Jamila's father, Reverend James Caraway. Our pastor gave the blessing and exchange of vows and rings. Our wedding day, how special it was to have our first Holy Communion together as husband and wife. The ceremony continued with Whit and I presenting gifts to our parents, watching with joy as married couples joined us at the altar to renew their vows, and hoping the guests without a relationship with Jesus would respond to Pastor's invitation to receive the gift of salvation and become disciples of Jesus Christ. After the pronouncement of Mr. and Mrs., the loving kiss that gets everyone smiling, and the jumping of the broom, the celebratory recessional was filled with joyful songs of praise as we made out grand exit under the six-man military saber bearers arch down the aisle, as husband and wife.

Immediately following the ceremony and the photo session, we headed in the limousine to our wedding reception at Fort Myers Officer's Club. We were delayed by unforeseen Saturday traffic. But upon our arrival, we were greeted by guests and strolled right on into the ballroom at the announcement of Mr. and Mrs. With the saber-bearers again in position, we walked under the military arch. As my husband I approached the end, I felt an unexpected tap of a sword on my behind. I looked back, smiled, and wondered why he did it. I found out it was a tradition done at military weddings.

Now on the dance floor with music playing by musician Jonathan Smith on keyboard, Whit and I embraced and moved into our first dance. So heavenly in love, I surprisingly fell limp in my smooth dancer husband's arms as he surprised me with the end of dance dip. We had no practice beforehand. The second dance was a first in my life, my Dad and I dancing together. Amazing how Scriptures inform us about our lives and why we should not be surprised by the trials and tribulations we encounter. The prophesy in the book of Malachi chapter 4 verse 6 and also similar in Luke chapter 1 verse 17 (NIV) the coming of the Lord is *to turn the hearts of the fathers (parents) to their children, and the hearts of the children to their fathers (parents) to make ready a people prepared for the Lord.*

My sister Sancheleresa, a pianist since age 5 serenaded us by singing and playing on a baby grand piano, Lionel Richie and Diana Ross' song "Endless Love." Another beautiful and much-awaited wedding day moment was my sorority sisters encircled around me to sing our beloved sorority "Sweetheart

Song." I was so very happy. Followed by the throwing of the bride's bouquet. Melissa, my co-worker who owned the mystery "crisis project" caught the bouquet and Mom's friend caught the garter.

I received a blessing I would never forget. I was very glad I had finally given the desires of my heart over to the Lord God and trusted Him to perform just what He said He would do. God's unfailing love toward me and my Prince Charming made me feel very special. Whit and I found real and unconditional love in the Lord God Almighty and He made it manifest on our wedding day. How much he loves His children. Our marriage ordained by God.

The Wedding Night and Honeymoon

Our relationship had already been filled with wonderful surprises by Whit. Yes, I did manage to surprise him at least once in the beginning of our relationship. It was a surprise birthday dinner cruise on the Spirit of Washington. So quiet naturally, the wedding night and honeymoon would be no different for him. He did it again. We spent Saturday night at the historic Watergate Hotel. On Sunday morning, we were back in church just like our second date to worship together but this time with family and friends. Then off to our surprise honeymoon destination on Monday. With packed bags, filled with summer clothing and swimsuits for the beach, probably too many, where were we off to? I did not have a clue. Until we spotted my Dad and Mona traveling on the same plane. From that point I guessed we were going west maybe somewhere in California. Not until we arrived in Chicago at O'Hare International Airport and said our goodbyes. My husband gave no hints until we approached the gate for our connecting flight to destination Honolulu Hawaii. Wow! Whit, no longer able to keep the secret said we will be staying overnight in Honolulu and the next morning flying to the Big Island of Hawaii. We will spend seven days there. Our God is truly amazing! God answers prayers and makes dreams come true.

Wait I say, wait on the Lord!

Because of the LORD's great love we are not consumed, for his compassions never fail. They are new every morning; great is your faithfulness. I say to myself, "The LORD is my portion; therefore, I will wait for Him" (Lamentations 3:22-24 NIV).

"It is the bridegroom who marries the bride, and the bridegroom's friend is simply glad to stand with him and hear his vows. Therefore, I am filled with joy at his success" (John 3:29 NLT).

I am the Alpha and the Omega, the First and the Last, the Beginning and the End (Revelation 22:13 NLT).

Truly, truly, just like me so were you born to become His Bride on Earth as it is in Heaven! *The Spirit and the bride say, "Come." Let anyone who hears this say, "Come…"* (Revelation 22:17 NLT).

A Love Letter from Your Heavenly Father

Dearest Daughter and Bride-To-Be,

    *Y*ou are Mine, and I am yours. When it is time, the husband I have created just for you will find you. I will keep My promise. When a man finds a wife, he finds what is good and receives My favor (Proverbs 18:22 NIV). As with the first family Adam and Eve, I created the woman for the man and brought the woman to him. The marriage covenant is a loving union between a man and a woman. For those who desire to be married not one will lack her mate. For it is from My mouth that gives the order, and My Spirit gathers both of you together (Isaiah 34:16 NIV). When the couple leaves the father and mother and unites with one another, they no longer remain two people, but the two become one flesh (Genesis 2:24, Ephesians 5:30 NIV). And what I join together, let no one separate (Matthew 19:6 NIV).

    Your marriage will be a part of the journey and path for becoming the Bride of Christ on earth as it is in heaven. When couples get married, husbands and wives, they are to submit to one another out of their reverence for Me. This is why wives, are encouraged to submit to your own husbands just as you submit to Me, the Savior and Lord. For the husband is the head of the wife as Christ is the head of the church, his body, of which he is the Savior. Now as the church submits to Christ, so also wives should submit to their husbands in everything. The husbands are to submit to Christ by the way they love their wives, just as Christ loved the church. Christ gave himself up for her to make her holy, cleansing her by the washing with water through the word, and to present her to himself as a radiant church, without stain or wrinkle or any other blemish, but holy and blameless. In this same way My command is for husbands to love their wives as their own bodies. A husband who loves his wife loves himself. After all, no one ever hated their own body, but they feed and care for their body, just as Christ does the church— for we are members of his body (Ephesians 5:18-30 NIV).

    My Son, Jesus Christ prayed to Me about all who would give their hearts and lives to Him and be saved so that I would protect you by the power of His name and you may be one as He and I are one (John 17:11b NIV). For this reason, a man will leave his father and mother and be united to his wife, and the two will become one flesh." This is a profound mystery—but I am talking about Christ and the church. However, the husband also must love his wife as he loves himself, and the wife must respect her husband (Ephesians 5:31-33 NIV).

Having created you female, to be loved and to give love was my deepest desire for you. I did it for you to experience pure innocence in your relationships. Wait on Me to bring you the mate I have specifically created for you. Be strong and take heart I know just the right mate for you (Psalm 27:14 NIV). Wait to receive him at the right time, and then you will be excited to hear My response, you have stolen My heart with one glance of your eyes, with one jewel of your necklace. How delightful is your love, my sister, my bride (Song 4:9-10a NIV).

I have made some to be married and some to enjoy the life of singleness. But, the Apostle Paul addresses important questions raised about marriage "It is good for a man not to have sexual relations with a woman before marriage. But since sexual immorality or impure activities is occurring, each man should have sexual relations with his own wife, and each woman with her own husband. He also writes about the blessings and challenges faced for the unmarried and single... sometimes I wish everyone were single like me—a simpler life in many ways! But celibacy (staying sexually pure and not getting married) is not for everyone any more than marriage is. God gives the gift of the single life to some, the gift of the married life to others" (1 Corinthians 7:7 TMB).

As I promised the chosen generation, the first requirement is for you to have a relationship with Me in love, reverence, honor and worship. Rejoice and be glad and give Me the glory! I also say it to those who believe that I sent My firstborn Son Jesus Christ to earth to be your Savior. For the wedding of the Lamb (Jesus Christ) has come, and His bride has made herself ready. Fine linen, bright and clean, was given her to wear."

Because "It is the bridegroom who marries the bride, and the bridegroom's friend is simply glad to stand with him and hear his vows. Therefore, I am filled with joy at his success" (John 3:29 NLT). Then the Spirit and the Bride say, "Come!" And let the one who hears say, "Come!" Let the one who is thirsty come; and let the one who wishes take the free gift of the water of life (Revelation 22:17 NIV).

You are becoming His Bride on Earth as it is in Heaven for My eternal Glory!

Your Eternal and Everlasting Bridegroom

Self-Discovery / Self-Reflection

Application

(1) Find photos to create your own wedding day, marriage, family, career, and a vision of becoming a bride of Christ on the vision board.
(2) Reflect and chat about the questions below with your mother or close adult female friend (mentor).
(3) Look up and write down on your vision board the Bible verses from this chapter that inspired you and use them to also answer the questions.

Thinking about Me: Marriage…Finally!

1. Why did God create marriage? What are the scriptures that address marriage?

_____
_____

2. Do you want to get married? Why or why not? What are about 10 character traits you possess for a godly marriage relationship?

_____
_____

3. Does a girl have to search to find her own husband? Why or why not?

_____
_____

4. What is the role of the woman and the role of the man in marriage?

_____
_____

5. What is the difference between the earthly bride and the Heavenly bride of Christ? Are you becoming a Bride of Christ?

_____
_____

Be somebody who makes everyone feel like a somebody.
—*Author unknown*

There is a purpose for everyone you meet. Some people come into your life to test you, some to teach you, some to use you, and some to bring out the very best in you.
—*Author unknown*

EPILOGUE

The Conclusion of the Matter . . . We are Our Sister's Keeper

The conclusion of the matter is better than the beginning. This epilogue is written for you, who are mothers, female teachers, counselors, teaching aides, social workers, therapists, behavioral specialists, psychologists, medical practitioners, politicians, attorneys, probation officers, mentors, coaches, business leaders, ministry leaders, clergy, and pastors. Because now that all has been said and heard, knowing who you are and your own identity in Christ is what makes you and me our best sister's keeper. Our duty is to *fear (revere) God and keep His commands, for this is the whole duty of all human beings, everyone (Ecclesiastes 12:13)*.

This resource book is for those of us who are raising and working with teenagers and young women. *"Dear friends, let us continue to love one another, for love comes from God. Anyone who loves is a child of God and knows God" (1 John 4:7 NLT). First, love God with all our heart and with all of our soul and with all our strength and with all our mind, and second love our neighbor . . . our girls, as ourselves. (Luke 10:27 NIV). We are all God's daughters!*

I believe you are the instrument God will use to address the problem of epidemic proportions in our local communities and around the world. Why? Because you know that "each child is a precious human being with great potential."[66] Yet, Phyllis Kilbourn brings to our attention that "girls are the world's most squandered gift . . . who are facing the double challenge of being female and being young."[67] Sixteen-year-old Jessica Inglis captured the issue in the last few lines of her poem: *"we'd better think hard about the future before our goals and our dreams disappear."*[68]

Something dramatic is happening to our adolescent girls in America and everywhere, something going unnoticed by those not on the front lines.[69] Therefore, this author is responding to psychologist Mary Pipher's alarm to "the National Weather Service bulletin from the storm center". . . *girls all around the world are lacking in positive self-esteem.*[70]

Our girls are experiencing an identity crisis. Girls, more than ever, are growing up in a society that needs women coming alongside them. Women who have prayerfully worked through their own self-discovery and received the love and healing of Jesus Christ in their own lives. A girl's self-esteem, self-identity, and ethnic identity problems and issues must be brought to everyone's attention. This should no longer be individuals, families, cultures, or ethnic groups working in isolation to solve these social problems. Women must come together, collaborate, be transparent, and prayerfully seek God for wisdom, understanding, and knowledge in order for the solutions to come. Each culture and ethnic group should come together to understand and acknowledge the role each one plays in this broken world. Because girls grow up and become women.

The fact is we were once adolescent girls ourselves, and we grew up to be the women we are. When women help others, women are helping themselves. The Bible refers to that as the body fitted together (Ephesians 4:15,16), which begins with relationships. Girls need positive self-esteem throughout their entire lives by being in healthy relationships, where they are loved and can freely give love. The best way for young girls and women to grow up with positive self-esteem, positive feelings about their ethnic identity, and healthy girl-and-girl and boy-and-girl relationships. Girls need to get to know themselves through the eyes of the loving Heavenly Father revealed to us in His Holy Scriptures.

Girls need more godly role models to help them to live in this world with confidence in who they are by seeking a love relationship with God first. Beverly White Hislop gives counsel in her book *Shepherding a Woman's Heart*.[71] She highlights the significance of negative change that has occurred in our society today. The increase in emotional pain and trauma is worldwide, and there is a dramatic need for women to shepherd other women and mothers their own daughters as well as other women mentors coming alongside of these mothers.

After having lived and traveled in many American states, Asia, and Europe, I have become familiar with many cultures and have also served as a lay-leader in military chapels, local churches, and communities. Now as a pastor, I can attest to the psychologist Mary Pipher's observations: "Girls and women are more alike than different" with the same common denominator of self-esteem issues.[72]

I know this truth because I was a girl who grew up and as a woman, I took the journey down memory lane under God's divine tender loving care to discover my past relationships were fraught with right and wrong decisions. My eyes, ears, mind, and heart have been opened by God to deal with my past in order for me to better understand what our young girls and women are experiencing. But one fact remains and it is worth broadcasting, whether I knew it or not, through the good, the bad, and the ugly, our Heavenly Father God and Savior Jesus Christ was always present and never abandoned me. He never rejected me. He never failed me. I learned to develop a relationship of love and trust in God and what Jesus Christ did to atone for my sins. It is a process, though. Despite the mistakes I made along the way, it was not until I was able to sit still with myself and with the Lord that I found the truth. Jesus said to the people who believed in him, *"You are truly my disciples if you remain faithful to my teachings. And you will know the truth and the truth will set you free" (John 8:31, 32 NLT).*

I meet girls and young women where they are and build nurturing and non-judgmental relationships with them. The journey to self-awareness is liberating even with God's corrections and rebuke from the Bible. *"I correct and discipline everyone I love. So be diligent and turn from your indifference" (Revelation 3:19 NLT).*

Together, we too can begin to love, accept, and guide girls and boys with intentionality in gaining positive self-esteem about themselves. We can teach and motivate them to build healthy relationships in and out of their home. The main ingredient for healthy relationships is with God and His Son Jesus Christ first, and with ourselves second because we know who we are.

Our girls need transparency and authentic relationships with you. I know it is difficult opening up our hearts to someone we do not know. However, I do believe our Creator is giving us new opportunities and ways to first rediscover ourselves. Through the journey with girls and young women you will come in contact with, God will be with you every step of the way. He needs you to invest your time, your talents, your treasures, and your testimonies of how He intervened and rescued you during challenging seasons of your life. Even if you may be thinking God did not bring you through and you did it all on your own, I would like to ask that you take some time to ponder that a little more. Ask in a prayer to God if He would reveal to you the first time you were ever exposed to the truth about His existence as God the Heavenly Father and God the Savior. Also, ask in prayer for His Son, Jesus Christ to reveal how knowing who created you is knowing yourself, loving yourself, and sharing yourself with others in an authentic way. *"Make allowance for each other's faults and forgive anyone who offends you. Remember, the Lord forgave you, so you must forgive others" (Colossians 3:13 NIV).*

Let it be with our heads, hearts, and hands that we help every young girl learn how to have healthy self-esteem and how to build healthy relationships. First with God, then second with themselves and with others. This is the only way. From the beginning of time until eternity, all relationships are interrelated. God mandates everyone to develop and maintain quality heavenly and earthly relationships. The heart of the matter is when human beings care for themselves as God created them to, they will live with an abiding sense of their own unique self-esteem, self-worth, and self-identity coming through none other than Christ Jesus, the perfect image-bearer.

This means we as leaders and confidants should go back to the basics of seeking the truth of who we are according to the greatest love story ever told of our Creator God. In the beginning, God made females to be loved. As God's image-bearers, you may want to ask yourself and reflect on five key questions in order to help each other: (1) who I am, (2) who loves me (3) who do I belong to, (3) who values me, and (5) who is my source of positive self-esteem?

Jesus Christ, our Savior and Redeemer can liberate all cultures of women to ignite a fire that will transform all teenage girls, whether two-parent family or single parent or from system-involved, human trafficked victims, or single mothers into successful businesswomen, educators, athletes, health, legal professionals and other choice professions.

This also would be the step in the right direction toward Dr. Martin Luther King Jr.'s vision of the *Beloved Community*,[73] which unifies people in houses of faith, churches and communities with the strength to love and build genuine relationships. "In a *Beloved Community* solidarity and trust are grounded in a profound commitment to a shared vision."[74] Everyone is his or her brothers' and sisters' keeper. It is a family affair of relational women contributing their resources of compassion, time, the ability to persevere and all being *accepted in the Beloved.*[75]

Will you join us in sounding the alarm and rallying to take concerted action? There are too many girls whose "development is limited and their wholeness truncated, leaving them traumatized."[76]

I pray that God is impressing upon your heart to courageously stand together for the truth of His Word and by the power of His Holy Spirit for the sake of our girls and young women. It does not matter how we may have failed to live a flawless life. I failed, but I know how very important it is to surrender my will to God and confess my sins to Jesus. He forgave and cleansed me from all my unrighteousness. *Now sisters, I know that you acted in ignorance, as did your leaders... Repent, then and turn to God, so that your sins may be wiped out, that times of refreshing may come from the Lord (Acts 3:17,19 NIV).*

Again, I am reminding you I have made some serious mistakes along this life's journey. However, the Lord looked past all my faults and saw just what this daughter needed. God does not have favorites. We all are equal before God (Romans 2;11, Ephesians 6:9 NIV). He gives favor to those who choose to seek a relationship with Him. *Therefore, let us confess our faults to each other and pray for each other so that we may be healed (James 5:16a NIV).*

Let's break the prevailing cycle of lack of self-esteem issues and unhealthy relationships in girls and women, alike. In order for our girls and young women to find their true identity in God and His Son, Christ Jesus, we should guide them in becoming more self-aware about who they are. *"Where there is no vision the people (girls and young women) perish" (Proverbs 29:18).*

We have a mission to accomplish. Through education, awareness, accountability, and practical application, we can together provide the best solution for God's daughters, young and old, to live fully and completely as His image-bearers. Let us unite as a cultural and ethnically diverse group of females that includes clergy, pastors, counselors, therapists, educators, probation officers, politicians, attorneys, parents, and others, who are knowledgeable about the cultural and ethnic similarities and differences among adolescent girls. Many women are sounding the alarm across the cultural and ethnic divide.

With the many women already sounding the alarm, let us recognize God has divinely placed girls in our lives and still others yet to come that we can help. Let's look at ourselves first for a check-up in our relationship with God, family, and others. We are our sisters' keeper called by God for such a time as this. Let's do it ...

Guide older (younger) women into lives of reverence so they end up as neither gossips nor drunks, but models of goodness. By looking at them, the younger women will know how to love their husbands and children, be virtuous and pure, keep a good house, be good wives. We don't want anyone looking down on God's Message because of their behavior (Titus 2:3–5 MSG).

All because "... *that is what the Scriptures mean when they say, "no eye has seen, no ear has heard, and no mind has imagined what God has prepared for those who love him. But it was to us that God revealed these things by His Spirit. For His Spirit searches out everything and shows us God's deep secrets"* (1 Corinthians 2:9,10 NLT)

May the grace of the Lord Jesus Christ, and the love of God, and the fellowship of the Holy Spirit be with us all. AMEN!

…We are in the Final Act!
And He also said, "It is finished! I am the Alpha and the Omega, the Beginning and the End. (Revelation 22:6 NLT).

Jesus Christ is Coming Back to get
His Bride, the Church!

Hallelujah! Amen!
To God be the Glory!

Appendix ~ Poem

Stop Searching
by the author

Stop searching! You won't find it through drugs, alcohol, riches, or sex.

That emptiness in your life is the need God has
put there for us to seek Him first.
Give glory and praise to our Father, our Creator.
He's our Creator and no one else.

We will only experience peace, joy, love, and
happiness in this life through Jesus Christ.

Don't succumb to the powers of darkness ...
indulging in alcohol, drugs, riches, or sex.

We're in a spiritual battle. Only through Christ will we see victory.
Christ is the light.

One of the biggest sins of darkness is fornication, yes ... sex.

Why do you seek to fulfill these lustful desires?
God gave us this beautiful gift but only to be shared
in marriage, and then will you be fulfilled.

How many relationships have you been in? How many times
have they failed? Were you always completely fulfilled?
Maybe momentarily, but other things weren't right.

Sex is not the answer. Adultery is not the answer. Drugs are not the answer. Alcohol is not the answer. Hearing the opposite sex say, "I love you," is not the answer. Riches are not the answer.

What are you searching for?
I'm a witness. It is my Lord and Savior Jesus Christ,
Whether you realize it or not.

Think about it. He's calling you from the powers of darkness.
That still, quiet, sweet voice you hear while indulging in sin ... it's Him.

Come to Me and you will never thirst, says the Lord.
Trust in Me. I *love you*.

You will have peace, love, joy, and happiness. I'm your Creator.

The only way you will be fulfilled is to put Me first in your life.

No other will fill that void you have, that emptiness you have.
I'm the way, the truth, and the life. I'm the answer.

Stop searching! Here at the door of your heart, I knock.
Whosoever shall let Me in will know Me. I am *love*. ~ *Stop Searching!* ~

Appendix ~ Poem

Why?

by the author

Why? Why is this world so cruel?
I know, I know because there is one who thinks he's greater than God.
That's why I believe in my Lord, the Prince of *Peace*,
Lord of lords, and King of kings.
I don't like this cruel, cruel world.
I want to live in peace, love, and harmony.
It makes me sad to see how he, the enemy of
our soul, tries to rule this world.
But I have news, I have the Good News.
Hey, we're going to tear his kingdom down.
We're going to tear his kingdom down.
This is my Lord and Savior's kingdom, by the Alpha and Omega, my God.
Oh, how it hurts to be and see those controlled
by him … the enemy of our soul,
But it was Jesus, the Christ, who shed His blood on Calvary
and died for all our sins, iniquities, sicknesses, and diseases and
after three days, He arose again that we might
live forever with Him and the Father. *Amen!*

Chapter Sources and Notes

Prologue

1. Walk Thru the Bible, Quote from *Daily Walk: Getting God's Word into Your Heart*, November 2010, 21.
2. Nikki Giant and Rachel Beddoe, *Surviving Girlhood: Building Positive Relationships, Attitudes, and Self-Esteem to Prevent Teenage Girl Bullying*, 14.
3. Robert A. Josephs, Hazel Rose Markus, and Romin W. Tafarodi, "Gender & Self-Esteem," *Journal of Personality and Social Psychology* 63, no. 3 (1992), 400.

Chapter 1

4. Teresa Wiltz, "Why Teen Women of Color Are More Likely to Become Pregnant," *Huffington Post*, March 5, 2015, updated December 6, 2017 (https://www.huffpost.com/entry/racial-and-ethnic-dispari_n_6799378).
5. Teresa Wiltz, "Why Teen Women of Color Are More Likely to Become Pregnant," *Huffington Post*, March 5, 2015, updated December 6, 2017 (https://www.huffingtonpost.com/2015/03/05/racial-and-ethnic-dispari_n_6799378.html).
6. "A Generation at Risk," Step-Family Association, http://www.griefspeaks.com/id113.html.
7. "A Generation at Risk," Step-Family Association, http://www.griefspeaks.com/id113.html
8. Jean Illsely Clark, *Self Esteem: A Family Affair*, 4.
9. *Oxford Dictionary of English*, 3rd ed., s.v., "self-identity."
10. Robert A. Josephs, Hazel Rose Markus, and Romin W. Tafarodi, "Gender & Self-Esteem," *Journal of Personality and Social Psychology* 63, no. 3 (1992), 400.
11. *Oxford Dictionary*, s.v., "love."
12. Kellee Terrell, "Smart + Strong: Building Self-Esteem in Young Black Girls" (March 4, 2009), accessed October 29, 2018, https://www.realhealthmag.com/article/Dove-selfesteem-survey-16222-6882.
13. Kellee Terrell, "Smart + Strong: Building Self-Esteem in Young Black Girls," March 4, 2009, accessed October 29, 2018, https://www.realhealthmag.com/article/Dove-selfesteem-survey-16222-6882.

Chapter 2

14 *Webster's Online Dictionary*, s.v., "love."
15 Jean Illsely Clark, *Self Esteem: A Family Affair* (Minneapolis, MN: Winston Press, 1978), 4.
16 Robert Rector, "Marriage: America's Greatest Weapon against Child Poverty," *The Heritage Foundation Leadership for America*, Special Report from Domestic Policy Studies Department, 117 (September 5, 2012): 1, accessed November 20, 2014, http://www.heritage.org/research/reports/2012/09/marriage-americas-greatest-weapon-against-child-poverty. Child poverty is an ongoing national concern, but few are aware of its principal cause: the absence of married fathers in the home. According to the US Census, the poverty rate for single parents with children in the United States in 2009 was 37.1 percent. The rate for married couples with children was 6.8 percent. Being raised in a married family reduced a child's probability of living in poverty by about 82 percent.
17 Adriana J. Umana-Taylor, Marcelo Diversi, and Mark A. Fine, "Ethnic Identity and Self-Esteem of Latino Adolescents: Distinctions among the Latino Populations," *Journal of Adolescent Research* 17 (2002): 304, accessed December 8, 2014, http://www.sagepub.com/thomas2e/study/articles/section2/Article56.pdf.
18 Jean Illsely Clark, *Self Esteem: A Family Affair*, (Minneapolis MN: Winston Press, 1978), 4.
19 Jean Illsely Clark, *Self Esteem: A Family Affair*, (Minneapolis MN: Winston Press, 1978), 3.
20 Alice P. Mathews, *Preaching That Speaks to Women*, (Grand Rapids MI: Baker Academic, 2003), 51.
21 Jean Illsely Clark, *Self Esteem: A Family Affair*, 4.
22 4-H stands for head to clearer thinking, heart to greater loyalty, hands to larger service, and health to better living; *Wikipedia*, s.v., "4-H," accessed on November 27, 2017, https://en.wikipedia.org/wiki/4-H.
23 https://www.brainyquote.com/quotes/sigmund_freud_138674
24 Kevin Leman, *The Birth Order Book*, 13.
25 Kevin Leman, *The Birth Order Book*, 13
26 Gail Gross, "The Achiever—First Born, the Peacemaker—Middle Child, and the Life of the Party—Youngest Child: How Birth Order Affects Personality," *Huffington Post*, http://www.huffingtonpost.com/dr-gail-gross/how-birth-order-affects-personality_b_4494385.html.

Chapter 3

27 Nancy Boyd-Franklin *"Black Families in Therapy: A Multisystems Approach"* (New York: The Guilford Press, 1989), 191.

Chapter 4

28. Jenn Savedge, Teen Challenges Seventeen to Stop Airbrushing Models, May 4, 2012, https://www.mnn.com/lifestyle/natural-beauty-fashion/blogs/teen-challenges-seventeen-to-stop-airbrushing-models
29. Jenn Savedge, Teen Challenges Seventeen to Stop Airbrushing Models, May 4, 2012, https://www.mnn.com/lifestyle/natural-beauty-fashion/blogs/teen-challenges-seventeen-to-stop-airbrushing-models
30. *Real Girls, Real Pressure: A National Report on the State of Self-Esteem*, commissioned June 2008.
31. National Institute on Media and the Family, http://www.heartofleadership.org/statistics/.
32. "11 Facts about Teens and Self-Esteem," https://www.dosomething.org/us/facts/11-facts-about-teens-and-self-esteem.
33. The Dictionary of the New Testament (TDNT) cites that "sin," in Greek *hamartano*.
34. Lee Grayson, Conformity in Teenagers, Feb 18, 2015 http://www.livestrong.com/article/559761-conformity-in-teenagers/
35. https://www.simplypsychology.org/maslow.html

Chapter 5

36. Orfanides, Effie, "10 Celebrities Who Saved Themselves for Marriage," https://www.more.com/celebrity/10-celebrities-who-saved-themselves-marriage/?page=5
37. 13 Celebrities who Chose to Save Sex Till Marriage, https://aleteia.org/slideshow/13-celebrities-who-chose-to-save-sex-till-marriage-8423/14/
38. Elizabeth Weiss McGolerick, "The Importance of the Father-Daughter Relationship," *SheKnows*, February 9, 2017, accessed April 17, 2019 https://www.sheknows.com/parenting/articles/821928/the-importance-of-the-father-daughter-relationship-2/
39. Iyanla Vanzant, 'Daddyless Daughters' http://www.huffingtonpost.com/2013/07/23/iyanla-vanzant-daddyless-daughter_n_3636568.html, accessed February 9, 2017
40. Life Application Study Bible footnotes s.v. "1 Corinthians 6:18."
41. Life Application Study Bible footnotes s.v. "1 Corinthians 6:18."
42. https://www.healthychildren.org/English/ages-stages/gradeschool/Pages/Helping-Your-Child-Develop-A-Healthy-Sense-of-Self-Esteem.aspx
43. Dannah Gresh, The Myth of "Friends with Benefits," CBN Family, https://www1.cbn.com/youth/the-myth-of-friends-with-benefits
44. Dannah Gresh, The Myth of "Friends with Benefits," CBN Family, https://www1.cbn.com/youth/the-myth-of-friends-with-benefits

45 Dating Abuse Statistics, Love is Respect.org https://www.loveisrespect.org/resources/dating-violence-statistics/ and Centers for Disease Control and Prevention, "Physical Dating Violence Among High School Students—United States, 2003," *Morbidity and Mortality Weekly Report*, May 19, 2006, Vol. 55, No. 19.
46 Dating Abuse Statistics, Love is Respect.org https://www.loveisrespect.org/resources/dating-violence-statistics/ Grunbaum JA, Kann L, Kinchen S, et al. 2004. *Youth Risk Behavior Surveillance—United States*, 2003. Morbidity and Mortality Weekly Report. 53(SS02); 1-96. Available at http://www.cdc.gov/mmwr/preview/mmwrhtml/ss5302a1.htm.
47 Joseph H. Thayer, *Thayer's Greek-English Lexicon of the New Testament*, s.v. "#3986 peirasmos (1 Peter 1:12)" (Peabody MA: Hendrickson Publishers, 2000), Accordance edition 9.5.7.
48 Jason Evert, "Theology of the Body for Teens – Parent's Guide.

Chapter 6

49 https://en.wikipedia.org/wiki/All_that_glitters_is_not_gold
50 Martin Nystrom, *As the Deer,* 100 EZ Praise & Worship Favorites (Word Music, 1999), 6.

Chapter 7

51 Life Application Study Bible, s.v. "Psalm 36:7."
52 Michele and Craig Borba. Self Esteem: A Classroom Affair – 101 Ways to Help Children Like Themselves. Minneapolis, MN: Winston Press, Inc., 1978, 19.
53 http://www.americanpearl.com/historyoyster.html
54 http://www.americanpearl.com/historyoyster.html
55 Wikipedia, s.v. "royalty," *Wikipedia online*, accessed April 19, 2019, https://en.wikipedia.org/wiki/Royal_family
56 https://en.wikipedia.org/wiki/Royal_family
57 D. G. Bloesch, "Sin," in *Evangelical Dictionary of Theology*, ed. Walter A. Elwell (Grand Rapids MI: Baker Books, 1984), 1012.
58 Zodhiates and Baker, s.v. "Old Testament #281 amartia (Gen 4:6)," 1583.
59 Zodhiates and Baker, s.v. "Old Testament #281 amartia (Gen 4:6)," 1583.
60 Erickson, "The Results of Sin," In *Christian Theology,* 2nd edition (Grand Rapids MI: Baker Books, 1999), 636.
61 Craig W. Ellison, 3. (These were the Remarks made in his Presidential Address for the Western Association of Christians for Psychological Studies, Westmount College, May 1975.)

62 Karen Mason, *When the Pieces Don't Fit: Making Sense of Life's Puzzles*, (Grand Rapids: Discovery House, 2008), 71.
63 Erickson, "The Results of Sin," 636.
64 Thayer's Lexicon, s.v. "#1504 eikon," (the image of one; one in whom the likeness of anyone is seen as to Christ, on account of his divine nature and absolute moral excellence (Col. 1:15; 2 Cor. 4:4), 175.
65 Thayer's Lexicon, s.v. "#3341 metanoia," 405.

Epilogue

66 Michele Borba and Craig Borba, *Self-Esteem: A Classroom Affair—101 Ways to Help Children Like Themselves* (Minneapolis, MN: Winston Press, 1978), Preface.
67 Phyllis Kilbourn, *Shaping the Future: Girls and Our Destiny* (Pasadena, CA: William Carey Library, 2008), 2.
68 David A. Hamburg, *Great Transitions: Preparing Adolescents for a New Century*, ed. Community Scribes (New York: Carnegie Council on Adolescent Development, 1995), "Poem Land of Diminishing Dreams," 2–3, accessed November 28, 2014, https://www.carnegie.org/media/filer_public/a4/d3/a4d397ae-74ea-4318-81f4-73ee6832d943/ccny_report_1995_transitions.pdf
69 Pipher, Mary. *Reviving Ophelia: Saving the Selves of Adolescent Girls*. New York: Riverhead Books, 1994.
70 Pipher, Mary. *Reviving Ophelia: Saving the Selves of Adolescent Girls*. New York: Riverhead Books, 1994.
71 Beverly White Hislop, *Shepherding a Woman's Heart*, (Chicago: Moody Publishers, 2003), 15.
72 Girls' Initiative, *Youth Policy Initiative: Report on High Risk Girls and Gender Specific Programming* (Boston: Black Ministerial Alliance (BMA), 2009), 44.
73 Dr. King's Beloved Community, accessed December 4, 2014, http://www.thekingcenter.org/king-philosophy. The Beloved Community is a global vision in which all people can share in the wealth of the earth. In the Beloved Community, poverty, hunger, and homelessness will not be tolerated because international standards of human decency will not allow it. Racism and all forms of discrimination, bigotry, and prejudice will be replaced by an all-inclusive spirit of sisterhood and brotherhood. International disputes will be resolved by peaceful conflict-resolution and reconciliation of adversaries, instead of military power. Love and trust will triumph over fear and hatred. Peace with justice will prevail over war and military conflict. The Beloved Community will not be devoid of interpersonal, group, or international conflict. Instead, he recognized that conflict was an inevitable part of the human experience. But he believed that conflicts could be resolved peacefully and adversaries could be reconciled through a mutual, determined commitment to nonviolence. No

conflict, he believed, need erupt in violence. And all conflicts should end with reconciliation of adversaries cooperating together in a spirit of friendship and goodwill. One expression of agape love in the Beloved Community is justice, not for any one oppressed group, but for all people. As Dr. King often said, "Injustice anywhere is a threat to justice everywhere." He felt that justice could not be parceled out to individuals or groups but was the birthright of every human being in the Beloved Community. "I have fought too long hard against segregated public accommodations to end up segregating my moral concerns," he said. "Justice is indivisible."

74 bell hooks, *Killing Rage: Ending Racism* (New York: Henry Holt and Company, 1995).
75 bell hooks, *Killing Rage: Ending Racism* (New York: Henry Holt and Company, 1995), 272.
76 KJV Ephesians 1:4-6 *"According as he hath chosen us in him before the foundation of the world, that we should be holy and without blame before him in love: Having predestinated us unto the adoption of children by Jesus Christ to himself, according to the good pleasure of his will, to the praise of the glory of his grace, wherein he hath made us accepted in the beloved."*

Author Bio

Dr. Sandra Gatlin Whitley truly loves the Lord! She is a prayer warrior, teacher, pastoral marriage and family counselor, author, military veteran, and TV host who has served over twenty-five years ministering in military and civilian settings. A native of Montgomery, Alabama and the eldest child of eight siblings, she has lived in different parts of the world during her father's and her own Air Force career. From her childhood prayers in the clothes closet to falling in love with Jesus, she discovered first-hand how much God really loves and values all His children. She is a worshipper and soldier in the Army of the Lord, who stands her ground on the Word of God. In answering God's call to *"Edify the Body of Christ,"* she testifies to what she has seen, heard, and accepted about God and certifies His truth to individuals, couples, and families.

In this book, Dr. Whitley takes girls and women on a journey of discovering who they are and how to live in healthy relationships with our Creator and Father, His Son and other human beings. She motivates, equips, and empowers girls and women in their own ethnic identity to dream and use their God-given talents in achieving positive self-esteem.

She is happily married to her God-sent friend and mate from Philadelphia PA Reverend Kenneth, also an Air Force veteran. They serve in ministry together and are both graduates of Gordon-Conwell Theological Seminary. Both share the love of travel, photography, music, people, God's Word, and spoiling their nieces, nephews and god-children. She also enjoys her walks with God, animal and bird watching, designing and sewing fashions, and trying to sing. She dreams of playing the organ and being on a triathlon team. Without a doubt, she believes it is *"but by the grace of God, I am what I am, and His grace to me was not without effect."*

CPSIA information can be obtained
at www.ICGtesting.com
Printed in the USA
BVHW031827210720
584254BV00001B/48